ON LOOKING

ELEVEN WALKS WITH EXPERT EYES

ALEXANDRA HOROWITZ

SCRIBNER

New York   London   Toronto   Sydney   New Delhi

SCRIBNER
A Division of Simon & Schuster, Inc.
1230 Avenue of the Americas
New York, NY 10020

First Scribner hardcover edition January 2013

SCRIBNER and design are registered trademarks of The Gale Group, Inc.,
used under license by Simon & Schuster, Inc., the publisher of this work.

For information about special discounts for bulk purchases,
please contact Simon & Schuster Special Sales at 1-866-506-1949
or business@simonandschuster.com.

The Simon & Schuster Speakers Bureau can bring authors to your live event.
For more information or to book an event, contact the Simon & Schuster Speakers Bureau
at 1-866-248-3049 or visit our website at www.simonspeakers.com.

Manufactured in the United States of America

1   3   5   7   9   10   8   6   4   2

Library of Congress Cataloging-in-Publication Data is available.

ISBN 978-1-4391-9125-5
ISBN 978-1-4391-9127-9 (ebook)

to Ogden:

look!

Contents

Contents

Sensory City:
Things That Hum, Smell, or Vibrate

ON LOOKING

Amateur Eyes

You missed that. Right now, you are missing the vast majority of what is happening around you. You are missing the events unfolding in your body, in the distance, and right in front of you.

By marshaling your attention to these words, helpfully framed in a distinct border of white, you are ignoring an unthinkably large amount of information that continues to bombard all of your senses: the hum of the fluorescent lights, the ambient noise in a large room, the places your chair presses against your legs or back, your tongue touching the roof of your mouth, the tension you are holding in your shoulders or jaw, the map of the cool and warm places on your body, the constant hum of traffic or a distant lawnmower, the blurred view of your own shoulders and torso in your peripheral vision, a chirp of a bug or whine of a kitchen appliance.

This ignorance is useful: indeed, we compliment it and call it *concentration*. Our ignorance/concentration enables us to not just notice the scrawls on the page but also to absorb them as intelligible words, phrases, ideas. Alas, we tend to bring this focus to every activity we do—not just the most complicated but also the most quotidian. To a surprising extent, time spent going to and fro—walking down the street, traveling to work, heading to the store or a child's (or one's own) school—is unremembered. It is forgotten not because nothing of interest happens. It is forgotten because we failed to pay attention to the journey to begin with. On the phone, worrying over dinner, listening to others or to the to-do lists replaying in our own heads, we miss the world making itself available to be observed. And we miss the possibility of being surprised by what is hidden in plain sight right in front of us.

It was my dog who prompted me to consider that these daily journeys could be done . . . better. Bring a well-furred, wide-eyed, sharp-nosed dog into your life, and suddenly you find yourself taking a lot of walks. *Walks around the block,* in particular. Over the last three decades, living with two dogs, my blocks have been classic city blocks—down the street and three right corners and home; they have been along sidewalked small towns and un-sidewalked, hilly villages. But what counted as a "block" was changeable. Heading out for what I imagined would be a quick circumnavigation, I often found myself led elsewhere by my dog: our "blocks" have become tours of city parks, zigzagging meanders through canyons, trots along the sides of highways, and, when we were lucky, down narrow forest paths.

After enough waylaid walks, I began trying to see what my dog was seeing (and smelling) that was taking us far afield. Minor clashes between my dog's preferences as to where and how a walk should proceed and my own indicated that I was experiencing almost an entirely different block than my dog. I was paying so little attention to most of what was right before us that I had become a sleepwalker on the sidewalk. What I saw and attended to was exactly what I expected to see; what my dog showed me was that my attention invited along attention's companion: inattention to everything else.

This book attends to that inattention. It is not a book about how to bring more focus to your reading of Tolstoy or how to listen more carefully to your spouse. It is not about how to avoid falling asleep at a public lecture or at your grandfather's tales of boyhood misadventures. It will not help you plan dinner for eight as you listen to books-on-tape and as you consult the GPS—all while you are driving.

In this book, I aimed to knock myself awake. I took that walk "around the block"—an ordinary activity engaged in by everyone nearly every day—dozens of times with people who have distinctive, individual, expert ways of seeing all the unattended, perceived ordinary elements I was missing. Together, we became investigators of the ordinary, considering the block—the street and everything on it—as a living being that could be observed.

In this way, the familiar becomes unfamiliar, and the old the new. My method took advantage of two elements. The first is inherent in each of us. We all have the capacity to really see what is in front of us. On moving to a new home, one's first approach is wide eyed—with senses alert to the various ways that this new block differs from one's old home: the trees provide more shade, or the cars are more plentiful, or the sidewalks are leaner, or the buildings are more deeply set back from the street. It is only after we have moved in, after we have walked the same street again and again, that we fall asleep to the block. Even the feeling of time passing changes on our walk: with less to notice, time speeds up. The capacity to attend is ours; we just forget how to turn it on.

The second element takes advantage of individual expertise. There is a certain bias in everyone's perspective that has been named, by the French, *déformation professionnelle*: the tendency to look at every context from the point of view of one's profession. The psychiatrist sees symptoms of diagnosable conditions in everyone from the grocery checkout cashier to his spouse; the economist views the simple buying of a cup of coffee as an example of a macroeconomic phenomenon. In the wrong context these experts are merely the people you try to avoid sitting next to at a dinner party. But applied to this project, these people are *seers:* able to bring attention to an element of a person's manner, or to a social interaction, that is often missed.

I live and work in a city—New York City—and thus have a special fascination with the humming life-form that is an urban street. To investigate, I took all the walks for this book in this and other cities, around ordinary blocks. My companions on these walks were people who have a distinct perspective on the world. Often, it was a perspective forged from explicit training, as with a doctor. For others, their sensibility was shaped by their passion—finding insect tracks or studying lettering, for example. Finally, for some, the way they see the world is part of their very constitution, as with a child, a blind person, or a dog. What follows is the record of eleven walks around the block I took with expert seers, who told me what they saw.

Well, *twelve* walks. I began by walking around the block by myself. I wanted to record what I saw before I was schooled by my walking companions.

The air was already drunk with humidity when I stepped outside on that first morning. I chose to walk the blocks around my home because they are not particularly special blocks; I have a certain fondness for my neighborhood blocks, born of familiarity, but even as they have grown familiar, I realize that I rarely look at them. Nonetheless, I was sure that I would be able to describe them well. My eyes were not altogether amateur: I was knowingly walking to "see what I could see" and, furthermore, professionally I study animal behavior using a method that is, in essence, *looking closely*. On this walk, I set off at a slow pace with a reporter's notebook in hand, planning to reconstruct the scene later. Feeling wide eyed, I turned down the block.

My eyes rested first on the bags of trash by our curb. Shredded, formerly private papers were visible in their clear recycling bags. A beagle pulling on a long leash trotted by and unceremoniously defined the corner of the trash pile by urinating on it.

I scribbled down something about flowers in a tree pit. When I looked up, I was at the corner, flanked by two large, somber apartment buildings. I briefly coveted a free parking spot, a gaping space between cars along the curb. There was no decoration in front of the near building save two pipes—one a humble water pipe, the other a mysterious two-headed gnome. I did not investigate. A child scurried by. I was passed by a series of dog-person pairs, headed toward the park that was now at my back.

The walkers trod silently; the dogs said nothing. The only sound was the hum of air conditioners. A pretty, red brownstone, with a gracious, curved stoop, sat between a large stone building and a handful of white- and red-bricked specimens. But I barely looked up. There was too much to see on the ground. Each building on the block was marked by its characteristic pile of bags of trash. Something dribbled from each: a Q-tip (how does a Q-tip escape? I wondered), a chicken bone, sundry crumpled papers. I saw another Q-tip, and started to wonder about the ear health of my neighbors. As I continued, the trash piles grew messier, or the sidewalk narrower, or both. Moving aside to let someone pass, I was nearly seated in a small alcove along a building—perhaps a place to sit, but it was lined with spikes. I did not sit there.

I approached the next intersection, Broadway, a wide avenue with traffic running both directions. An older gentleman was resting in the median, unable to make it across both lanes of traffic in one go. As he resumed, he teetered, and I swung widely around him so as to not knock him off course.

Across the avenue, continuing east, a few commercial stores had escaped onto the side street: a small grocery, a rash of crushed cigarette butts outside its door; a hair salon, with a long awning to its entrance, oddly formal for a haircuttery. A stream of cars reversed its way down the block, some vehicles pulling into parking places and some backing heedlessly onto the avenue. I smelled trash. The sounds of a garbage truck straining to crush its load wafted from up ahead. A spill of spaghetti, cooked and sauced, formed a sunburst at my feet, attended to by a cluster of pigeons.

The garbage truck was out of sight, but it left a path of garbage leavings—marking the meals, cleaning habits, and unwanted memories of the hidden local inhabitants—from sidewalk to street. I took in the impatience of the drivers, all straining to see ahead, as though if they got a clear view of the impediment, it would dissipate. Watching them, I arrived at the building at the end of the block and turned right onto another busy avenue. Traffic came in waves as each scrum of cars caught the lights timed together running uptown. Every building had a storefront on its first floor, and at this early hour most of them were shuttered. Forgettable, indistinguishable signs topped the stores, advertising pizza and cleaners. Walking as I scribbled down notes, I missed whatever was on the next corner as I turned it. But I saw I had turned onto a tree-lined block, with one half providing an assurance of shade. I headed to it. Newly laid asphalt, deep black and glowing proudly in the morning's heat, gummed the soles of my shoes. Up ahead I saw, and then heard, a film-set truck. The block was taken over by those creating a simulacrum of the block for the day. The truck was a hub of human activity of an unidentifiable nature. Piles of metal rods, racks of poles, and stacked platforms, readied for work, sat on wheeled carts by the truck's rump. An audience of curious onlookers idled away the morning on brownstone stoops.

Each residence had its own one or two distinguishable features. At one building, there were rolled-up, rubber-banded newspapers just sitting on the step outside closed doors. I marveled, for the umpteenth time, that delivered newspapers do not just go missing every morning. Another building had ivy trained over its steps, forming a hopeful arch. A third presented a well-ordered set of trash cans underneath a metal fence.

Clustered along the curb were the loitering film crew and their loitering trucks, generators loudly generating. The crew wore badges or headsets, and nearly everyone held a coffee cup, some kind of early-morning security blanket. They stared at me: they had nothing to do, and they were not in their own neighborhoods, where eye contact is brief and polite. The smells of a nearby caterer caught me: breakfast. The front of a church I had never been in had become a gaping hole, its many doors propped widely open, as men in long shorts hoisted crates inside.

In the middle of this hubbub a honey locust tree sat broken. A recent furious storm had felled its top half, now folded messily next to its trunk. Passersby simply stepped around the police tape unhelpfully slung across it.

A breeze lured me from down the street and I reflexively pursued it, continuing back across Broadway. This block climbed ever-so-slightly up and then down a hill, which seemed to give it great character: the row of identical houses looked more intriguing at slightly different altitudes. On the second floor of one building an old dog studied me through the rails of a balcony. His ears dangled becomingly over his face, and he wagged as I greeted him.

Dominating the street was a single-family mansion, a true anomaly in this city. From behind its wall popped a squirrel, who headed across the street in fits and starts, pausing under a car and in the middle of the road before scurrying across and into a bush.

I turned my final corner, toward the mansion entrance, gazing up at its pair of stone lions waiting patiently for royalty that never arrives. A wooly caterpillar, his head crowned with four fearsome green horns, moved lazily on the first step, heading nowhere good for caterpillars. I scooched him onto a finger and deposited him in a nearby potted tree. I arrived back on my doorstep. The newspaper that should be rubber-banded outside my door had been stolen. I turned the key and was home.

I had waltzed out my door with considerably more self-consciousness than usual, not unaware that I was out to take a "typical" walk around the block. I reveled in my naïveté, pleased to be embarking on a walk whose limitations I knew I would spend the rest of this book delineating. But I also thought to myself that I might just impress myself with my uncanny observational skills. After all, in my professional life I am an observer—of dogs in particular. That skill should translate to observing my own behavior, and certainly to observing my own block. Hadn't I heard how observant I was, from those many friends onto whom I'd lobbed surely unwelcome observations?

So on my return I felt plenty pleased with myself and my walk. Surely I had seen all that really mattered on the block. Not a car passed without my gaze upon it; nary a building got by un-ogled. I had stared down the trees; I even knew one's name. I had eyeballed the passersby; noted a daring squirrel; spied a wooly caterpillar. I was consciously looking. What could I have missed?

As it turns out, I was missing pretty much everything. After taking the walks described in this book, I would find myself at once alarmed, delighted, and humbled at the limitations of my ordinary looking. My consolation is that this deficiency of mine is quite human. We see, but we do not see: we use our eyes, but our gaze is glancing, frivolously considering its object. We see the signs, but not their meanings. We are not blinded, but we have blinders.

My deficiency is one of attention: I simply was not paying close enough attention. Though *paying attention* seems simple, there are numerous forms of payment. I reckon that every child has been admonished by teacher or parent to "pay attention." But no one tells you *how* to do that.

The consensus is that it is in some way taxing. Gustave Fechner, a nineteenth-century German psychophysicist, claimed he felt a physical sensation when attending: "a strain forward in the eyes," and when listening, "one directed sidewise in the ears." The American father of modern psychology, William James, reported that when attending to a memory, he felt "an actual rolling outwards and upwards of the eyeballs," as though fixing on the striations of neurons in the interior of his head. In researching what people perceived attention to be, psychologists found that schoolteachers instructed their students to pay attention to an image by "hold[ing] the image still as one would with a camera." To concentrate, to *pay attention,* is viewed as a brow-furrowing exercise. Sit still, don't blink, and *attend*.

Given a thorny sentence to read, or asked to listen to a whispered secret while a truck rumbles by, you will quickly be brought to that mind-straining place that James and Fechner described. We take on a characteristic attentive pose. In reading, you might frown slightly, your eyes narrowed as though contracting the words into finer focus. In listening, you may lean toward the speaker, looking down to avoid visual distraction, your mouth falling slightly open. You hold something tensed—a flexed foot, fingers curled into a loose fist, shoulders raised protectively. You are surprisingly still, as though the noise of your muscle movement might drown out a whisper.

This may do for a moment of concentration, but it is not the way to better attention in your daily life. For that, we need to know what attention is. The very concept is odd. Is it an ability, a tendency, a skill? Is it processed in a special nugget in the brain, or by your eyes and ears? The psychologists have no clear answer. Since we all feel comfortable using the word, it has been customary to agreeably nod when someone starts talking to you about attention, but is it coherent to discuss something that we cannot even define, much less locate?

Surely "everyone knows what attention is," claimed James over a century ago. *Maybe,* but it is notable that James himself then spent sixty pages of his psychology opus largely theorizing about what exactly it might be. If we are unsure what attention is, we are bound to have difficulty honing it.

The longtime model used by psychologists is that of a "spotlight" that picks out particular items of interest to examine, bringing some things into focus and awareness while leaving other things in the dim, dusty sidelines. The metaphor makes me feel like a headlight-wearing spelunker who can only see what is right in front of her in the darkness of the cave. Such a comparison can be misleading, because in fact one can still report on what was within one's peripheral vision at rates better than chance. And despite that spotlight, we seem to miss huge elements of the thing we are ostensibly attending to.

A better way of thinking about attention is to consider the problems that evolution might have designed "attention" to solve. The first problem emerges from the nature of the world. The world is wildly distracting. It is full of brightly colored things, large things casting shadows, quickly moving things, approaching things, loud things, irregular things, smelly things. This cacophony can be found right outside your house or apartment. Should someone see us standing quietly on the sidewalk in front of an apartment building, and ask us, "What's up?" we might be hard-pressed to respond accurately: "My eyes are being tickled with a splendid display of colors; we are surrounded by improbably large stone towers; occasionally a storm of metal and plastic roars by me on the street; soft-faced irregularly-moving forms come near me and pass by; smaller tight-bodied things move by my head in the air; there is a rumble from somewhere, intermittent jabbers from the soft faces, continual hums from these stone towers; my nose is attracted and repelled by something ripe and rotting . . ." we could begin.

Instead, we say, "Nothing much."

And "nothing" is more or less what we notice, in fact. One way to solve the problem of the "blooming, buzzing confusion" an infant confronts on entering the world is to tune much of it out. As we grow up, over the course of days and months, we learn to deal with the confusion by paying little of it mind. By the time we are old enough to walk outside to the sidewalk, we have organized the perceptual melee into chunks of recognizable objects. After a few years, we learn to see the street scene—without really seeing it at all.

The second problem is that, even ignoring most of it, we can only take in so much of the world at a time. Our sensory system has a limited capacity, both in range and in speed of processing. The light we see, "visible" light, is an impossibly small snatch of the solar spectrum; similarly, what we hear is but a fraction of what there is to hear. Our eyes, like other sensory organs, can process a finite amount at once: the neural cells that transduce light to electricity effect this through a change in their pigment. In the time that this is happening, the cell cannot take in any more light. We do not *see* what cannot get past the eye. And, too, though with our highly fancy brains we are massive parallel distributed processers, there is still a limit to our computational capacity. The world's best computers do not (yet) think like humans do, but they are much, much faster at processing information. Happily, not everything out there in the world is equally informative or important. We do not need to see everything.

If only we had a system that let us take in what we *do* need to see—

—and of course, we do: that system is attention. Having a way to tune out unnecessary information, to sort through the bombardment of visual and auditory noise, solves these problems. Objects in the world may seem benign, impotently hoping that your glance will light on them, but they are competing with each other for your regard. Attention is an intentional, unapologetic discriminator. It asks what is relevant right now, and gears us up to notice only that. Why bother sorting out all the elements of a visual scene? Evolution has a simple explanation. Some things are good to eat, and some things are trying to eat you. At the most basic level, an organism needs to be able to discriminate between these two categories of things from the rest of the world. Indeed, for a simple organism, that could be nearly *all* that is noticed. The bacterium does not care if your orange shirt clashes horribly with your pink slacks. The subtle but important difference between the smell of sweaty feet and the smell of Limburger cheese (actually not so different to all but the cheesemongers) is lost on the brave bacterium that would happily lounge on either. For an early hominid on the savanna, detection of, say, a lion would be of paramount importance. As a result, modern humans still have a type of attention—*vigilance*—which helps keep the body ready to look out for that lion, and dash off if he appears. More recently, what is relevant for modern man is being able to nod at the right times to the person animatedly talking to you at a cocktail party, while blocking out all the other conversations around you (noticing if one of them mentions you, though). We have got another kind of attention—*selective attention*—to do this job for us.

When we can, we try to offload this work on the world: bringing attention by changing it—circling the key words of a book's pages; marking with bright color anything to be noticed; keeping your preferred knife not among knives but among the poor defenseless spoons. Hence the commercial success of highlighter pens, bright orange construction cones (or, even better, construction cones in neon green, for contrast with the old orange), and advertising that blinks at you from its billboard.* Indeed, the singularity of one unexpected element in a visual scene is so remarkable that the item can serve as just a marker for some other thing, tangible or intangible: to do the laundry or to call your mother. It is the string-on-the-finger phenomenon: in noticing the string, you do not head into a reverie about strings. Instead, you are reminded that there is something that needs remembering.

If you overuse this trick, though, you simply become accustomed to having strings on your fingers, and the strings no longer serve to do anything but keep you armed for tying knots at a moment's notice.

The most successful spotlighting of any situation usually involves directions from upstream, in the brain. Your brain ties strings on fingers all the time, without wasting a single strand. Your own internal monologue about what you are doing in any given moment actually affects what you will see in that moment. If you *know* you are looking for the knife, it will be easier to find.

At a basic level, then, *paying attention* is simply making a selection among all the stimuli bombarding you at any moment. It need not be concerted or difficult. But it does require some direc-

---

* Before I had a child and the floor of our home became an in-progress canvas of wooden toys, squeaking balls, and plush animals, I could drop the single item I needed to remember to take with me the next day by the front door. There it would wait for me, utterly forgotten, until I spied it on my way out and stashed it in my rucksack.

tion from the brain. Simply to be reading these words at all is to be narrowing your range of mental field to the words on the page. Other sights, thoughts, sounds, and smells still fly by in your periphery, the suburbs of your mental viewfinder. They are a sub-level of attention, a kind of attention that we might not be aware of (until one of those sights or sounds migrates into our mental field of view). These are things we will quickly, and almost surely, forget—but that are ready for consideration. Later today, reflecting on the time spent sitting and reading this book, you will not remember an image of what was to your left or right, what was in your visual field above the top of the book's pages, the tune flitting through your head, or the ambient sound track of muffled footsteps or car traffic that accompanies your reading.

Psychologists call this the *selective enhancement* of some area of your perceptual field and suppression of other areas. And therein lies my approach to "paying attention" to the block: each of my companions on these walks serves to do the selective-enhancing for us, highlighting the parts of the world that they see but which we have either learned to ignore or do not even know we *can* see.

This is not to say that everyone I walked with saw everything. Moments into my walk with one of the world's foremost researchers on the science of paying attention, she stepped over sixty dollars lying in her path on the street.

She simply did not notice it.

A half-step behind her, I, and my eyebrows, expressed surprise. For this, an early walk for this project, I had headed out of town by train to walk with a psychologist who thinks a great deal about attention. We had just been talking about the psychological idea of being "mindful"—aiming to bring active attention to our daily lives by noticing new things. And we were on one of the prototypical elements of daily life, a neighborhood jaunt with dogs.

But the mindful psychologist walked mindlessly by the cash.

It was her dog and I who saw it (well, I am guessing the dog smelled it). One twenty-dollar bill, bereft of owner. A footstep later, another twenty. I goggled at seeing a third bill lying forlornly to the side of the first two. They bore the creases of having been folded with the same hand, in possessive quarter-folds, though they were now unfurling with their freedom. They must have leapt from a pocket together, parachuted to the ground at different speeds, and landed a stride apart. I stopped, reached down, grabbed the loot, and managed to mutter, *"Look!"*

She smiled broadly as she registered the money resting on my outstretched palms. The dog stood beside me, proudly quiet, nose pointed at the ground. But then I thought, *Wait, did I miss another one?*

In this book, I am looking for what it is that I miss, every day, right in front of me, while walking around the block. "The block" includes the physical elements of the street—from the sidewalks to the buildings—and their history. My first four walks attend to this *inanimate city*. The block includes who (or what) is on it now and who (or what) has passed before; the next three chapters attend to this *animate city*. The block is full of things we miss seeing, smelling, or hearing—and it holds untold stories of the things we *do* see, smell, or hear. The final three chapters attend to the *sensory city*.

The result of all this walking is not a master's degree in the details of any one city or any single block. It is a tale about what there is to see in any environment, urban or rural. These walks re-awakened in me a sense of perpetual wonder in my surroundings—a perceptual skill typically available only to experts and to the very young (not yet expert in being people). Perhaps they will awaken wonder in you, too.

William James suggested that my experience will be "what I agree to attend to." And so I headed agreeably to my first walk around the block, mind in my hand.

Inanimate City:

The Material of the Landscape

"You can observe a lot by watching."

(Yogi Berra)

Muchness

"There was no decoration in front of the building save two pipes—one a humble pipe, the other a mysterious two-headed gnome. I did not investigate."

By taking in my hand the small, soft curled fingers, and a good chunk of frayed wool jacket hem, both belonging to my nineteen-month-old son, I came to learn about the acute isosceles triangles on my block.

Before we even met the triangles, I was to have the conceptual foundations of my world rocked. When I headed out for a "walk" with my son, I was already being presumptuous. For me, to go for a walk is a simple matter, almost too simple to describe. But because my understanding of a walk was upended by a toddler, I'll try. I thought a walk was a navigation of a path—sidewalk, street, or dirt—from point A to point B. I suppose that, if pushed, I would relent on "path": it needn't even be a true path, just a route along which to place my feet, one after the other, in going from somewhere to somewhere else.

How wrong I turned out to be. On a late afternoon on a late-spring day, we prepared to go for a walk around our block. At this age, my son had been walking on his own for seven months, but a walk outside—where he would be doing the walking, not being walked—was an unusual outing. He was still small and young enough that many expeditions were undertaken attached to Mama's belly with an infant carrier, or to Daddy's back in a ret-rofitted backpack. But today he was to lead *me* on a walk. Even more, I was going to ask him to tell me what he saw.

His response would, of course, require some amount of transla-tion. Although he was a prodigious collector of vocabulary words—besides *ma-ma, peek-boo, daddy,* and *apple,* he was very fond of *belly button, helicopter,* and, after witnessing an impressive collapse of our liquor cabinet, *catastrophe*—he was not yet a conversational-ist in the way that could be recorded on audiotape. On the other hand, he communicated all the time—with elaborate gestures, with expressions that spanned his face, with rudimentary sign lan-guage, and with emotion. On our walk, I would be listening to him reporting on what he saw by following his interests—and trying to imagine being in his six-inch-long shoes.

Buttons were buttoned, zips zipped, knots tied and double-tied. With no small amount of excitement, we headed down the elevator to "Outside!" as he exclaimed. My son ran through the lobby to our apartment building's front door, weighted heavily in glass and iron—and gigantic relative to his small body. Together, we peeled it open slowly, as though to admire its solidity. Hand in hand, we turned left and started our walk.

Then we stopped. We had not even turned fully to our left. Poised half off the bottom step and half onto the sidewalk, my son squatted—a young weight lifter's pose, or the spring-loading of an infant rocket. There he crouched. And stayed there.

"Let's go for a walk!" I prompted.

Nothing.

"Okey-doke!" I said, in my best *off-we-go!* voice.

Maybe an eyelash batted.

Eventually he reached out his hand again and I grabbed it with mine.

This was the beginning of my realization: to him, we *were already* "taking a walk." As we proceeded, I began to get the details of his definition. A "walk," according to my toddler, is regularly about not walking. It has nothing to do with points A, B, or the getting from one to the other. It barely has anything to do with planting one's feet in a straight line. A walk is, instead, an investigatory exercise that begins with energy and ends when (and only when) exhausted. It began in the elevator, continued with running through the building, opening the door, and then being poised on the step. It began before the elevator, tying shoes—and before that, doing a going-to-tie-our-shoes march down the hall. To him, we were miles into our walk.

A walk is exploring surfaces and textures with finger, toe, and—*yuck*—tongue; standing still and seeing who or what comes by; trying out different forms of locomotion (among them running, marching, high-kicking, galloping, scooting, projectile falling, spinning, and noisy shuffling). It is archeology: exploring the bit of discarded candy wrapper; collecting a fistful of pebbles and a twig and a torn corner of a paperback; swishing dirt back and forth along the ground. It is stopping to admire the murmuring of the breeze in the trees; locating the source of the bird's song; pointing. *Pointing!*—using the arm to extend one's fallen gaze so someone else can see what you've seen. It is a time of sharing.

On our block, my son has shared his discovery of the repeating motif of lights under construction scaffolding (they come in fluorescent, yellow, red, and bare-bulb white, I am happy to share with you). Of the numerous intentional or unintentional letter *O*s—his first spoken letter, enunciated carefully and long, lips pursed and eyes beaming with pleasure—on signs and walls (on the STOP sign, of course, but also on license plates and the zeros of no-parking signs—and by the way, nO parking, buster); on the circle-pocked grating of a window air-conditioner; in a round call button; in an egg-shaped sidewalk crack; on an iron gate with *O* filigree. He has shared the feature of our building that, to him, distinguished it from its neighbors: the lion's head, mid-roar, above our entrance. I had never noticed it, over thousands of entrances and exits.

Was he fixated? Obsessed? A lightbulb, letter *O,* or lion savant? No. My son was but an infant. And the perceptions of infants are remarkable. That infants reliably develop into adults, who for all their wisdom or kindness are often unremarkable, blinds us to this fact. The infant's world is a case study in con-fused attention. A newborn, freshly plopped into the world, is unwittingly enrolled in a crash course in sensory experience. In some respects his biology takes care not to overwhelm him too much. Though all sensory organs—including those compellingly large, naive eyes; the ears the size of his hands; the perfectly soft, unblemished skin—are intact, the messages they receive from the world do not all get to the infant's brain. At least not in an organized way. What the infant sees, for instance, is something quite fuzzier and more dazzling than what the normal adult sees: babies are very nearsighted and they lack the clouded filters that take bright light down a notch. Even more critically, the world is not yet organized into discrete objects for these new eyes: it is all light and dark, shadow and brightness. To the newborn infant, there is no "crib," no "mama" and "daddy," no floor no wall no window no sky. Much of this can be seen, but none can yet be made sense of.

Information taken in by the eyes might be processed in any part of the brain—it could be the visual cortex, leading to an inchoate "seeing"; but it could also be the motor cortex, leading to a leg kicking; or the auditory cortex, in which case a nearby teddy bear may be experienced as a bang, or a ringing, or a whisper. There is good reason to believe that this kind of *synesthesia* is the normal experience for infants. Synesthesia—literally "joining of sensations"—is a somewhat rare and highly improbable form of perception in adults. Synesthetes experience things from one sense—say, vision—overlaid with experiences from another, such as taste. Of course we often experience two or more sensations at once—it is hard to eat near a spewing sewer; we can locate the person who is speaking to us by looking at lips.

In some people, though, sensory overlays are less functional and more extreme. The nineteenth-century Soviet psychologist A. R. Luria wrote about his encounter with a synesthete, introduced as "S," in *The Mind of a Mnemonist* (the patient also, not coincidentally, had an extremely good memory). In asking him to memorize lists of words, Luria became aware that S. was visualizing the words in his head, and that this "seeing" was not straightforward. For if someone coughed or sneezed when a word was being read from the list, S. reported that a "puff of steam," a "splash" or blur, appeared on the images he was forming in his mind. For S., sounds came in colors and flavors: pink, rough, or tasting like pickles. Many synesthetes experience numbers and letters with distinctive overlays—a "gloomy" number *3*; the letter *h* as a "drab shoelace"; an *a* reminiscent of "weathered wood."

While tasting sounds or smelling letters is viewed as aberrant (if conducive to creativity) among adults, those eminently creative infants may sense the world with crossed wires all the time. Heinz Werner, a German psychologist of the early twentieth century, called this the "sensorium commune": a primordial way of experiencing the world, pre-knowledge and pre-categorization. Researchers have found remnants of this perceptual organization in adults: on being shown drawings of curly lines, adults tend to characterize the lines as "happy"; descending lines, "sad"; sharp lines, "angry." To *feel* a tone, as though one were inside a vibrating bell, is to see glimpses of your vestigial sensorium commune.

But mostly, we ignore that feeling; we do not label lines as being happy or vexed or gloomy. One theory of synesthesia holds that the synapses connecting neurons identifying shapes and those leading to the experience of taste get snipped sometime in the first few years of life. This may be the simple result of our lack of attention to the connection. Few persons talk about the green-apple sourness of a triangle, and so the individual who experiences it may eventually stop attending to it. Snip.

The possibility of this way of perceiving the world makes more sense when we remember that the brain is but a soup of specialized cells—neurons—that communicate with one another electrically. These cells' communications form connections called synapses across the brothy gap between cells. It is not a stretch to say that at some level, every experience that we have—from feeling a stub of the toe, to trying to remember someone's name, or uttering a sentence—is the result of the activity of certain neurons, communicating over certain synapses.*

Attention—from "trying" to remember a name to "pondering" how to complete a sentence one is uttering—as well as sensory processing must be a kind of synaptic activity. To a brain without many synapses, like the newborn's, there is, thus, not a lot of direct attention. As the synapses start forming—and *Bam!* the ringing telephone lights up a row of *Zap!* neurons in the visual area, and *Whoop!* tickles a motor neuron into prompting a leg to kick— we can see attention beginning. Confused, random, involuntary

---

*Which neurons, and which synapses, is another, wooly question, one yet to be answered. And how neural activity comes to *feel* like a stub, or like remembering, may be unanswerable.

attention, but attention. Visit that infant two months later, and watch as he looks you in (or near, or around) the eyes, and follows your head as it moves to his left and out of range. That is attention, visual attention, beginning to unconfuse itself. At nineteen months, my son was largely but as yet not entirely unconfused. Thank goodness.

I was just getting used to the idea that we lived, apparently, on a block with an epidemic of Os. But I was unprepared for the triangles. We were heading west down the street, only fifty yards (but dozens of minutes) from our front door. Since we had not gotten far, I was hurrying my son along, gently tugging his arm instead of balancing between my left step and right step to wait for his little legs to catch up between long Mama-sized steps. But he was pulling back and I finally let him follow his magnet. I was on the street side of the sidewalk, and he was angling away from me. I looked in the direction he pulled. I saw . . . nothing.

While the Os were a linguistic tic displaced onto the world, in the physical world my son was drawn to edges, linings of routes, and low railings. On the corner of the block beamed a large building, of the typical prewar size and gravitas for Manhattan. The street travels up a steep hill, and the building's easternmost apartments seem to tower above the westernmost. At a glance, I had the feeling of the sort of apartment building it was, having visited or lived in dozens of them in my life. I studied the building for any personality in its facade that would allow me to see beyond the foreknowledge I had of it. I was coming up blank. While I was doing this, my son was bearing down his weight, pulling my hand harder to slow me to a stop. He had found a railing, of a sort. The building had a prewar moat: a basement-level cavity surrounding the building, more likely to allow storage of trash bags than to keep armies at bay. The moat was edged with a foreboding railing, anchored by heavy balusters. I had certainly attempted not to notice this. It was not a lovely part of the building.

My son had noticed it. He was blessed with the ability to admire the unlovely. Or, I should say, he was blessed with the inability to feel that there is a difference between lovely and un-. The balusters were planted on a parapet just wide enough for a toddler to fit on. He tiptoed along the low wall, hopped down, and clambered up the next. It was in this way that I learned of the triangles. As my son's route intersected with the sidewalk, the two paths created a long, sharp triangle between them. It was a small step up, and a big step down. Were the triangles friendly? I asked. Yellow? "Green. Bubbly," he said, solemnly, as I looked at the very nonbubbly, nongreen triangles. I nodded. Who am I to snip that synapse?

Part of normal human development is learning to notice less than we are able to. The world is awash in details of color, form, sound—but to function, we have to ignore some of it. The world still holds these details. Children sense the world at a different granularity, attending to parts of the visual world we gloss over; to sounds we have dismissed as irrelevant. What is indiscernible to us is plain to them.

We humans share our understanding of "what is out there" in the world, but we are not entirely born into it. We all begin in a kind of sensory chaos—what William James called an "aboriginal sensible muchness": a more or less undifferentiated mass of sounds and lights, colors and textures and smells. When we are growing up, we learn to bring attention to certain elements and to ignore others. By adulthood, we all agree on what is "out there." But let's focus on what we ignore: so much! The patterns of pebbles embedded in asphalt, the pitch of a radiator's hiss, our own heart beating tangibly in our fingertips and temples. The infant has a mind untrammeled by experience: he has no expectations, so he is not closed off from experiencing something anew.

Neither is he a blank slate, of course. Humans have built-in mechanisms that improve the chances that even in those precarious first moments of life outside the womb, an infant will find his mother (by the smell he's been entrained on in utero; by the orientation of his eyes to her face; by the bull's-eye that is a nipple on a breast). Still, the infant does not yet know to ignore the sound of crumpling paper in the hand of the person across the room, or the jangle of a full-body shake of a dog rising. In not knowing what is interesting and what to attend to, he also does not know what we all consider uninteresting: whatever the bottom of the chair looks like; a blank stretch of wall; the corner of a picture frame. We don't stare at each other's knees—they just aren't terribly fascinating—but the baby doesn't know that yet (and is, of course, at knee height). He ogles away. An infant's brain is still very early in sorting out what is a whole object and what is only a part: what the edge or limit of an object is. Nor is he yet inculcated in where one is "supposed to" look and where one is "not supposed to" stare. He doesn't know that the triangles formed between the balusters and the sidewalk are not the least bit interesting.

Or are they? Cézanne suggested that all natural forms are at essence combinations of cubes, cylinders, cones, and spheres. My son's *O*s are just cross sections of cylinders or spheres; his triangles are lopped-off corners of cubes. Cubists did a lot with these simple structures, deconstructing and reconstructing the shapes we have become familiar with and forget to notice. The infant toys that Froebel, the inventor of kindergarten, designed for his charges were all variations on these shapes. For a baby, even a soft ball delights: it rolls, but it can be caught. For an older infant, a hard ball represents the moving of things away from them and *by* them—and the cube stands in contrast, resistant to rolling, but pushable, stackable, pileable. Imagine the possibilities when a cylinder joins the party. For my son, the blue cylinder is easily a pretend cup, hat, or fleeing mouse; a "smushed" ball or "too big" marble.

As adults, we are conspirators in designing—*asserting*—what we see in the world. My son was still seeing the shapes of the world that I had stopped seeing. I missed the parapet triangles for the building behind it; the cylinders and cubes that make up the body of a mouse, for the mouse himself.

This is not to say that the world can be seen in infinitely many ways. There is a logic to the images we see; but the logic the child sees is as yet uninfected by the logic of the world seen through an adult's eyes. Though William James invoked the "blooming, buzzing confusion" a newborn faces in the visual world, the blooming forms a pattern; the buzzing beats a rhythm. Researchers in signal processing who try to reproduce the work of a natural visual system in an artificial (computer) system are faced with the question of just how to represent the world. It turns out that natural images are not at all *random*. That is to say, you could not concoct a natural-looking scene by throwing paint at a wall. This non-randomness means that natural images are fairly predictable: you can guess what is in the next "pixel" of visual space by looking at the pixel right in front of you. The world is highly structured, coherent, with large correlations between what is in one place and what is in the next. So it is not exactly visual white noise that we need to make sense of when we first turn our eyes to the world. Instead, perhaps that simple geometry of cubes and spheres—or pyramids—serves as the structure for building all other things that we will see in our lives.

• • •

It took us a good long while to move away from those triangles. I traveled back and forth beside them as my son traveled up onto and down off of them. I took the lead in alternating held hands and smiling apologetically when passersby were forced to weave around us. Each trip between balusters he walked "up, up, up!"—imagining climbing mountains, scaling to the top of unthinkably large vehicles like fire trucks and trains, or clambering all the way up from Mama's toes to her tip-top. Many people smiled at our game. These people, I determined, were parents.

Finally, for no reason I could see, he tired of the repetition and we headed on our way.

For four steps. Then he stopped, agog. I already knew that my son was extraordinarily keen on finding the "new" thing in a scene. Bring in the mail while he is napping, and he beelines for it on awakening. If I slip a watch on my wrist while he is looking away, it gleams brightly in his eyes as he turns back. On many occasions he has found—and brought to me with the gravity of an investigator at a crime scene—the speck of fluff left on the carpet after vacuuming, an impossibly tiny crumb alighted on his cuff, or another microscopically small particle. I know that cancer-sniffing dogs are in vogue, but I feel confident that any unusual growth on my skin ("dot!" he proudly proclaims) would be found by my son before our pup.

And here, too, he dropped my hand and pointed at the ground, and I knew that there was something new.

"Pebbles!"

An elm tree had disgorged hundreds, maybe thousands of small green seeds on the sidewalk. They looked like flat, circular petals dyed the faintest spring green. "Many, many!" he cried, sweeping his hands back and forth excitedly. They colored the sidewalk cracks, traced its edges, defined the five-inch altitude change from curb to street. From my son's enthusiasms, I knew when these petal-pebbles had arrived from their branchy haven: overnight. My son's neophilia—love of the new—was strong enough that he would have seen and announced them had they arrived earlier. It was through his eyes that I began to see how the sidewalk and street are refreshed, each time we leave or arrive home. There is a constant rearrangement of things on the street and in the air that is seen only by those who do not know that gazing at the cars parked on the street is boring.

In childhood, all is new. With age, we see things as familiar. We have *seen it all before*: in our daily lives, we are sure what we will encounter, and in a city, the cool resident will not even bother to slow his stride for the crowd of people gathered around some unusual occurrence on the sidewalk. Vacations are the adult exceptions. There, two things happen: we actually do see new places and second, we bother to look.* I suspect that some of our fondness for so-called vacation locales (which are, after all, someone else's home—as your home may be someone else's vacation) is due to this *simply looking*.

Soon, though, we acclimate. Familiarity begins following us around. Before we know it, we have become entirely accustomed to how that vacation spot looks. We have routines, we know the way—and we stop looking. Still, that vacation has changed us temporarily. Returning home, we have a small window in which we can use our newfound vision to see our old environment anew. When I travel outside my home in New York, the streets just *feel* different. It is on returning home that I can identify why. Compared to the width of the streets where the primary mode of transport is automotive, and where there is space to provide a generous sidewalk, my familiar sidewalks and streets suddenly look terri-

---

* The proliferation of McDonald's and Starbucks in far-flung locales notwithstanding. Chain stores abort vacation-vision.

bly narrow when I come back from a drive outside the city. When I have returned from abroad, they seem comfortably wide, compared to the much more ancient sidewalks that always force you to step into the street when people are passing. An ordinary street scene now appears crammed with uncountable objects on which the eye could fall. The sidewalk is temporarily unnavigable; I bump into people, fall out of step. Even the slope of the street surprises. In the Midwest, streets are designed to grade gently downward near the curbs to lead rainwater into gutters and avoid puddling. My, how non-gently-descending my NYC streets are!

This new perception of the peculiarness of my hometown lasts exactly one viewing. After seeing my block once, my visual system is rebooted and restored to its ordinary self. Same old block. Seen it all before.

In childhood, then, attention is brightened by two features: children's neophilia and the fact that, as young people, they simply *haven't* seen it all before.

Exhibit A of this convergence was about to appear.

"Dump truck!"

We had turned off our residential side street onto the avenue. Broadway. For me, the avenue meant waves of pedestrians, noise, and grocery stores. For my son, it meant *trucks*. Now that he had called my attention to it, I had to admit it was quite a truck. I admired the dump truck, out of scale with the city, its tires curling taller than my child stands and its dumper bright blue and enormous. Having a number of scale models of dump trucks on my dining room table at that very moment, I felt qualified to say that this one looked quite sound.

My son gaped at the truck, pointing redundantly. Trucks were his newest love, but he had long been vehicularly inclined. The first "new thing" he had noticed, many months prior, was airplanes: each one was unaccountably exciting. I quickly learned that planes appeared in our skies, flying north along the Hudson River lining the city, every three to five minutes, descending for their landings nearby at LaGuardia Airport. This reliability had air-traffic-controlling significance, but for me it was deeply satisfying, as it provided periodic but ever-increasing pleasure to him to spot them.

After planes, my son expanded his transportation interests broadly. Helicopters were fabulous, but even cars would do. Motorcycles! The thrill of finding a motorcycle parked on our block was surpassed only by the thrill of a motorcycle roaring down our block. He would not let a bus pass without comment. Now, trucks. One might think he had been bred for vehicular spotting, given the sensitivity to and alacrity he had in locating and identifying a truck in the greater New York City area. No sooner had he discovered the category "truck" than he identified subcategories, highlighting what made each one different and new and glorious. With his current vocabulary the categories included "big," "little," "dump," "fire," "garbage," and, a catch-all which was surprisingly apt, "funny."

Like all dump trucks, rare species in the city, this one passed us all too quickly. We proceeded along, looking down toward our feet. I became increasingly aware of the accoutrements of the street that beckon suggestively to someone with eyes two and a half feet off the ground. Tree guards, impotent iron fencing or enclosures which surround a tree pit, are not only of interest to dogs, familiar with their odorous messages, but also to the child whose hand can run smoothly along the railing. Mushroom-hatted fire hydrants are silent sentries at child height. The urban child is, unfortunately, trash height on garbage day; my son initiated *blech* as a spontaneous commentary before I got a chance to express it myself. The furniture of the street—the appointments of the sidewalk—is scattered hither and thither and coordinated by no master architect. It is visual cacophony. Over time, this furniture proliferates, "whelp(ing) whole litters of new objects," as one landscape architect bemoaned. Where one newspaper box beckoned, three more have sprung up; light poles are scooted aside for traffic-light and sign poles. These keep company with the tree guards and fireplugs, and also mailboxes, bicycle holders, bollards, pots. Our block, well whelped, even has benches—and a telephone booth, now an ancient relic in the city.*

It was none of these items that my son found on our walk, though. He approached a pipe extending from a building's outer wall, and he patted it on (what appeared to be) its head.

Its two heads, actually. A protuberant two-headed hydra, the pipe was gloriously red and capped at the end. A short chain dangled from its belly. My son's new pet was a standpipe.

 I had seen standpipes before, of course. You have seen them. We *see* them. They are everywhere, growing off of sides of buildings and sprouting from the sidewalk on short stalks. They are red or green or yellow or proudly shiny brass. What I had never done was look at them.

---

* It is almost reason enough to have moved to our current block that on its corner sits one of the last handful of telephone booths in the city. Seldom used but by children shooed inside by their parents, it is nonetheless a fine anachronism in a city filled with phones unboothed and tethered to our ears.

I can now tell you that there are five standpipes on our block, as we have five tall buildings on our street, and a standpipe is required in New York City for any building above six stories tall. Should there be a fire, the pipe provides a backup high-pressure stream for firemen's hoses. Along the city streets there are dozens of varieties of standpipes gargoyled on buildings or lying flush along their walls. This overlooked bit of outdoor plumbing is only used in an emergency: it runs into the building and is tied into the building's water supply. In an apartment building's stairwell you may see the pipes running to and from a rooftop water supply: the actual upstanding pipes.

As we moved away from the standpipes, after much petting and admiring of its component parts, my son turned and waved, *Buh-bye!* To him, the standpipe was as much a fellow creature as the bipedal primates peering down at him. His understanding of others was limited, and inculcating him with the rituals of wishing farewell was the beginning of getting him to acknowledge others. That "others" included standpipes now was fine by me. He greets and asks after the health of his trains; he tells his stuffed bunny that it "won't hurt" when he listens to the bunny's heart with a stethoscope; he kissed and bandaged our bedroom wall when he knocked into it with his head. Someday my son will need to learn about the organization of the actual social world. He will attend preschool, where the mandate is mostly "socialization," allowing kids to leave their independent satellites and start figuring out other people—and distinguishing people from standpipes, stuffed bunnies, walls, or trains. Someday he will need to learn about what built the city in which he lives, about who governs it now; about the people living in his neighborhood and the people living in other neighborhoods. He will learn about people who want things from him, or who will do things for him, or with whom he will compete or cooperate.

Someday, he will appreciate others' perspectives, have an idea of their histories, their motivations, their choices, their moods, their own childhoods learning these kinds of things. He will be sympathetic. He will be kind and, we hope, polite.

But not yet.

He is quietly but plainly rude. He gapes. He points with abandon. His behavior on the street is baldly impudent. He stares fixedly, penetratingly, at people as they approach, as they sit near us, sometimes even as they smile at him. He pivots fully around on his toes in order to stare at passersby. The infirm, elderly, and decrepit already register with him as *unusual,* and he stares even more at them. Walking down the street with him recently he extrapolated from our talking about the various colors of the parked cars to suddenly say "White! White!" while indicating the three (yes, white) people innocently going about their business near us.

On this day, a profoundly limping man, destitute and dressed too warmly for the weather, was clearing a path ahead of us with his presence. He was gesticulating and making exclamatory pronouncements to himself. He lurched around, the picture of menacing. Other people on the sidewalk were not simply not looking; they actively engaged themselves in other activities—a sudden phone call, a fleet-footed maneuver to step into the street—that preempted any possibility of looking. I swallowed my urge to abruptly change our path.

Instead, I peeked down at my son. He held his lips tightly closed, curved around his teeth. He slowed and grasped my fingers tightly in his fist as the man approached us. This lurching, menacing man stopped in front of us and stared at my son, taking him for an audience. My son was silent and attentive. It read as a critique. After a beat, the man transformed: he smiled at him. In front of my son, he was unable to keep up his normal routine of an outsider among adults.

And I learned a new way of dealing with crazy-looking strangers on the street.

On a typical walk with a toddler, every person must be stopped for and stared at. But my son did not discriminate against nonhumans. Each dog deserved giggled commentary and a proffered hand for sniffing; pigeons were to be run after; squirrels, to be bemused by their magic disappearing acts on tree trunks. Nor did my son discriminate against nonanimals. Indeed, he treated social encounters as if they were with inanimate objects, and he treated inanimate objects, like the standpipes, as though they were social players. His attention was only dislodged from the departing limping man by the sudden emergence of another man out of a building's side entrance. He was an employee of the building, dressed in overalls and lugging a trash bag behind him. He swung the bag summarily ahead of him; it plopped unprettily by the curb. The man then reached forward and placed a single shoe on the bag before retreating inside. We were agog. At least, my son was.

"Shoe!" My son pointed. This was not one of his first few dozen words, most of which had to do with family, animals, and food, but it was one of the few words in regular rotation in his speech.

I nodded. "Shoe."

He gave me a look. I recognized the look: the unhappy-pig face from a children's book by Richard Scarry we often read together. This particular unhappy pig was occasioned by a catastrophic pile-up of cars and trucks, many leaking tomatoes, eggs, mustard, or other messy truckloads, and all driven by clothed animals. One pig truck driver, in particular, turned upside-down by the crash, was making a face that my son found satisfying to mimic: the unhappy-pig face, we called it. At this point in his development, before speaking regularly, my son was wildly expressive nonverbally. It seemed he employed every muscle in his face to make commentaries and convey emotions. He used his whole body to gesture: extravagant sweeps of his hands, shoulder-shrugs and head-tilts, at once comic and dramatic. All this nonverbal communication was infectious, and I reproduced and exaggerated his gestures and faces—which in turn caused him to mirror and riff off of me.

I knew I did not have long before words, enablers of thoughts but also stealers of idiosyncrasies, muted his theatricality. And so our family had together created a fluid vocabulary of expressions, facial and bodily, that could be applied to a new situation. The unhappy-pig face represented something sad, forlorn—but also a little bit funny. Just as parents do with their children's early words, I created meaning out of his expressions. An infant saying "Mama" is interpreted as saying the more complete thought, *I want Mama,* or *Where is Mama?* or *I need Mama right now!* The child is communicative, but not fully versed in how to use language, so we interpret her utterance in a way appropriate to the context. I saw my son use the unhappy-pig face in sad-but-silly contexts, and so that is the meaning I gave to his use of it.

But wait. It was a shoe. Was my son really saying that the shoe was sad? That its situation was melancholy? Well, it *was* in a bad way: without a mate, all alone now, the shoe was being tossed. It had lost its laces and was quite smushed. It was a rather unhappy pig.

I was seeing a glimmer of animism in my son, the attribution of life to the inanimate. Psychologists describe a child speaking about the "happiness" of a flower or the "pain" of a broken chair—or noting the sadness of a single shoe on the trash pile, to say nothing of patting a standpipe gently on its head—as making *animistic errors*. Jean Piaget brought the concept to broader attention when he published his studies of his own children's language. In addition to observing his children, noting their utterances, he also asked them pointed questions about their knowledge of the world and recorded their answers. One of his daughters proclaimed to him, in her early years, that "the sky's a man who goes up in a balloon and makes the clouds and everything." Another explained to him that "the sun goes to bed because it's sad" and that boats pulled in from a lake at night are "asleep." Piaget was hooked. For years, he interviewed children, younger and older, about their knowledge of the world. He found them highly animistic. The moon and the wind are plainly *alive,* these children claimed—because "they move"; a fire is alive "because it crackles." A two-year-old brought a toy car to the window with him for it to "see the snow"; another claimed a car "knows" where it goes because "it feels it isn't in the same place"; that an unraveling string turns and twists "because it wants to."

Piaget thought of animism as indication of the child's cognitive immaturity and poor biological understanding. More recent research has belied this claim, showing very clearly that children can distinguish between animate and inanimate things from an early age. Indeed, Piaget himself saw some early understanding brewing: children regularly attribute vitality to the sun, for instance, because it travels through the day, but they would rarely claim that the sun could feel or be hurt by a pinprick.

So what are children thinking about the sun, or the boats, or the shoe? In my mind, animism results from making a perfectly reasonable inference about a new, incompletely understood object: it might be or act just like the things the child knows about already. The concepts and words one has learned are stretched to see if they fit around this new thing. The newly minted language-user is playing with the applicability of new words. In some ways, quiescent boats *are* asleep; the trash-top shoe is forlorn-*looking,* if not itself feeling that way. There is a richness in the child's analogies that we lose when we learn to be obsessed with "appropriate" word use. It is a sign of smallness of mind to think of this appreciation for the shoe's situation or the blooming flower's emotion as an error.

While much is made, in scholastic circles, of how to develop a child's moral understanding, I sense that this built-in animistic tendency gives children a sensitivity that adults cannot teach. The child might, upon collecting a flower, collect several others to keep it "company"; or she might adjust a stone's position on a path to give it different views to gaze at; or feel obliged to put a stone back where it was found, so that it should not "suffer from having been moved." Compassion emerges from imagining the world alive. I myself felt I was losing the sensitivity to broken chairs left out on the street that I once had. When I was a younger adult, I insisted on adopting these chairs, taking them in, mending the weave on their broken seats or the fractured leg. I'd give them a fresh paint and introduce them to the rather large population of chairs already living at my house. Soon, though I had no couch for guests to loiter on, I could host a Thanksgiving dinner for twenty on mismatched chairs. I now pass them by. Maybe my son will renew our collection.

We were nearing our leonine home again. Following my son, our route had zigged, zagged, and doubled back, covering the same street going west and then east. Now we were heading past elm petals and a parked funny truck: already, these were old news. Now he was nineteen months and three hours, and he was too cool for those infant entertainments. He ignored these finds and instead insisted that we walk backward. For my son, backward, sideways, and serpentine routes were just as good (maybe preferable) to a forward gait. Behind us, the setting sun cast long shadows, and it lay our own shadows at our feet, hounding us.

"What's that?" he asked, pointing at his shadowy doppelgänger on the sidewalk.

"That's Ogden's shadow. And there's Mama's shadow. Hello, shadow!" I waved. My shadow, probably six feet taller than I am, waved back.

My son was something between alarmed and transfixed. I encouraged him to talk to his own shadow. He did and, to his delight, the shadow returned his greeting. Passing a cast-away bookcase on the street, left on the curb for trash pickup, his shadow leapt onto the bookcase, crisp and dark against its white painted pine. This shadow was shorter, almost matching the height of my son. As he went to examine it, the shadow got shorter still; stepping back, it lengthened and enlarged.

And that was how we spent the next ten minutes: running up to the shadow ("Little!") and scooting backward ("Big!"), accompanied by the guileless laughter of a toddler discovering another way the world works.

Even between the bookcase shadow and home, I noticed more shadows. A perfect silhouette of a water tower (I thought of its standpipe comrade) was graffittied on the familiar tall building down the street. Every object on the sidewalk had a shadowy appendage. The shadows reminded me of the complexity of our landscape, the sheer numbers of objects on top of one another in the city.

At the steps to our building, my son roared in recognition and prepared himself to step up. I looked at this small, wondrous boy facing a too-high stair and lifting his knee to his chin to climb it. I held his hand tighter. This was a walk I did not want to come to an end.

"To find new things, take the path you took yesterday."

(John Burroughs)

Minerals and Biomass

"A pretty, red brownstone, with a gracious, curved stoop, sat between a large stone building and a handful of white- and red-bricked specimens. But I barely looked up. There was too much to see on the ground."

Find yourself pushing past a man stopped on the sidewalk to examine the stone slabs under his feet, and you might have just missed Sidney Horenstein. This would be a shame, for what this man knows about that bluestone, you want to know. A geologist by training, Horenstein began teaching college, eventually dropping the teaching but keeping the field trips that he had developed in his classes. He has spent forty years coordinating environmental outings for the American Museum of Natural History in New

York City. And he can still be found enthusiastically leading small walking tours around the outcroppings of earth found in upper Manhattan.

I found him at the staff entrance to the museum on a chilly day in autumn. Horenstein approached me smile first. With my reporter's microphone over my arm, I was recognizable as the person who had telephoned him yesterday on a whim; and he was as easily recognizable as the geologist who answered his own phone after one ring and who had agreed to meet me in as much time. Bespectacled, he was dressed comfortably for a stroll, in layers under a light jacket, his voluminous gray hair curling out from underneath a baseball cap. He epitomized the rumpled, unpretentious, slightly distracted scientist of childhood books and my imagination.

Don't be fooled, though, by the casual cap and easy manner: Horenstein is a man who knows vastly more about the past, oh, four hundred million years of the city than you do, and is about to gently let you in on how little you know. He began introducing me to his enthusiasms gradually. As we left the building, before officially setting out on our walk, I made an offhand comment about the paving stones underfoot in the vestibule to the museum, assuming that asphalt would be less interesting to him than a "pure" rock or stone. He glanced at me from under his cap and grinned.

"Well the thing is, there are only two things on the earth: minerals and biomass [plants or animals]. Everything that we have got here has to be natural to begin with—so asphalt is one of those things."

After all, asphalt pavement is a mix of a viscous residue from petroleum, with mineral aggregate thrown in—that is, just rocks, sand, and sticky stuff. Such a concoction is "pure"; it is even recycled. To Horenstein, the buckling of the stones revealed something of the natural topography of the earth underneath. Then he pointed out how even the shape of the paving stones alluded to a natural phenomenon. Hexagonal, they were modeled after the stones used in the long, straight ancient Roman roads. These were made up of basalt in the surprising six-sided shape that naturally forms when lava cools and shrinks.* Back in our vestibule, we did not need to move an inch to see geology in the city: it is just exactly where you are now.

What an epiphany to reconceive a city—which feels just like a jumble of man-made objects—this Horensteinian way. When we think about geology, we think about what is underfoot. But Horenstein maintains, yes, it is what is under us—but it is also what surrounds us: we are inside of the geology of the city.

"What I *see*," he said, gesturing at the museum and its moat-like landscaping around it, "is this: this [building] is a big giant rock outcropping, and this is a grassy plain in front of it, with scattered trees."

In other words, an ersatz natural landscape writ small—mountain and steppe—repeated a dozen times on every single block. Each building is, of course, forged of stone or hewed from a once-living tree. So-called man-made objects are just those that began as naturally occurring materials and are broken apart and recombined to form something customized to our purposes.

Viewed with this lens, the city feels less artificial. The cold stone is natural, almost *living*: it absorbs water, warms under the sun, and sloughs its skin in rain. Like us, stone is affected by time, its outer layer softened and its veins made more prominent. And viewed as a natural landscape, the city feels less permanent: even the strongest-looking behemoth of an apartment tower is gradually deteriorating under the persistent, patient forces of wind,

---

* A remarkable example of the natural paving of the land is visible in Northern Ireland, at a place called Clochán na bhFómharach, where a volcanic eruption left tens of thousands of columns of basalt standing like letterpress type well packed in its shelving.

water, and time. Weather continuously wears at the building, carving its influence by subtraction. Dirt stains; rainwater leaves a trail of salt tearing from a sill to the ground; a decorative copper touch oxidizes—and then its greenness washes onto the stone below it; steel rusts earthly red. Little is as convincing of the naturalness of the city as the process of weathering. Stones become covered with moss; ivy creeps up, disjoints, and eventually obliterates brick; wood darkens with moisture and lightens with age, then gets worn into a soft-cornered version of its former self. Eventually, this town—all towns—will dissolve and become fodder for another generation's construction.

Together we climbed up a few marble stairs out of the museum. Each step was irregularly concave, worn down by the footfalls of countless visitors ascending, and rounded at their leading corners, from countless descents. This erosion is petrified human activity. Each of those steppers toed the marble and pushed seventeen (or so) of its molecules forward, or to the side. After millions of steps, these gentle shovings changed the shape of the rock from tabletop flat to soft undulance. I reached for the handrail, a shiny stripe streaking along its top. The brass was polished by the oils from the sebaceous glands of the millions of hands matching the feet. While I was mulling over the effects people have on rocks, Horenstein brought me back to considering the effects rocks have on people.

For Horenstein is a geologist, after all. As we walked together, he was at once there and not there: walking *with* me but also discreetly smiling and nodding at his "friends," as he called the various stony spirits we passed on the street. And we were surrounded: when you begin to look at stone, it is varied—and everywhere. On the building, on the street; the sidewalk, the sidewalk curb; around tree pits, as fences, as walls. Steps and ramps and overhangs and decorative finials. "Every rock has distinctive characteristics: minerals, grain size, the overall look," Horenstein said. "And so you come to know them like friends. When I walk with people, I don't pay much attention to [the rocks]; it's not courteous. When I walk by myself, I pass these places and they greet me." These friends are well traveled. In a sentence, Horenstein named more than sixty different kinds of rocks he spied on the face and interior of his stately museum. Red granite from Missouri sits next to Rhode Island granite, which is next to stone from the Thousand Islands, a result of quarries closing during the extended construction of the museum building. Inside, a coral reef from the Midwest communes with nearly four-hundred-million-year-old German stone.

Keeping them company by the curb were bollards of iron ore (age unknown) and the relative newcomer, the gingko tree. Horenstein and I stopped to admire the tree, a bright spectacle of yellow leaves and orange fruits on a gray November morning. It had dressed for autumn, yet in its very dressing seemed more robust and lively: it was living and changing on our time scale, quite unlike the iron and granite nearby. Viewed with geologist's eyes, the *Ginkgo biloba* is a most appropriate tree for a city of rocks. The gingko is known as a "living fossil" because it is mostly unchanged from possibly two hundred million years ago. I, and any New Yorker who has walked outside of his house, know the tree for a different reason. Its fruit smells, as a number of early horticulture books gently suggest, "disagreeable."*

Horenstein and I waited at a street corner, and the cold-absorptive property of the stones underfoot were beginning to make themselves known to the soles of my feet. But Horenstein

---

* This is understating things. The fetid seeds, innocuous-looking yellow cherries, fall seasonally and are mashed underfoot. The butyric acid in their skin makes them, smashed, single-handedly responsible for scores of people stopping and visually investigating that odor coming from the bottom of their shoes. The female tree is the responsible party; the male simply turns delightfully yellow in fall and rains its fan-shaped leaves on merry fall-color-seekers.

seemed unaffected by the transient cold. He was looking into the past: across the street lay Central Park. While everything, even the asphalt pavement, is natural in some sense, "no part of Manhattan island is truly nature; everything's been modified," he said, as if anticipating a question about the park's origins. To most city visitors, the park feels like *the* natural element in the city; but Horenstein pointed out that, in fact, the park was constructed, just as the buildings that line it were. Or, looked at another way, one might say that both are equally natural: it is all stone, after all.

The short version of the story of the design and construction of Central Park by Frederick Law Olmsted and Calvert Vaux is well reported on. A rectangular plot of eight hundred forty acres in what is now more or less the geographic center of Manhattan, the park was at the time of its completion north of most of the city's population. It began opening for strolling and recreational business in 1858, replacing fields of sheep and pig farms and bone-boiling mills, and displacing hundreds of squatters who had set up more or less permanent camp on the open territory. Although it looks like a natural landscape, this is by design. The park epitomizes landscape *architecture*: it is a constructed naturalness, with only bits and pieces of the original, undulating topography remaining.

Indicating with his head toward a boulder peeking over the retaining wall to the park, Horenstein said, "Well, right there, that's a natural outcropping." The rock was enormous. Rising from the ground at a sharp angle, it could have looked fearsome, but time had smoothed and softened it. I could see two children playing on its other side, mere parkas-with-legs as they clambered up and down its shoulders. "That's what this whole area would look like [before] they removed some of the hills."

"You can see where they went," he added. He nodded toward the short stone wall that surrounds the park. Those hills that did not fit Olmsted and Vaux's plan were leveled, beheaded, and lopped—and transformed into blocks that formed the wall.

"So they're cousins?" I asked. The liveliness of stones that Horenstein experiences was beginning to rub off on me, and the relationship between park and park wall vaguely, and unpleasantly, reminded me of seeing chickens eating meal made of other chickens.

"Yep."

Those rocks were schist. Manhattan schist. Well, to quote another geologist, "very massive rusty- to sometimes maroon-weathering, medium- to coarse-textured, biotite-muscovite-plagioclase-quartz-garnet-kyanite-sillimanite gneiss and, to a lesser degree, schist."

Yikes! Here I must pause, anticipating a collective drop in reader blood pressure. One risks, in writing about geology, numbing one's readership with the terminology. Schist, gneiss, phyllite; metamorphic, sedimentary; siliciclastic, schistosity. It can be dizzying. I sympathize. I hear "Paleozoic" and I nearly drop right into a deep sleep. Perhaps the time scale of geology (hundreds of millions of years) combined with the amount of multisyllabic jargon used (thousands of terms) has some kind of cumulative soporific effect.

Of course, this is not an exclusively geological effect. What my Paleozoic response indicates is that I am a geology naïf. It is much easier to follow the details of a topic when one knows the least bit about it. When that least-bit develops into a great pond of knowledge, one may rightly call oneself an "expert"—and have the brain to prove it. Expertise changes what you see and hear, and it even changes what you can attend to. Neuro-imagery shows us how expert and naive brains look when attending: fundamentally different. Watch the brains of dancers while they watch a dance performance, and you will see considerably more activity than you would find in the brains of nondancers. Expertise leads to the ability to acquire more expertise.

This is why, listening to Horenstein wax eloquent about geology, I began to think about chess. In the field of cognitive psychology, there is a large amount of research on expertise: how it is acquired, retained, and applied. Since the 1970s, the preponderance of studies have scrutinized the behavior and abilities of one group: chess grandmasters. The reasons are simple. Master chess players have incredibly good memories, for one; and, helpfully, the compact, folding, packable chessboard is a tidy way to investigate the extent of those memories. And those memories are extensive: as soon as expert chess players see a game in progress, they see something quite different from what a novice chess player sees. Their eyes fixate on the board differently than the novice's; they actually see *more* of the board in one glance. They can see not just where the pieces are but also where the pieces came from and where they are going. Often, they can see a dozen moves ahead—perhaps to checkmate—or a dozen moves behind, to the opening gambit.

Grandmasters remember phenomenal amounts of chess. It is estimated that a typical chess master remembers on the order of 50,000 to 300,000 "chunks"—arrangements of five to seven pieces placed normally, not randomly, on a board. They might know, unconsciously, 100,000 opening moves. These memory stores allow them to recall the precise positions of a large number of pieces on a series of games in progress, having seen them once. Sometimes this ability even extends to random piece placements, since a randomly placed piece is surprising, and distinctive, to someone who can see the logic in the piece placement of a game underway. By contrast, when a novice chess player looks at a board, he sees a jumbled arrangement of black and white pieces. If he is attentive, he might later be able to remember a few squares of the board, or a handful of pieces neighboring one another. Nothing else.

The difference is that the scene is *meaningful* to the chess master but not to the novice. To the expert, every piece relates to the others, and every arrangement of pieces on a board relates to previous boards the player has seen or made. They become as familiar as the faces of friends.

The comparison to faces turns out to be apt. For quite a while, neuroscientists have known that there is a brain structure, subsequently named the "fusiform face area," which is largely responsible for our perception and recognition of faces. Humans can quickly distinguish a face in a scene, find a familiar face in a crowd, and remember uncountable faces even after very brief exposures. Indeed, infants' perceptions are face-centered from the beginning. On our walk, my son aimed his gaze at people's faces with a bald interest that seemed to unnerve some people. More recently, researchers have found that this same fusiform face area is also active in chess masters not only when they see faces but also when they are playing chess. Chess objects do not have any facelike features to them, so it appears that this area of the brain helps to process those visual scenes at which we have become expert "lookers." We are all experts at seeing and recognizing faces*; to experts at viewing other scenes, those scenes are just like the faces of friends and family.

I glanced over at Horenstein, who was himself looking at his rock friends. For a split second I swear I could see his fusiform face area pulsing with recognition.

---

* Well, not all of us. A disorder called prosopagnosia manifests in the inability to recognize faces at all—sometimes even, incredibly and embarrassingly, the faces of one's parents, children, or spouse. Oliver Sacks wrote about the strangeness and severity of this condition in one of his early books of essays. The book's title, which has almost come to stand in for the singular Sacksian approach, alludes to an event that occurred to a sufferer of face-blindness: *The Man Who Mistook His Wife for a Hat.* In a very strange subsequent development, Sacks has since revealed himself to be prosopagnosic, a condition he was not himself aware of for many years before writing that book in the 1980s. I cannot do justice to his reflections on his condition in a footnote (though many of his most surprising revelations appear in his own footnotes).

•   •   •

Back to the Paleozoic. I do suspect that others share my (naive) reaction to geology, which is why I spent several eye-crossing days trying to sort out, simply, what schist is. Follow me here: your brain will begin to change as you do.

Schist is metamorphic rock. *Schist* comes from a Greek word for *split*; metamorphic simply means "it changed forms": and in these word histories lie almost the entire story. For schist, the change of form was monumental. It started as mud or clay on the ocean floor. A couple of hundred million years ago, in an era that shall remain nameless, continents collided, land split, and that mud was pressed down toward the core of the earth, squeezed and heated and squeezed some more. For a very, very long time. When it was pushed back up again, it was in a form ultimately re-christened schist. Minerals pushed into the schist give it the layered look that distinguishes it from gneiss, which is more grainy metamorphic rock.

That's it for schist. But that's not the end of the story for us. Schist is the bedrock of my city. Skyscrapers are built on foundations embedded in schist; indeed, for many years the story of the Manhattan skyline, famously tall downtown and Midtown, but short in the streets between, was explained by the need to drive the foundations of especially tall buildings into bedrock. Schist lies right below the surface downtown and Midtown, but is buried more deeply on the intermediate streets.* Here and there, schist pokes up above "ground"—the convenient name for the surface

---

* This story of the dip in the city's skyline, long told by geologists and retold by John McPhee, was recently called into question by a trio of economists who found, perhaps unsurprisingly, economic forces more explanatory of the city's building patterns. They also found the bedrock less invariant than previously described. Perhaps, as is often the case, both stories have some truth.

on which we have placed roads and houses—and silently occupies an entire lot. Central Park is erratically polka-dotted with these peekabooing rocks. Olmsted and Vaux left some in place for natural color, and also moved around some slabs to make a hill from which to appreciate the newly designed view.

On this day, the schist of the city shined with the mica embedded in its layers, playing with the afternoon light as Horenstein and I gazed at it admiringly. I ran my hand across its striped surface. "That's the glaciation," Horenstein said. I must have looked puzzled, because he elaborated: long ago, "glaciers moved over these rocks, ground them down." New York City was covered by glaciers—and though they retreated thousands of years ago, they have left calling cards. We owe the shape of the coastline and the height of the seas to the glaciers' final, inglorious melting retreats. They also left us, on the schist, evidence of their passage. Glaciers move slowly and powerfully over rock, pushing along smaller rocks and rasping the surface. The striped surface I was petting was the result of the ice rasp it received. Horenstein pointed out that the stripes of the rock showed the direction of the ice's movement, in a southeasterly (advancing) or northwesterly (retreating) way. In theory, should you find yourself lost in Central Park, you can find your way out by seeing the schist stripes as a slightly skewed compass of the park: they point you to the southeast and the safety of Midtown. Those piggybacking rocks, "erratics," are the boulders peppered like modern art around the park and the city.

Back on the streets, we were honked at for jaywalking and nearly swiped by a bus. I felt for a moment that we had left the geology behind us, but I was quickly disabused of this notion. A few buildings in from the avenue, we reached a knee-high retaining wall in front of a row house: a short, unlovely white wall separating the sidewalk from the building's trash storage. Horenstein stopped, to my surprise. Apart from a few bright yellow leaves on its surface, the wall was not something to attract me: it looked filthy. Not to Horenstein: to him it looked like gold.

"Limestone. This is a limestone from Indiana. Right here, these are worm burrows."

He fingered a long squiggle on the surface of the wall. It did look like a place a worm had been trapped. But—in the rock?

In the rock. "This rock was once loose stuff"—sediment—"on the sea floor—and you have sea worms going through it and leaving their trails." When the rock was soft sediment, ancient marine worms burrowed through it, eating their way along. The worm-shaped traces Horenstein was pointing out were their paths, chemically changed from passing through the worm's digestive system and fossilized after the worm moved on. On the very next building down the street, he found some of the sea worms' old pals: "Oh, and here's a crinoid! And that's a bryozoan. And that's actually a pelecypod right there."

These were not familiar animal characters to me, but as I started to parse the variegated surface for signs of past life, Horenstein explained who we were seeing. Limestone, a popular building material, is full of the shells, remains, and other traces of ancient animals. In fact it mostly *is* these fossils and fragments. Like schist, it formed in the Geologically-Long-Ago era, on the floor of the oceans—and this ocean was where the Midwestern United States is now. The movement of ocean waters broke up the shells of the small invertebrate animals—snails, scallops, other tiny organisms. Crinoids were little creatures with stems of repeated discs, stacked like wafers. Bryozoans were sedentary animals, shaped like fans, much like coral. Pelecypods, scallopy things, left a trace of the familiar seashell-by-the-seashore.

The crinoid wafers looked like small coins with *O*s in their center, ancient subway tokens for the sea. Suddenly I saw them everywhere. The worm traces read like ancient graffiti down the length of the building. Taking this in, my view of the street was entirely changed: no longer was it passive rock; it was a sea graveyard. I was nearly speechless.

"That's a surprising thing to see on this retaining wall, three-hundred-million-year-old worm tracks," I managed, as though Horenstein could make this fact logical and ordinary.

He did not attempt a response. Instead, he indicated for me to follow him. As we continued down the block, Horenstein was constantly talking. If you think of the city as geology unearthed, it is nonstop: he pointed out features of the sidewalks and streets; walls, roofs, and stairs; atriums, cornices, and decorative rosettes. All were stones; all were known to him. Just this one block, a random sample of any block in this city or any city, contained the history of geology across eras and locales. But it began to look to me like a mash-up history written by lunatics, where red granite from Missouri sat next to stone from Knoxville, Tennessee, and immigrant limestone from France rested alongside the Midwesterners, both politely quiet on the other's accent. Between these sightings were a half dozen of the city's famous brownstones—actually sandstone, I learned, from two hundred million years ago. Underfoot, concrete, made of heated limestone, cement, and pebbles, nudged slabs of quarried granite from Maine and bluestone from Vermont.

We stopped at the bluestone. "It's from Proctor, Vermont," he specified. "It shows a very interesting thing, which we never think about. You see the feathers?"

I laughed. Clearly a trick question.

Wrong. "See right here? See these lines radiating out? . . . That is where the stone mason hit the stone to split it."

The stone has multiple stories to tell us, for it has had multiple lives. Every stone has a parent—for the limestone, it is the creatures of the sea—and even in this latest, most quiet phase of its last hundred million years, it has seen some things. Quarries, created to pull stone out of the earth by the tonful, each have distinctive characters, and the people who know stones come to know the quarries from which they have been sourced. Different techniques of harvesting the rock, splitting the rock into workable sizes, and treating the rock result in characteristic pocks and colors. One method of splitting a rock like bluestone into manageable slabs is to use a "plug" and "feathers"—just a rod and flanking shims, which, when hit into the stone at even intervals, causes the stone to split naturally in two. The lines of the split can be seen (Horenstein called both the tool and the mark it left by the same name), and sometimes even the round hole that housed the plug is clearly visible.

The bluestone's neighbor was a brownstone building whose first-story stone face was textured with pocks. These were the marks of the tools of the stone mason: hammers and chisels used not just to break apart the stone but to decorate it. Two blocks of stone adjacent to each other might have very different pocking, because they were done by different hands.

By the time we reached the end of the block an hour later, I was almost afraid to look around me. This vision of the city as vertical geology had made me dizzy. I could no longer see, and dismiss, a city block as simply a row of uniform buildings neatly snuggled together between avenues. Now the block and its contents appeared to me more as a jumble of geological time and place. Even a single building on West Seventy-sixth Street became a wildly anachronistic historical painting, on examination: Italian marble stood proudly aside 330-million-year-old Indiana limestone, atop 365-million-year-old bluestone from the Catskills and next to boulders of Manhattan schist, some 380 million years old and revealed by retreating glaciers only twelve thousand years ago.

Horenstein smiled in his gentle way. "There is so much to entertain you, you know." He had bestowed on me the ability to be entertained by rocks—not a trivial gift. A street full of rocks, made buildings, becomes a whirlwind tour through eons. I now saw Horenstein, too, changed by his own expertise. He can never walk down a block and not see its geology. We all have our own chesslike expertise in our heads, the place we know impossibly well, the images with which we are intimately familiar, the fine motor skill or athletic grace we can recognize in other people. Horenstein's brain, I thought, is full of rocks, arranged on a chessboard of his own reckoning. He shook my hand, turned away, and walked back to the museum, surrounded by his friends.

"To see is to forget the name of the thing one sees."

(Paul Valéry)

Minding Our Qs

"Forgettable, indistinguishable signs topped the stores, advertising pizza and cleaners."

Paul Shaw shuddered. We were standing in front of an architectural gallery's storefront and facing the quite ordinary-looking, quite benign sign that reported the store's name, mailing address, web address, and opening hours. I read the text. Shaw read not only the letters, but the *lettering*. "Helvetica: the usual thing you'd expect"—that is, the kind of typeface architects like to use— "followed by avant-garde Gothic with *italic*. Eww." Shaw crinkled his forehead. "And then Adobe Garamond, *italic* . . . and then with bad spacing. . . ." He trailed off, sounding bemused.

Shaw is afflicted with the disorder of knowing too much—in this case, about the design of letters. It is a disorder that makes one, as Shaw is, a formidable typographer. He is a professional letterhead. Shaw creates lettering—custom lettering and logos, whole typefaces—and studies it, as a writer and on foot. He leads an elaborate, meandering tour through Italy for a small group as keen on contemporary Roman graffito as on medieval and ancient inscriptions. In New York, he has taught calligraphy and typography at Parson's School of Design for over two decades and has stalked Helvetica (and the various non-Helveticas) in the subway system. This malady, this *literaphilia,* makes one seek, and see, letters. In a city, letters are everywhere.

One trouble with being human—with the human condition—is that, as with many conditions, you cannot turn it off. Even as we develop from relatively immobile, helpless infants into mobile, autonomous adults, we are more and more constrained by the ways we learn to see the world. And our world is a linguistic one, fashioned in and then described with language.

Early in life, an infant will make certain noises that have special resonance to parents. The varieties of cries, from fussy to outraged, are matched by the round warm coos of satisfaction. The infant vacillates between being a catastrophist and a purring kitten. Soon, though, nearly regardless of what his parents do, as long as they talk around him, that infant will start making different sounds. These hums, burbles, and yammers will be the sounds that make up the language or languages he hears floating above his head. His young brain magically distinguishes the parents' language from the hums, roars, and crashes of nonlanguage sounds in the world.

For the first five years of life, it is said, children learn approximately one word *every two hours* they are awake. This fact is intended to impress, and it does. From an adult's vantage, the prodigiousness of the infant mind is enviable (even though we have all had that mind). Most of us struggle to remember that new, curious word we read just this morning in the newspaper. In theory, I would like my brain to sponge up words like an infant's does, but in reality, I also find the child's progress terrifying. Every hour, children are losing more and more ability to think without language—and without the cultural knowledge that language passes along. Every hour, children are less able to not notice words. And to me, the *lack* of language is what is enviable.

Don't get me wrong: I am appreciative of the language that allows me to write that I am appreciative of language. I love, covet, and collect words—silly words and finely formed words and words I'll never use but just feel glad to know. My husband and I own hundreds of dictionaries, whose main roles in our lives are first, to wait uncomplaining until they are thumbed through by us, and second, to then offer up such masterpieces of grace and charm as *omphalos, amanuensis,* and *picklesome*.

Few of these words, though, will I encounter in an ordinary day. By contrast, every day, when walking in a city, driving along a highway, or existing anyplace but deep wilderness, we are beset by dull, tedious words. Signs and storefronts and billboards and computer screens barrage us with text that we, with our language-besotted minds, cannot help but read. As I write this, I hesitantly peek out my office window, and, without my willing it, my eyes track quickly and inevitably to the text on the side of a taxi: NYC TAXI, it reads. $2.50 INITIAL FARE. On its roof, an advertising billboard commands, BE STUPID. As the taxi passes, a stenciled POST NO BILLS is discernible on the scaffolding hulking over the sidewalk. Words are the ample cleavage of the urban environment: impossible not to look at.

Worse still, every city is dense with surfaces, and at some point in human history someone discovered that surfaces are great places to put words and other symbols. Ancient Egypt slaveowners plastered walls with papyrus posters offering a reward for the return of runaway vassals. Greek and Roman merchants placed symbolic signs—a wooden shoe; a stone soup pot—above the doorways of their shops. And the ruins of Pompeii, which in its ashen burial preserved a day in the life of AD 76, has walls covered with notices and inscriptions for real estate ("To rent from the first day of next July, shops with floors over them, fine upper chambers . . ."), advertising gladiatorial games, and promoting electoral candidates (or opposing them: "The whole company of late risers favor [the election of] Vatia")—as well as plain old graffiti and personal messaging: "Health to you, Victoria, and wherever you are may you sneeze sweetly" is still inscribed on one wall, at least two millennia after Victoria stopped sneezing for good.

Today we rarely encounter a public surface completely without words. In New York City, signs identifying shops have migrated from the shop face and door onto awnings, banners, and placards thrust into the line of vision of a passing pedestrian. Should you hope to escape the linguistic attack by ducking into the subway, you will be sorely disappointed. The support columns, stair risers, and banisters in the subway system are plastered with advertisements, excited text and airbrushed photos vacantly hollering as you weave through the crowds. Before freestanding billboards came into urban spaces, a building's windowless wall might be painted with an ad. The faded remnants of the paint still peek out from between more recent developments. (The products advertised, the lozenges and carriages of our grandparents' time, are usually as faded as the paint.) In much of New York City, the mere presence of a stretch of wall *without* words on it is all the prompt a graffitist needs to spray-paint some onto it. Rarely are they wishing Victoria sweet sneezes.

So I had no concern, on heading downtown to meet Paul Shaw,

that we would not see any letters. Still, I wondered, is there any other way to see these words than as linguistic? En route, I gaped at the language that tracked me as I walked down my block, onto a bus, and through a pocket park between avenues. Everything was lettered. Officially, "lettering" describes letters specially "drawn, carved, cut, torn," or otherwise assembled for the purpose of being displayed. More recently, the words *type* and *font* have become lay synonyms for lettering, although you can cause eye-rolling or lip-pursing in a typophile if you use them that way.* What I was seeing were mostly just *letters.* I saw letters on street signs and commercial signs; on flyers, telephone booths, and lampposts; as building names; on T-shirts and knapsacks with logos, affiliations, and statements of purpose; on trucks, declaring their master's and their maker's name. Underfoot, the text on the manhole cover *(Con Ed, NYC)* and discarded potato chip bag *(Lay's, 150 calories)* lay alongside a mouse-sized flag announcing the application of mouse poison to this area. I waited at a bus-stop shelter with the stop name and bus line printed on it, which lettering was overpowered by an advertisement for a television show, which itself was partially covered by a flyer ("room to rent . . . from July 1st . . .") and marred by a graffitied "DOOR" etched into the plastic wall of the shelter. The sides of trash bins say things now. The heels of sneakers. Even my toddler son noted that the holey ventilation grate on the business end of window air conditioners is really just a concatenation of letter *O*s. Instructions, directions, labels, assertions, names, descriptions, suggestions, and commands abound.

Perhaps I should have challenged Shaw *not* to see letters. But I was walking with him not to find more letters but to see them in a different light. Shaw is in love with letters—with finding

---

* *Font* is meant to refer to the set or assortment of letters you are using when you type; the *typeface* is the style of that font.

them, making them, and, as though they were rare shy marsupi-als seen only at night, "investigating their habitats." This love may come from some intrinsic Shawness, but it also comes from being a designer and researcher of letters for so long. To me, the TAXI sign says, well, "taxi." To a typographer, it says *disaster*. When the current version of taxicab signage first appeared, there was a low murmur of outcry among those interested in lettering. Among other missteps noted, the NYC and TAXI are set in two separate type-faces, the kerning (spacing) on the former is so tight as to make the letters almost illegible, and the word TAXI, which features a circle around the contrast-colored *T,* really reads "T-Axi." There was an art—a *lack* of art—in those letters. There was a political or personal choice, an anachronism, a misapplication of type font to signage, a readability study gone awry. There was a history in the letters, and Shaw knew it.*

We met on a sunless day in February. As I approached him, grinning and waving, Shaw's shoulders slumped and his hands dove into his pockets. His hair was dramatically unkempt. Although he glanced at me in greeting, his eyes were scouring the surfaces around us: the walls, the fire escapes, the streets, the lampposts and telephone boxes. He was, as always, looking for letters. Shaw himself was linguistically neutral: his jacket and bag had no visible letters on them.

We had decided to walk down a series of blocks across town from where we both lived, down streets unknown to us. Yet I sensed that these streets already had familiar elements to Shaw. Just as architectural styles identify a city, so too is a city recognizable by the type of lettering that predominates. Putting aside the rash

---

* The typographers' complaints must have reached the taxi powers-that-be, for at press time, a new logo began appearing on taxi doors: simply the *T,* unbothered by any fur-ther letters. One might think that a single letter would be unproblematic, design-wise, but if so, one has not met Shaw.

of newer, computer-font signs now topping identical cell-phone stores and delis, the lettering that exists and remains on buildings represents when a city was built, how it has evolved, and whether that evolution involved destruction or restoration. New York City's style is hodgepodge, but with a distinctive early-twentieth-century twang. The regularity of Art Deco and Art Moderne lettering tells us that the 1920s and '30s saw a lot of construction in the city—construction of a scale and of a quality that has largely survived. Sans-serif Gothic from the late nineteenth century also appears around town, in raised stone letters on the face of a building, for instance. Like building styles, lettering goes through fads, trends: what looks modern now will look antiquated soon enough; what is brash may soon be ordinary.

The block on which we began was chock-full of letters. I tended to see them as words, though, not just strings of letters: I *read* them. GALLERY HOURS, AUTO SERVICE, WHOLESALE LIGHTING, 24-HOUR DRIVEWAY, the always-perplexing HOT DOGS PIZZA combination. We stood in front of a gallery named "Storefront for Art & Architecture." It has a locally famous facade, with irregularly shaped wall panels that pivot on hinges opening over the sidewalk. Exhibits bleed out into pedestrian space, and passersby are swept into the art merely by the act of choosing to walk on the north side of the street. Less famous is the lengthy signage spelling out the gallery's name, which runs along the forty or so feet of storefront. Standing directly in front of it, Shaw noted that the lettering appeared unnaturally broad and tightly squeezed between two horizontal planes. The legs of the *A*s and *R*s were widely splayed; the ampersand had become a squat croissant. Then he realized, they were not meant to be read by us. At least, not by us standing where we were. We took five steps backward toward the street corner: yes, that was more like it. The letters were designed to be read *in approach*: they were stretched and distorted so that from an angled approach, they all looked to be the same size. From this vantage, the gallery name was perfectly legible.

As I loitered, admiring the gallery's way of luring people closer, I mumbled something to Shaw. But Shaw was gone. Indeed, Shaw was continually going missing from my side, pursuing some new letter, as we walked together. He darted to the curb to take in a second-story shop sign from a proper distance; he stopped cold to add to his collection of photos of NO PARKING signs, an unglamorous but very common sign in this city of more-cars-than-parking-spots.

"I look at everything," he said in response to my query about whether he had a preference for a kind of lettering—on a sign or on the ground, deliberate or inadvertent. "When I do walking tours, I forget to look where I'm going." With all the signs, a person could get lost.

We passed a yellow NO PARKING sign painted on a pull-down garage door. The door was topped by red lettering for an auto-service shop: PARK IN AUTO SERVICE. To the side, there were more letters, climbing up the building: small printed signs on the sides of fire escapes at each floor. All were unlovely to my eyes: a verbal mess, part of the visual cacophony of the city. But Shaw stopped to admire them, to look at them directly.

"It's from the forties," he said. It took me a minute to realize he was talking about the awkward auto-service sign. I looked. The letters were jaunty, in the way that uneven, improperly spaced lettering can be, like a child's handwriting. It looked like a bit of a mess to me. But not to Shaw. If we looked around us, most of the shop signs were computer-printed vinyl signs, undistinguished and undistinguishable from one another. Given the ubiquity of the generic shop sign these days, this odd sign became more interesting. "It's hard to find anything that's unique. And somebody had to cut these letters out of wood or something." He paused, finally conceding, "They're all strange."

Their strangeness became more clear as we peered at it. "The *U*" [in AUTO] "appears backwards." Now that he said it, I could see it: the right leg was heavier, thicker, than the left leg. I realized that I knew—without explicitly knowing it—that the thicker leg of a letter *U* is usually the leading leg. I impulsively enlarge and embolden the font I am typing in, Garamond. Its left leg is subtly thicker. Cambria, too. Times. Palatino. One of Shaw's creations, Stockholm. They all wear an asymmetry that we know about but have never seen.

"The *V*"—in SERVICE—"is backwards, too," Shaw continued. "The *R*s are very high waisted."

He was on a roll. The diagnoses came fast and furious now. "The *E* is not high, but the *A* of course can't be. The *A* has to be lower. The *N* has a serif in the lower right, which you often don't find, but in this particular, I won't call it *style,* but with these sort of triangular serifs, that is one place that you do find serifs. It seems to be a piece of wood, but it could be cut out of metal, so . . . they probably were using some kind of blowtorch. And that might explain why the kerns are a little bit different. . . . And the *S* is in two pieces: it has very nice curves."

Shaw's ability to find interest in this splendidly dull, unattractive sign was humbling. I was not only dismissive of the sign, I had a dismissive response built in to my perceptual system, to allow me to avoid even seeing this kind of sign to begin with. Now that I looked at it, I still did not find it attractive. But it had its own character, animated by Shaw's attention. I felt pleased for the sign that it stood boldly individualistic among boring vinyl-awning lettering. Good for you, Auto Service!

This is not to say that Shaw was not judgmental. As we proceeded, I was treated to his verdict on various letters on our route.

This verdict was usually rendered as a version of "That's *awful!*" loitering on the *awww* to emphasize the emotion behind that assessment: it *hurt,* it was so awful. As I learned, the ways that lettering awfulness can happen are various. In one case, a sign's typeface looked to have been stretched on the computer, distorting the letters; in another, the type had been unnaturally squeezed, making the letters plainly uncomfortable. Here, a random final letter was made larger, for no reason (the awfulness of arbitrariness); there, it was the wrong typeface for the building (the awfulness of unsuitability). Another was awful for being mechanically cut, not hand cut. A further awfulness used two versions of a letter form in the same word. We saw, of all things, a shop that makes and sells signs. Its sign was particularly awful.

Shaw looked despondent. This despondency lasted approximately three seconds.

"Look at that!"

I looked. If you are interested in letters, there is a lot of awful about, but there is always something else to see. Shaw was facing a shop whose sign read "PACIFIC AQUARIUM & PET." It was what I, with my non-professional sign vision, would have called "an ordinary sign." Red lettering attached to a long stretch of yellow plastic announced what was probably a desultory array of fishbowls and small birds inside. The sign did not tell us much else. If pressed, I could probably have said that the sign was not new: its style seemed dated, and the whole thing looked to have been battered by weather. My interest was waning, but Shaw's was percolating.

"It's a *Q!*"

The lettering was all in capital letters. I followed his gaze to the *Q* of AQUARIUM. There *was* something different about it. My eyes were slowly adjusting to seeing letters in this light: it was plainly not as *Q*y as *Q*s usually are. We stared up at it, our Adam's apples flashing the passersby, who followed our gaze and looked back at us for the explanation not forthcoming. Still, it took me a surprisingly long time to see what Shaw had presumably seen immediately. Then I saw it: "The *Q* has an internal limb," I exclaimed happily. The flourish of a leg that makes an *O* a *Q* was turned inside, instead of pointing out. It was an inverted belly button.

Shaw smiled approvingly. As if in explanation for his grin, he elaborated: "What looks like an ordinary sign from the past, is not. That *Q* is perfect for it." It was a *Q* he had never seen before.

Was it beautiful? I like *Q*s as much as the next person, but I had not been particularly moved by this one. Still, its eccentricity plainly animated an otherwise unremarkable sign. The *Q* was probably specially designed so its tail did not extend into the phone number sitting below it. I began thinking about *Q*s and the problems that they might present.

It was hardly only *Q*s, though. Over an hour's walk, we encountered lots of problems, and Shaw was happy to enumerate them.

Of a Park's Department sign: "Well, lettering on brick is a problem. . . ."

Of a sign that sat away from the wall: "Well, it's made worse from the depth—there's the shadow problem. . . ."

Lettering around a curve: "It's hard to make letters with straight serifs going around a curve and it's worse if you don't space them out further," which they had not.

The "horrible gap" created in the space between a *T* and an *h*: like *This* and *That,* which can be partially solved by a ligature: Thusly.

Problem letter combinations: "the double *t* in *settlement.* Always a very tough thing . . ."

". . . And the problems with the *R*s."

The problem with the *R*s?

The more we looked, the more problems with letters we

found. Any time I felt my gut twist on seeing a sign, I could just turn to Shaw with a plaintive *Why so bad?* look, and he would diagnose the malady. I realized that I had been blithely walking by undiagnosed lettering disasters my whole life—fairly like the hidden psychological frailties of passing strangers, I supposed.

Shaw's whole perception—his ability to see the art of the letters, and to be moved by the awful or glorious—is evidence of an element of his own psychology. We all have an aesthetic, even emotional reaction to particular scenes or objects we see. Some researchers theorize that we have an innate hunger to pursue visual stimuli that give us pleasure. When we sate that hunger, a flood of the brain's natural opioids is released. What, exactly, gives us pleasure? Things rich with information, packed tight with perceptual pudding that calls forth the knowledge we have and associations we have made with similar experiences in the past. In this way, Shaw's expertise allows him to get a kind of natural high from seeing a beautiful letter.

Over the course of our walk, it was cold enough that my fingers lost their normal flow of blood and the batteries in my tape recorder quietly stopped generating a charge. Shaw, by contrast, seemed to get more energy as we went. As he explained what it was that I did not see, his eyebrows were working, raising and lowering in emphasis, his blinks fast and spirited. At times it seemed as though he was talking *to* the letters themselves, as though they were animate, living creatures. His language about letters certainly evoked a kind of humanity.

An *O,* squished between an *S* and *N,* looked "uncomfortable." Another letter was "jaunty." In prose and speech, Shaw appropriated the language of the human body to highlight anything unusual about the characters he found: an ampersand was "pregnant"; an *R* "long-legged" ℝ; and an *S* "high-waisted." On the web, lettering and typography discussion boards sprinkle animistic characterizations among the professional jargon: an *S* "is a bit depressed," another is "complacent"; an *R* "curtsies," a *G* is "tipsy" ℭ, a *J* "suicidal"; one letter design "needs more humanisticness." There is a lot of humanisticness to borrow, in fact. As Shaw and I passed by people on the sidewalks, I started mentally reckoning which of their features I could use to describe the letters we were seeing. I pictured a "squinty," small-holed *B*; a "large-nosed" *P* wearing a heavy top; a "short-necked" *f* with its crossbar squished at its top.

Most of the letters we saw on our walk were plainly visible, if not usually so closely examined. But it has become the sport of some city buffs to find letters that are mostly invisible: ghost signs. These signs have been intentionally removed, painted over, replaced, or neglected to the point of nearly—but not quite—disappearing altogether. Discovery of one is pleasurable in the way that finding that a cashier has handed you an old Indian-head nickel is pleasurable. I keep these nickels, little totems of the past. And I mentally collect ghost signs, nodding up at them from the street as I walk by. When new construction causes the demolition of an old, tall building, I scan the sides of the adjacent buildings now freshly exposed for evidence of dormant advertising on their broad, windowless walls. To find the occasional nickel, to spy large painted capital letters heralding CORRUGATED BOXES • BOUGHT AND SOLD on a building's flank, makes me feel that if only my eyes were really open all the time, I would see these glimpses of the past everywhere.

On our walk we came across a double-ghost: at least two ghost signs overlapping. A real estate concern and an ad agency both had named telephone exchanges—Canal 6–1212 and Orchard 4-1209—indicating that they dated to the mid-1900s. The signs were romantic and yet horribly ordinary. It is hard to believe that today's signs may be tomorrow's beloved ghosts, but sure as my 1970's polyester tritone shirt and my plebeian 1964 Volvo are now "classics," it will likely be so. For Shaw, the ghost signs were more informative than nostalgic. While you might expect an architectural historian to be able to date a building by its window-frame style or the kind of brick used, Shaw was just as good an architectural detective, using only the evidence from the lettering.

And indeed, a half hour into our walk, we came across a strange architectural dig of a building. Regal but squat, wider than it was tall, it featured a limestone facade (crinoid rich, I now suspected, after walking with Sidney Horenstein) and a central, arching display window. Were there car showrooms along the street, I would have expected they would look something like this building. Shaw went straight into letter-assessment mode.

"This is really cool."

Then he slipped into letter-*detective* mode. What caught his attention first was a delicate and colorful stained-glass sign, miraculously intact, protected by a plastic cover. For a big building, it was a very small building sign. We barely looked at what it *said*; instead, Shaw immediately identified its style: "That is Art Nouveau all the way: all the curves. The *B*, the *E*, the *R*, the *Y*, and the way everything fits together."

Each letter had enormous character. An *A* swaggered; the *B* had a great belly; the *R*, a proud chest; *O* was apple shaped. They were golden colored and segmented, backed by a wash of sea-green glass. It was unlike any other public sign I had seen in the city.

Art Nouveau is a late-nineteenth-century style, and rare in this city: Shaw thought this was a replica. He stood on his tiptoes to try to get a closer look and found a *T-M* embossed on the ironwork. Stepping back from the building, we saw TREE-MARK SHOES engraved into the stone at the top of the building facade—"copying classical Rome," he said, indicating dots carved between each word. Between all of these clues, he guessed the building's date: early twentieth century with a late-twentieth-century revision.

At its edge was a *6,* the building's numbered address. I looked wordlessly at Shaw, who responded: "That's tacked on . . . from a hardware store."

Make that . . . twentieth-century revision with a twenty-first-century hardware-store number.

A simple set of signs, unseen by even those who look at them, is a story of the past. To complete the story, I consulted newspaper archives and city guides. I found that 6-8 Delancey Street was constructed in its current form, first housing a theater and then a retail shoe shop ("shoes for abnormal feet," their ads proclaimed), in 1929. Before that, it held residences, was the scene of a locally famous robbery implicating some New York City detectives, and then wound up as the euphemistic "disorderly house."

It was now a rock club.*

Give or take a decade or two, Shaw's detecting got us a fair biography of the building. There was nothing about the criminality of the police, of course. But it was lettering that led me there.

Three hours of walking with Shaw later, I felt relieved, for the moment, of my compulsion to read what was readable, to parse text when I saw it. Surprisingly, this relief came not from avoiding

* The Bowery Ballroom.

text, but from seeking it out—only to zoom in on the details held within. It was a vision that let me miss the forest and see the trees. Rather than words, I saw the components of words. Some small part of my brain (the linguistic part) rested; the shape-identifying part hummed with activity.

Shaw and I parted ways under a beautiful neon sign, and I doubled back to the spot where we began our walk. It looked much the same. I felt a letdown that my quick immersion in lettering did not enable me, suddenly, to recognize the typeface on the street sign, or identify what was wrong with the spacing of the lettering glaring at me from an awning.

I glanced down from the architectural storefront's name to the paneled wall. It was winter; the panels were closed, quiet. But then I saw something: letters. Each of the panels, far from being a random shape, was cut in the shape of a clumsy, enormous, serifless letter, as by a giant with a blunt X-Acto knife. I had caught Shaw's disease, I realized, *I saw letters*.

As a college student, long ago, with a new Macintosh computer, the type whose screen was dwarfed by its computer case housing, I became a Tetris player. Do you know the game? If you do, I have just induced a nostalgic bubble to pop in your brain. Perhaps only one or two computer games came pre-loaded on the Mac, and this one had an addictive quality. Four simple shapes floated down from the top of the screen, and all one had to do was rotate them and send them scurrying to the left or right in an attempt to fill all the bins at the bottom of the screen before the shape landed, clumsily, on its edge. Tetris players know what happens after hours of playing this game. Objects in the *real* world all turn into variations on these shapes. Entering the library, I saw the jagged pieces that needed to be rotated vertically and set onto a matching shape. I felt the satisfaction of *L*-shaped pieces when looking at intricate floor tiling patterns. A long rectangular restroom sign placed above a square handicapped sign made me thoroughly uncomfortable.

This is a real perceptual phenomenon, not just limited to video-game enthusiasts. The thing you are doing now affects the thing you see next. In conscribing my percepts to that computer screen for hours on end, I began heightening my ability to spot just those shapes that danced across it. Psychology research studying subjects playing Tetris (because psychology research can get away with studying *anything,* it seems) for seven hours over three days reified this "Tetris Effect." The researchers kept the subjects in the lab overnight and woke them up when their brain waves indicated they were entering hypnagogic sleep, unofficially known as "just dropping off to sleep." All of the subjects who did not poke or punch the nasty researchers, but who reported that they had been dreaming, were dreaming of falling Tetris pieces. Even amnesic subjects, who had no recollection of playing the game during the day, reported dreaming of the shapes: they could not explicitly remember what they had been doing, but their dreams told them.

A walk with Shaw left me with a Letter Effect. Now that I saw the storefront panels as letters, I couldn't not see them. Together, they clearly spelled out a nonsense word, heavy in *P*s, *Q*s, and *U*s. Walking back to the subway, I glanced down at my feet as I crossed the street. LOOK was painted on the sidewalk where I stood. I will—but I feel sure that now, my vision changed, the letters will find me.

> "The world is full of obvious things
> which nobody by any chance ever observes."
>
> *(Sherlock Holmes)*

Into the Fourth Dimension

"The front of a church I had never been in had become a gaping hole, its many doors propped widely open."

"If you are ever bored or blue, stand on the street corner for half an hour," writes Maira Kalman. She does not say what she expects will happen to you, your boredom, or your blueness after a half hour, but I now feel equipped to take a stab at it. On a humid, still day in late summer, I stood with Kalman, my friend and sometime co-conspirator in celebrating the ordinary, on a number of street corners for many minutes. We even stopped and sat on a bench at the median of two intersections for a solid thirty-five minutes. Not only was any glimmer of boredom vanquished, but I'll be darned if I didn't grow less azure by the second.

Kalman is an illustrator: her gouached, fantastical drawings are widely published—and then torn out of their magazines and newspapers and taped to office doors and walls. She is also a hoarder, in the finest sense of that word, of both experience and image. Whereas typical hoarders accrue unreasonable quantities of physical—frequently nonessential—items, Kalman restricts her collecting to the noncorporeal.* She does not seem to favor the beautiful or the refined; nor is she only interested in the grotesque or curious. She collects the ordinary, the things that you trip over but have forgotten to look at. Her portrait of a pair of scissors has them planted jocularly (if scissors can be jocular) across a red background. They are not just any scissors, but that's the rub: they *were* just any scissors to begin with. What changed them, or the cakes, tape dispensers, bottles, and lunch trays she has drawn, is that Kalman has looked at them, set them just so—and made us look, too.

I suspected that the reason the street corner is such an unboring, unblue place to stand with Kalman is that a lot of ordinary happens there all at once. I asked Kalman to walk with me so that we could look avidly at the ordinary. One perceptual constraint that I knowingly labor under is the constraint that we all create for ourselves: we summarize and generalize, stop looking at particulars and start taking in scenes at a glance—all in an effort to not be overwhelmed visually when we just need to make it through the day. The artist seems to retain something of the child's visual strategy: how to look at the world before knowing (or without thinking about) the name or function of everything that catches the eye. An infant treats objects with an unprejudiced equivalence: the plastic truck is of no more intrinsic worth to the child than an empty box is, until the former is called a toy and the latter is called garbage. My son was as entranced by the ubiquitous elm seeds near our doorstep as any of the menus, mail, flyers, or trash that concern the adults. To the child, as to the artist, everything is relevant; little is unseen.

* Though she does have more ladders than one would ordinarily expect of an apartment dweller, and is drawn to rubber bands . . .

Once you look at what seems ordinary long enough, though, it often turns odd and unfamiliar, as any child repeatedly saying his own name aloud learns.* I had the suspicion that walking with Kalman would be the ambulatory equivalent of saying my own name aloud a hundred times. An inveterate walker, Kalman was happy to wander the blocks of our shared city with me. We met just off an intersection—an auspicious start for a walk with a person who declaims about street corners.

As we began, our attention went in different directions at once. While I was beelining down the block, Kalman was loitering. The vines peeking through an ornamental gate impressed her. Overhead, she noted that the signage of the scaffolding company featured one of her repeated illustrated motifs, the pyramids. Already, we were in familiar but odd territory. I thought of the German biologist Jakob von Uexküll, known for trying to imagine the sensory world of animals, whose approach has inspired my own research into the perspective of a dog. He observed that we are lazy in imagining the perspective of other *people,* too. "The best way to find out that no two human *Umwelten* [world-views] are the same," he wrote, "is to have yourself led through unknown territory by someone familiar with it. Your guide unerringly follows a path that you cannot see."

Following Kalman's path, I was led straight to a discarded couch on the sidewalk. She spied it and just about leapt out of her skin with excitement.

"Oh my god. That's like the bonanza of bonanza—there it is—it's a sofa on the street, I cannot believe it."

All too familiar with the twice-weekly trash piles that accumulate on city sidewalks as New Yorkers shake their houses

* And so I try it! *horowitzhorowitzhorowitzhorowitzhorowitzhorowitzhorowitzhorowitzhorowitzhorowitzhorowitzhorowitzhorowitzhorowitzhorowitz* . . . and my last name becomes a pulsing, throbbing vowel-crushing machine.

upside down until the dregs fall out, I could believe it. The subject of Kalman's excitement was a long wooden couch set ungloriously near a mound of trash in front of an apartment building. Alfred Kazin, writing about walking in early-twentieth-century New York City, spoke of the "nude, shamed look" of furniture left outdoors as trash. I felt for the sofa: it belonged inside, partnered with stuffed armchairs and flanked by end tables, not exposed to weather and upturned dog legs. But Kalman loved it for the boldness of its naked arrival on the curb. She pulled out a small digital camera and snapped a photo, continuing to intone: "One cushion—it's extra bonanza." The single cushion beckoned the weary passerby to spare a moment to recline. One could see it had been well reclined upon in its previous life. Though the couch's edges were worn and one leg was buckled, it had the look of former elegance: clean lines, no surfeit of frilliness, a proud back. Under our gaze it seemed for a moment to turn elegant again, lightening my heart burdened with the thought that it was now simply trash, unattended by side chairs and a coffee-table manservant.

We walked along, carrying the sofa with us in Kalman's camera, where it would join her collection of photos of spent and discarded chairs and sofas.

"Once you start looking," she advised, "they are everywhere."

We had thrust ourselves off the corner. The real magic of the walk happened then, when we stopped standing there and began to actually amble. With Kalman, walking around the block entered a fourth dimension.

Of course, I—and each of my fellow walkers—had been in four dimensions all along. Still, the progression of the walks was decidedly three-dimensional: always up, down, and along sidewalks. Except when disabused of this notion by my son, I had defined each walk as a straightforward journey along a path between two points, A and B, the beginning of the walk and its end. What we manipulated was the time it took to cover that path: many of my co-walkers had slowed down to look more carefully at something underfoot or overhead. Occasionally we sped up to catch a glimpse in a store window before a shutter was pulled down, or we briefly galloped, as though someone were lighting a match to our tailcoats, to avoid becoming a pedestrian-automobile accident statistic.

But with Kalman, the definition of the space changed. She walked straight off of the sidewalks. I don't mean she floated, in her blue canvas sneakers, hovering inches off the ground. (Though the image suits her, and matches many of her charismatic drawings that pose the subject, be it a pleated skirt or a robin, frameless on the page.) No, Kalman climbed not a tree. Instead, she veered. She abandoned the course. She left the route and wandered into buildings that interested her. Over the course of five blocks and two hours, we went off course a half dozen times. We knocked on the door of the local halfway house. We meandered into a church. We descended into a basement senior center that advertised itself as being specifically for "black social workers." We made it into the anterooms of an odd small museum of Russian art and a Buddhist temple, only stymied by ongoing renovations in each. Eventually, we made it from A to B, but not before visiting all of the later letters of the alphabet.

Beyond this, she implicated others in our walk. We spoke to a mailman, various policemen, a couple of movers, numerous passersby who Kalman for unknown reasons thought might be able to tell us the name of the man featured in a horribly done plaster bust set in a first-floor window, folks working at the halfway house and senior centers, people entering and leaving the church, people who had simply stopped in their walking (for reasons of infirmity or tourism) somewhere near where we had stopped, and an office worker and two cooks doing work behind windows open just enough for Kalman to call in to them and for them to acknowledge us.

Kalman's boldness was matched by my admitted discomfort. I try, as an accredited city resident, to manage coexistence with millions of strangers by keeping pretty much to myself on the street. I had not spoken to this many people on the street in my last hundred ventures from my house. Kalman forced me, reluctantly, to remove my invisibility cloak and read the social-workers sign as though it were really inviting us in. Her frank interest in others made me think about the feeling of privacy we carry with us from our homes into public, where there is truly no privacy. I had not noticed, until forced to by Kalman's sociability, how I was engaging in a fundamentally social activity by walking out in public.

Still, we all have a sense of the "appropriate" personal space around us—a kind of zone of privacy that we wear, even on the social sidewalk. Indeed, we have many coencentric circles of personal *spaces,* plural. The Swiss zoologist Heini Hediger, elaborating from studies of animal behavior, proposed that the personal zones around us fall into a few categories. Those with whom we do not mind "inescapable involvement"—as our loved ones—can broach the closest zone and get nearer than eighteen inches to us. At that proximity, we can smell them, feel the heat of their bodies, their breath, hear the small sounds they mutter or emit. We can whisper together. Most social interactions take place in a comfortable zone about one and a half to four feet away—closer in some cultures (Latin American) than others (North American). Friends can waltz through; acquaintances can hover on the edge. We have a social distance up to twelve feet from our bodies for more formal transactions, or for those we don't know well. Beyond that is a kind of public distance in which we use our "outdoor" voice. All of these zones are artificial, varying with differing relationships, based on context and the physical setting—but we have a bodily sense of the reality of these spaces. Violate them, and we may feel stressed and anxious.

Kalman minded people's spaces, but she seemed to see *personal space* as an indication that there was a *person* in that space to engage with. Of course, the persons had to be willing to be engaged with. We make judgments about people—their trustworthiness, their intelligence, their beauty—in glances that take less than a third of a second. All those quick glances aimed at Kalman and me must have added up to many seconds' worth of judgments over the duration of the walk. (Apparently, we were judged to be basically nonthreatening.)

These engagements and our path-veering led, ultimately, to various curious episodes. Our first foray off course was into the halfway house. It did not identify itself as such—but its entranceway distinguished it from the austere residential buildings on either side. In the vestibule there was but one sign. Not an identifying placard—at least, not directly. "Please remove your hats on entering the building," it read.

Kalman immediately looked for an *informant*. She inquired of the weary, uniformed man sitting behind the window at the facility's entrance about the sign's provenance and meaning. We were clearly the first to ever so ask. He looked at us with a long, steady gaze. I looked away, but Kalman happily persisted. As they chatted, I looked around at the anteroom of the building. This space was roughly seventy feet as the crow flies from my own living room; I had never been inside. The same is almost certainly the case with all of the buildings in the vicinity of your own home. Though we become accustomed to the look of our neighborhood from the street, it is but the skin that we see. Though this building looked residential, the entryway revealed its business core: Plexiglas set off the guard's post; the elevator was of the industrial varietal, and a handful of visitors stood in solemn observance of its slow travel. The room was unlovely but eye opening. We went no further. Back outside, my vision was changed: I noticed that more than a usual number of people edged the tree pit outside; cigarette butts by the curb now indicated to me the presence of many people forced to go outside to smoke. I imagined that every hatless pedestrian was headed into that building, probably feeling a little naked of pate.

As we left, I swung around to watch the building click from its old, familiar face to this new one, informed by what I now knew of its inside. The door settled into its jamb. Through a window I could see the guard's eyes following us. So much for being invisible. When Kalman wanted to get the guard's attention, she looked him in the eyes. Now we were the subject of his gaze. This may seem trivial: gaze and eye contact are the most simple of acts. But they sit squarely at the center of our advanced social intelligence. There is a reason we can imagine others' perspectives, have empathy, infer others' goals, communicate—and it begins with a shared gaze.

It could be a happy accident of pigmentation, this interest in each other's eyes. The sclera of our eyes lost its dark coloration somewhere on the route between chimpanzee and human. With the whites of my eyes as backdrop to my bright blue irises, the direction of my gaze suddenly becomes plainly distinct. I cannot avoid being spotted looking at you by turning to the side and sneaking a peek out of the corners of my eyes. (Not only can you see me looking, I would look sneaky.)

Even worse, as our ancestors came out of the trees and onto the plains, the entire shape of both our faces and our eyes changed. Our faces flattened: while the human face allows us to smush it fully against a windowpane or to receive a coating of pie from a pie tosser, the monkey's face has a prominent snout, more like other mammals. The architecture of the human face is centered on the eyes, not the mouth or nose. Our cheekbones are conspicuously high—right below the eyes. The forehead and eyebrows complete the framing on the other side. Even the nose gets in the action, serving as an indicator of where our faces are pointing. Unlike most mammals, we have highly developed facial musculature, including around the eyes and even in the eye itself. What we lost in expressive potential when we lost tails is made up for by our ability to squint an ironic half smile—distinct from a full-bore joyous grin or a grimace. Along the way, too, the shape of our eye opening got squashed, revealing more of the whites.

What pure disappointment these evolutionary developments might have been to their first bearers. Just when they thought that their attention was private, now everyone else could read it on their faces. It could be no worse if a Magic Marker traced a circle around your genitals when you felt attracted to someone, or your forehead scrolled the text rambling through your head in private thoughts.

But our ancestors dealt with this change, and it was the harbinger of the development of the so-called social brain of present-day humans—one keen on others' faces and eyes, and on the personhood behind those features. There is no one area in the brain that organizes our social understanding; instead, it is a network of regions in the cortex and subcortex, but especially parts of prefrontal cortex, right behind our forehead. There is something lovely about how eyes, windows to the mind, are contemplated in the space nearly right behind them. But they get there indirectly: the occipital cortex, processing raw data received through the eyes, is at the very back of the head.

In that extra loop through the cortices of the brain, gaze gained meaning—lots of meaning. Gaze reveals that we are attending, and we react physically to seeing someone gazing at us. The sympathetic nervous system, responsible for revving up our bodies to run when we spy that lion, and for calming us when we are sitting down digesting dinner, treats gaze as something of interest. It reacts in the way it would if we saw a lion—just more moderately (unless it is a lion's gaze). Adrenaline starts coursing through us, our heart pitter-pats, our breath subtly quickens, and we begin to sweat. How we feel about that rush of excitement depends on what we think the gaze means. And this depends on context: is it our lover gazing at us (I must really love him back) or is it that creepy guy across the subway car (I've got to get out of here)? Fear and sexual attraction are in the head; the body prepares the same way for both.

In all events, the gaze is salient. We notice it, and we notice it from day one. Newborn babies can do very, very little when they first appear in this world, but they are already making one choice clearly. They prefer to look at a face looking toward them than one looking away. Later, this mutual gazing between oneself and others will be a way to convey a sense of closeness or understanding. Indeed, the easiest way to get an infant to smile is to simply let them see you looking right at them.*

From those first gazes on, we look at the ones we love, and we tend to love the ones we look at. Or those who look at us: researchers have found that in a controlled setting, we like unknown people who gaze at us more than those who do not. When we are in an audience, we are delighted by eye contact with whoever is on stage. Not only do we rate them as better speakers or performers, we think they are stronger, more competent, more attractive, and more credible.

---

* It's not you, alas: any egg shape with eye shapes within it that you show to an infant will elicit coos and smiles of delight.

Unless they stare. A fleeting glance can, if it is less fleeting, turn sinister. The gaze of a stranger is unwelcome. Even the gaze of an oil painting can be disconcerting. Part of the animacy of Renaissance portraits is that the eyes seem to follow you, half-flirting and half-glaring as you shyly try to duck out of its gaze. It is the cues of the face that cause us to feel this way, since they never change: if the subject's eyes are locked on the viewer's from one vantage, they will always be so locked, wherever that viewer goes.

My solution to get out of this eye lock with the building guard? Walk out of his view. A block away, though, Kalman found the senior center, another place to enter. I had passed this place for years and never more than glanced at it. A few short stairs later and that story was changed. We walked through heavy gun-metal doors that looked too heavy to be propped open by the wooden shims at their feet. The room beyond was certainly a public space—its sign and open doors indicated that—but not a beckoning one. As we entered, we took on the mode of visitors to a church: quiet observation, neither talking nor conspiratorially whispering together. Inside, there were established games of bingo underway; *O47* and *N4* excited a number of players to dutifully stamp the array of cards laid out in front of them. The walls were decorated with admonishments and instructions. One hand-stenciled sign told us that lunch was $1, a bargain on the west side of Manhattan. A man's onion-chopping cadence sounded like it might be a Ping-Pong game, and Kalman's face brightened at the possibility. A connection between Ping-Pong and onion-chopping was thereby forged in my brain. We watched the onion performance, were handed an "Activities calendar" by an employee, and aged fifteen years before we decided, by mutual head nod, to turn back to the street.

Approaching an intersection (a *corner*), we slowed, instead of hurrying, when the *Don't Walk* sign blinked at us ominously. Getting stopped allowed us to notice the miscellany that was hanging out at the corner all the time. I learned from my son how much happens when you are waiting for the thing that is supposed to be the big event. He never complains about waiting for the subway: simply the platform provides thrill enough, with trains screeching and zooming by, flashes of lights and rumbles underfoot, swells of people entering and exiting. Kalman slowly passed a line-up of newspaper bins, considering each one as though they were displayed for sale at a flea market. I followed the arc of a tossed crumpled paper bag that failed to pass the lip of its target huddled by the streetlight. Together, we gazed, bemused, at a sign giving instructions for the *Walk/Don't-Walk* street-crossing signals for pedestrians (weren't they self-explanatory?).

The light turned, and we followed the instructions, feeling dutiful. Kalman spotted a church up ahead. At this point into walking with her I suspected what would happen next: we would be going in. Of course, this church, too, I had never visited, despite its open doors, shaded interior—so alluring from under the watch of the sun of summer—and occasional hallelujahing chorale. Once inside the church, we wandered down the middle aisle, as churches seem to allow anyone to do regardless of denomination, personality, or number of cameras around one's neck. From inside, the street was visible, but seemed suddenly distant. As we walked, our cadence slowed, and we were no longer proceeding at New York pace. We were walking leisurely, at a tourist's pace, because we had become visitors in our own city. The street signs were in a foreign language and the churches were all to be checked off on the map. After a tour down and back the aisles, we met again by the exit. Kalman spotted a wooden sign over a recessed area in the wall. POOR BOX, it read—a label at once no longer valid (there was no box) and also apt: *Poor box! Gone missing from its alcove!* She snapped a photograph.

Back on the street, Kalman was church-prompted into talking about her own churchgoing. This was a definite fourth-dimensional fact for me to learn about this New Yorker born in Tel Aviv. But she loved the music of the congregation at Saint Thomas Church on Fifth Avenue. And she marveled at their permissiveness in letting even a non-believer warm their benches: "You can do whatever you want—well, maybe not anything you want. But you can come and go. You can do *anything* and you don't have to *do* anything."

I was beginning to see what Kalman saw. She did not see a space as defined by an edge, but as an infinitely explorable openness. The church may seem to be about religion, but for her it was about music and company and freedom of allegiances. The senior center might seem to be for seniors, defined by its name to exclude us, two nonsenior non-social workers, but its doors were open and that was all it took for Kalman to wander in. Take a left turn where you ordinarily take a right; open the gate to the block garden you have never visited; view the passerby as a person who is waiting for you to speak to him.

Kalman's movements and behavior also highlighted, however inadvertently, the multiple claims to space in a city. Cities are filled with a variety of private and public spaces, spaces one can enter and spaces one must be invited into. In the latter case, an open door may be the only sign that the public is invited in (but owners reserve the right to take a look at you and boot you back out). At times the dividing line is non-obvious, but most urban residents instinctively mind these boundaries and do not cross into private space. City sidewalks present a great confusion of private and public: they are generally public space, which means they are owned by the city—which in turn means that anyone who wants to plant his stake on the sidewalk must pay the city and get a permit. With municipal permission, a restaurant, under private ownership, can take over a portion of the sidewalk for outdoor seating. The newspaper stands pay for the right to appear on the sidewalk, as do food carts and other vendors. Should you just want to walk and speak loudly, declaring your protest of this or that, or should you want to display art or be art on a public sidewalk, you need a permit. But sidewalks are also the responsibility of the abutting building's owner. These owners must repair, clean, shovel, and generally maintain the sidewalks in front of their buildings—but they are not "theirs."

Urban buildings, by contrast, are generally private spaces, often owned by one party (a landlord or corporation) and leased by another (a tenant). In buildings owned by cooperatives, the corporation owns all the space up to the rooms themselves, including the interior of the walls. In New York City, there are also "privately owned public spaces," which developers create and maintain in exchange for the right to build taller buildings.

What struck me about Kalman was that she moved through all the spaces with ease. Had she opened a mailbox on the street (federal space) and lifted out a letter, I would not have been surprised. Sure, she didn't climb any walls, but her ability to transcend the social and cultural knowledge of where one is allowed to go felt like a superpower.

Is there something about Kalman's brain that leads her to see more *possibilities* on the street than I do? Simply put, yes. Neuroscientists are just beginning to put together a picture of what exactly it might be. The difference is not simple, nor is there a canonical "creative brain" that can be spotted from the outside, as if using a phrenologist's chart to identify the bumps of a creative person's skull.

One research team, though, reported a correspondence between the brains of those who seem to be especially creative thinkers. Certain people, they found, have fewer of one kind of dopamine receptor in the thalamus of the brain. These people also performed well on tests of "divergent thinking," in which people are asked to concoct more and more elaborate uses for ordinary objects, for instance. The reduction in receptors might actually *increase* information flow to various parts of the brain, essentially allowing them to think up new and interesting solutions. "Thinking outside the box might be facilitated by having a somewhat less intact box," the researchers wrote.

Objects and people on our route became possibilities for interaction, rather than decoration or obstruction, as the urban pedestrian might define them. With that in mind, Kalman and I approached a streetlight. I cannot say I had ever approached a streetlight before with such anticipation. I had walked by streetlights, run into streetlights (then cursed streetlights), watched my dog spend precious minutes smelling the urine on their bases. You have seen these lights in your city. Indeed, in New York there are two or three on each side along every city block . . . wait, have you really seen them? *Yes, of course I have,* you say to me impatiently. And so you have. So you know that the most common streetlight typically extends from a pole that is round or octagonal—not rectangular—or is hooked like an inverted *J*; that the legs of these poles are thirty feet tall, more than three times as long as the arm holding the cobra-headed lamp; that there are white and yellow sodium lightbulbs (and that we feel calmer under the yellow), which are typically one of two streetlighting wattages; that there are a variety of possible pole bases, none of which is entirely impervious to dog urine. But you are getting restless, I see, since you have seen streetlights, and you know about them already.

This streetlight pole was festooned. Someone had decorated it with a few half-hearted flyers, attached at eye height with serious packing tape. An advertisement for clarinet lessons stopped Kalman in her tracks. The bottom edge of the paper was cut into strips cut and bent hopefully for easy grabbing by clarinet-interested passersby. Kalman grabbed one. She had begun to learn the clarinet the previous year, she revealed, as part of a project for a class she teaches at the School of Visual Arts. For her curriculum, everyone was tasked with learning a new instrument, then taking a walk by themselves, writing down "what was going on in their minds," Kalman mused, looking at the wee bit of paper in her hand. "Then one of the students took all of the texts that they wrote and made them lyrics for a song using all the musical instruments." They were to perform the music on the street but kept being thwarted by the weather. She sighed. "So we never performed it out on the street where it was meant to be; it was meant to be walking music."

We left the flyer otherwise intact, its strips fluttering in the breeze. I did briefly consider taking up the clarinet. I could hear someone practicing piano awfully through an open first-floor window. We walked down the street to this music. The street provided the accompaniment.

ANIMATE CITY:

Everything That Won't Stand Still

"'Tis very pregnant,
The jewel that we find, we stoop and take't
Because we see it; but what we do not see
We tread upon, and never think of it."

(Shakespeare)

Flipping Things Over

"A wooly caterpillar, his head crowned with four fearsome green horns, moved lazily on the first step, heading nowhere good for caterpillars."

If you do not get excited about finding a blowfly paralyzed by a parasitic fungus on the bottom curl of a leaf tip, or upon spotting the globular, smooth-edged holes in a leaf that are the characteristic sign of a munching tortoise beetle, then perhaps a walk around your block with Charley Eiseman is not a good idea. But for anyone who as a child marveled at the metamorphosis of a homely caterpillar into an iridescent butterfly, or who has admired the tenacity of a slug or snail assiduously consuming their tomato plants, this sort of walk will open your eyes to the unnoticed population underfoot, overhead, and, alarmingly, onbody.

It is time to consider the bugs.

Even when you see no bugs before you, even when the ground looks still and the air looks clear, they are there. Millions upon millions of bugs. And there are even more signs of bugs past: on vegetation; in leaves and bark; in characteristic leavings; in egg sacs, cocoons, spent exoskeletons, and built structures; on brick, dirt, clay, and on your own skin. Their ubiquity does not make them inherently interesting, of course. In fact, as a culture we tend to value the rare over the common, in our sensibilities and in our policies. We mourn the passenger pigeon, hunted out of existence a century ago, but vilify the pigeon on every city street; we keep bunnies and mice as pets yet kill rabbits and mice not born in pet stores. Of course, there are hundreds of rare—federally named as endangered—insects: the "superb" grasshopper; eleven pomace fly species; assorted weevils, ants, beetles, and midges. But the prevalence of bugs (or, better, *Arthropoda*—true insects, arachnids, and otherwise) only highlights our obliviousness to them . . . most of the time: we certainly notice when a cockroach darts across our dinner table or when a male mosquito, covering for his blood-thirsty mate, buzzes in our ear.

The insects' advocate is Charley Eiseman, a young man with a calm manner and a trim beard befitting the naturalist that he is. Though I had not met him before, he proved easy to spot: wearing a plainly genuine expression and a flannel shirt on a sixty-degree day, he stood out among city folk. Eiseman has the quiet footfalls and unassuming presence often found in native New Englanders. He smiled broadly in greeting, but he also looked at me a bit like he was trying to determine what kind of insect I was.

A field naturalist by training, Eiseman confessed to having an overweening sensitivity to all living things. While working out of doors teaching tracking classes and conducting salamander surveys, he began noticing "little mystery objects"—the spoor and leavings of insects and other invertebrates. Wanting to have a field guide to these tracks, and finding none, he and his friend Noah Charney set off on a fifteen-thousand-mile, forty-day journey to document evidence of invertebrates—what is called sign—in all the major ecotypes in North America. The result of their travels and research was *Tracks and Sign of Insects and Other Invertebrates: A Guide to North American Species*. The book is a marvel: a rollicking, seemingly plumbless guide to the innumerable indicators that insects leave of their presence.

Eiseman met me on an early-September afternoon in a parking lot in Springfield, Massachusetts, an industrial city that never had an urban reincarnation and is very unpromising for walking, as far as I was concerned. But it was near Eiseman's hometown, which is not urban at all, so this was where we converged. I asked that we meet in a parking lot on the strength of a mention in his book. In the introduction, Eiseman writes that he and Noah stopped on their invertebrate tour to visit Noah's mother in Tennessee. Five hours after they said their good-byes, Noah's mother left her house to find the fellows still in the driveway. Turning over sugar maple leaves and flipping logs, they had found enough insect sign to postpone, for the time being, their trip to the "wilderness" where real nature was to be found.

I was secretly hoping that we would not make it out of the parking lot ourselves. If a driveway holds an ecosystem, what of a parking lot? Perchance a universe. Sure enough, we were barely ten seconds into our walk before he spotted a few beautiful orb weaver webs, followed by a handful of funnel webs along a hedgerow at the lot's edge. He did not know the name of the orb weaver ("An arachnologist might be able to tell you," he said unhelpfully for those of us having no arachnologist readily available), but here, as throughout our walk, it was clear that the specific naming was not the point. Instead, the fun is the discovery of the thing at all.

The funnel webs turned out to be a repeating motif of our walk.

Once we saw one, it was as though they were imprinted on us, and we were unable not to notice another. The characteristic dense white web shows up again and again—at the top of a row of hedges in front yards, along intersecting brick walls. If you look more closely, you will see the titular funnel: a smoothly rendered spout in which, if you are lucky, the spider is hiding, waiting for some walking insect to happen upon her lair and submit to her jaws.

To look at insects up close is to see the hasty cycle of birth, violent killing, and death. Few insects are humanitarians, and even herbivorous insects work great damage to the leaves, buds, grasses, and stems they eat. But Eiseman and I were looking less for insects, and more for the traces of insects past. In following their tiny footsteps, we were forensic insect hunters, looking at the evidence of their criminality they have left in their wake. Insects are messy eaters, like to storm a place and live it up, and rarely clean up after themselves (except those polite larvae that eat their own egg cases). They shed their skin, excrete willy-nilly, plunder and pillage, and move on: the insect equivalent of a mad party with only hastily removed clothing, broken bottles, and other detritus left behind. Positively uncivilized.

I could have loitered over the funnel webs for a while, but Eiseman had darted off. An urban walk with Eiseman is decidedly nonlinear: one minute he is beside you, the next he has veered over to a tree pit, or to a piece of street furniture—a fireplug or lamppost—and is scrutinizing its surface for bugs. We did leave the parking lot, but over the next two and a half hours, we managed to cover but two-thirds of a mile. At that rocketing pace— about a quarter-mile in an hour—we could have been overtaken by nearly all the species we saw on our walk, including some of the larvae. This was a typical pace for Eiseman, who, as a healthy young man, takes about ten hours to complete a five-mile hike, waylaid by logs whose undersides need examining and snakes demanding pursuit. He has spent uncountable hours in a quarter-acre vacant lot in Burlington, Vermont, where he once lived: a few dozen photos for his insect guide came from that single plot.

Over those hours, on the most ordinary of city blocks, we saw nearly all the categories of insect sign mentioned in his book: egg cases (the egg sac of a common house spider along a brick wall); exuviae—a fancy word for the discarded exoskeleton of a fly (a mayfly, attracted to and molting on a streetlight); parasitism (gruesome blowflies overtaken by a paralyzing fungus); droppings (earthworm droppings, a large constituent of what we call "dirt"; jumping spider droppings, black speckles in white dots); webs ("*everything* has a spiderweb on it," Eiseman advised); cases (spider "retreats"—structures for temporary spider-hanging-about); leaf mines (the work of the oak-shothole leafminer, whose larvae fashion rounded holes as they eat their way into adulthood); galls (small deformities on a grape plant leaf, inside of which we found uncountable secreted orange aphidlike things); mounds (small hills with burrows in their middle erupting out little brown "sidewalk crack" ants); and even sign on vertebrate (a mosquito bite on my own calf that swelled excessively).

Though this listing belies it, our walk did not start out auspiciously. After the initial web excitement, we headed down a block that looked terrifically dull. Desultory, underwatered sycamore and London plane trees lined the edge of a tired concrete path. Nothing moved; the afternoon was hushed. We were alone on the street, with not even a bored, idle squirrel for company. But Eiseman beelined to the trees and flipped over a leaf.

"This jumped out at me," he said as I followed him, vexed. What *this* was was not obvious. He twisted a leaf between his fingers just overhead. I looked up at it: it looked vaguely unhealthy. Then my eyes adjusted, as if coming into a cool, dark room after a summer's afternoon outside. Suddenly I looked *through* the leaf—

and that was when I began to see what he meant. The green tissue was peppered with black and yellow spots, "the characteristic feeding signs of the sycamore lace bugs," Eiseman explained. "They don't make holes; they just suck the green juice out and make it turn yellow." These lace bugs lived on the underside of the leaf, which, on close examination, was splattered with their excrement—those black spots. Nearly indistinguishable from the excrement was a bevy of nymphs. "They are very beautiful bugs," he said, pulling down the leaf for my examination, and in the process, raining little nymphs and young adult lace bugs all over his hair and shirt. If I squinted, and suspended disbelief, the adults were indeed almost pretty, their transparent wings crisscrossed with raised and darkened veins.

I considered these little guys while Eiseman regaled me with lace-bug trivia. The bugs are specialists, often preferring just one tree: there are sycamore lace bugs, birch tree lace bugs, and oak lace bugs. They are what is called, sweetly, *true bugs*: of the large order *Hemiptera,* which includes all sorts of bugs that do not have chewing mouthparts. Instead, the lace bugs have beaks, and invent creative ways of getting out of eggs. The oak-tree varietal grows up in tiny flip-top egg lids that pop open when they are ready to hatch.

As we moved on, I pointed out the young adult bugs now speckling him. He did a perfunctory brush at his hair and smiled: "It doesn't matter." For the rest of the walk a few lace bugs cruised happily on Eiseman's chest.

As we headed down the sidewalk, every new species of plant we came across became an opportunity: an opportunity for new evidence of an insect. In an ordinary tree pit encircling its featured tree, a few plants at its base, and tree detritus (fallen leaves, twigs, seeds or nuts or seedpod), there might be thousands of bugs and spiders and other things to munch on the bugs or spiders. Soon I was a co-participant in what seemed to be the major investigative strategy of the Searcher for Invertebrate Sign: flipping things over. *Flipping-Over* behavior marked Eiseman's approach to most things, "if things aren't jumping out at you," he said (and hopefully they're not). Eiseman was continually turning over leaves, which were often his first approach to a tree. "If you're looking for an insect specific to a tree," he suggested, "the leaves are the place to look." Sure enough, nearly every single tree we passed bore the sign of some bug. *Holes* were rife. Just as the beginning arborist begins to use a leaf to identify a tree, it is soon clear that the *holes* of a leaf can be used to identify the hole-*maker*. In the motley array of trees, tree-pit plants, and wild weeds growing roadside and between sidewalk squares on our walk, we saw a dozen different kinds of leaf holes. Apart from the tortoise beetle and shothole leafminer holes, we saw large ragged holes like those a katydid or grasshopper might leave; punctuative holes that mimicked commas and semicolons; and birch leaves with neat, hole-punch circles, the sign of the aptly named leaf-cutter bee. The bee builds its nest elsewhere, but mines the leaves to make cylindrical cells for her eggs.

Other leaves were intact but unusually shiny. A resolute shiny streak indicated that a slug had been sliming along the leaf overnight. A slap-dash shining job was probably a wash of "honeydew," the clear excrement of aphids, which itself draws other bugs and birds to feed on the sticky stuff. Holes and slime are only the beginning. A single leaf, nonchalantly fanning itself in the breeze, might be the repository of one of dozens of types of sign.

"Here's something," Eiseman said—and repeated on our walk together. There was always something. In this case, it was a browned, curving scribble on a leaf. "This is a leaf mine of a fly larva," he explained, ending with a period. He must have sensed that I thought at least ellipses were due, and elaborated: "The fly inserted its egg there"—he pointed at the base of the trail—"and the larva is living between the epidermal layers, and is munching along and making a wider trail as it grows bigger."

My mind boggled a small boggle. The strip of denuded leaf we were looking at was a path cleared by a young fly who was growing up sufficiently quickly that the path he left in his wake had widened over the course of his living on that one leaf.

These leaf mines, I learned, are left mostly by moths, beetles, and flies, whose larva create a visible trail as they plow along, chomping leaf tissue. They spend their whole larval life in one leaf and then emerge as an adult. Many of the mines are very particular to the species of insect: the female always inserts her egg in a particular place, such as at the leaf's edge or base. As a result, by looking at the starting point of the mine one can (if one knows quite a bit about insects) determine the larval species that is living there. The *type* of trail is species-specific, too. Some leave serpentine trails that draw an inscrutable image along the canvas of the leaf. Other mines cruise along the veins of the leaf. Still others are more blotch than trail, growing pools of ungreen leaf. We saw mines that followed a serpentine course and ones that hugged the leaf's perimeter: leaf-as-jogging-track.

It is not mines but *galls* that are the crowd-pleasers of the insect-track-and-sign world. "Some of the galls are what draw people in first," Eiseman said with a straight face. This was initially hard to believe. A gall is a growth, a plant tumor, caused by a critter burrowing into the tissue of the plant when it is developing. The small lump, fold, or pouch that results serves as shelter and often food for the nymphs that the midge, sawfly, moth, aphid, wasp, or mite (not technically an insect) lay in it. To my eye, many galls looked a bit cancerous, the leaf blighted or with an embarrassing skin condition.

"How do the plants endure all this?" I wondered aloud. "Most of it seems so destructive."

"Being deciduous helps: they get to refresh their leaves every year. Galls are a sort of agreement that's been worked out, concentrating the damage to one spot. It gives the insect shelter and food."

"The tree doesn't get anything."

"It gets less damage."

Most galls do no serious harm to their tree hosts. Some galls are almost picturesque—and adorably named. I could imagine trying to hunt for the fuzzy red "hedgehog" gall; the flamboyant "sea urchin" gall, boldly pink and spiky; or the "wool sower gall," a soft dotted pom-pom that reaches outward like a flower.

Each of these winsome galls actually holds tiny wasp larvae that reside on oak trees. If your city has oaks, you could find galls down the street. When I returned to New York City, I was barely out of the train before I come across an oak and quickly found a gall, green and pealike, on a leaf.

I started to wonder about wasp aesthetics: their galls are architectural beauties. If not inspiration for humans, there is a theory that galls might have served as a sort of inspiration for trees. As Eiseman described it, the theory suggests that galls kick-started trees into bearing us the fleshy fruits we now cultivate greedily, such as peaches and plums. If that were the case, fruits are really just evolutionary extensions of galls, developing because of wasps laying their eggs in the plant's flowers, eventually altering the plant's genome to produce galls that become bigger and more nutritious over time.

Galls are also a very particular sign: gall insects usually choose a specific place to induce a gall, as at the midrib, edge, or underside of a leaf. Most are on leaves, but some insects choose branches, twigs, or even flowers. You can open one up to reveal the tightly packed, sleeping larval species inside—or you can just infer the species from the shape and location of the nub.

• • •

Surprisingly, those leaves that have no sign, no holes, no smattering of excrement, are themselves sign of something else. They indicate that the tree is probably not from around here. Although some bugs are generalists, knocking about in our faces or homes or wherever they can find nourishment, many are extremely plant-specific. They might be born, grow, eat, mate, and die on the same plant. One type of plant—or even one individual plant—may be their entire universe. Plants native to North America have their own community of North American bugs that have evolved to live on and with the plant. However, non-native—what are increasingly called invasive*—plants are often new enough to the area that no native bug has yet evolved to specialize in them. As a result, the invasive plants do not need to put any of their resources into defense chemicals or strategies; they can put all their energy into growing and reproducing. That is why invasive plants invade so well: they can spread quickly while native plants, struggling against the bugs, are lucky to maintain their numbers.

You can, thus, make a reasonable guess as to whether a tree is native by checking out its insect population. Walking by the lovely Norway maples, five-fingered leaves robust and hole-free, I suddenly realized that the "Norway" was not a rhetorical turn. The tree I was accustomed to seeing throughout New York City is an immigrant. Even the city Parks Department logo is a silhouette of what is probably a maple (or London plane, another non-native tree) leaf. The trees we passed looked gorgeous, each leaf custom-printed, dry-cleaned, and pressed. And largely sign-free.

• • •

* As a member of an invasive species myself, the tone of this descriptor seems unduly harsh.

Though Eiseman had not given any urban insect-sign tours, I was starting to think there may be a call for them. One might imagine that a typical city does not host too many bugs (outside of cockroaches and bedbugs); this walk was convincing me otherwise. Eiseman flipped over a stone and rocked a log with the toe of his shoe, causing shiny dark bugs to move quickly under the nearest leaf litter. In some ways, he suggested, cities are not *un*natural so much as they are *concentrated* nature. On his cross-country tour, highway rest areas turned out to be gold mines for bug-tracking. "It almost seems like in someplace like that, where there is just a little scrap of nature, life is more condensed." Upon entering Texas, they discovered the Texas leaf-cutter ant at the parking lot where they had pulled over for a pit stop. Then, on going into national parkland, "we barely saw anything," he said. The density of insect life was not the same, or maybe the method of exploring—wandering along waiting for something to pop up, rather than poking into every crevice at the rest area—is not conducive to finding sign.

Certainly if a rest area provides opportunity to find sign of insect life, a city must. Eiseman cataloged some urban elements that lead to good insect-sign hunting—beginning with the city's tendency to never shut down. When Wabash, Indiana, was the first town to light itself up at night with electric light, onlookers were flabbergasted: when the lights went on, "people stood overwhelmed with awe," the local paper reported. "Men fell on their knees, groans were uttered at the sight, and many were dumb with amazement." We have grown accustomed to the ordinariness of nighttime lighting, but many insects are still in its thrall. Lit all the time, cities attract insects whose compound eyes are specially tuned to the short wavelengths of UV light, found in incandescent lamps and many fluorescent lamps. City streetlights are now usually a more energy-efficient sort, such as high-pressure sodium vapor lamps, which emit less UV light but are still a siren call for various fliers. Insects use these light waves to find and choose mates, navigate, hunt, even migrate. So they must get very excited to find UV radiating toward them at every address and along every street. The UV-seekers include moths, of course, but also beetles, lacewings, things lacewings eat (aphids), various flies (caddis-, crane-, hover-, true-, scorpion-, damsel-, dragon-, even butter-), and wasps. About a third of them will perish in their excitement to touch the light. They hit the hot light, circle around it until exhausted, or make enough of a ruckus that a predator (bird or bat or other insect) gobbles them up.

Other urban elements are conducive to the insect hunt. If there is a waterway near a city, you can expect that there are all kinds of mayflies and stoneflies nearby, who lay their eggs on the lampposts, and, as we saw on our walk, often molt their white filamentous skin and leave it there, quivering in the wind like the clarinet lessons Maira Kalman plucked from their flyer. Walls, especially brick walls, provide nooks that house cocoons or nests. On the first brick wall we approached, we saw jumping spiders—and jumping spider "retreats," which sound like summer homes for spiders but are just the places where they hide but do not lay eggs. We found an egg sac of a common house spider. We found bee and wasp nests punched into tiny holes in a wall. If you are lucky, you might see a leafcutter bee nest, which features the packets of leaf bits that they have collected, each with a ball of pollen, nectar, and an egg inside. If you are less lucky, you might find a paralyzed cricket stashed by a wasp in a hole stoppered with grass or mud.

Abandoned places, something cities provide in abundance, are "promising" in Eiseman's eyes. A dusty, unpeopled overpass is a great substrate for insect tracks. Old Dumpsters attract cocoons and spiderwebs. "I did see a grasshopper munching on the paint on the corner of my house one time," he added. We were poking around a Dumpster together. Eiseman naturally got much closer than I would. It was only when perched on its wall that he spied a downy woodpecker on a nearby tree making a rhythmic racket.

Sidewalks have sidewalk-crack ants. A graduate student who recently cataloged the ants in the medians of the long avenues in New York City found cornfield ants, thief ants, pavement ants (a warmongering, pavement-loving species), and a Chinese needle ant, a stinging ant that is not from around here. He also found that the ant diversity on the Upper West Side of the city was greater than on the Upper East Side—presumably a function of that great environmental condition, "number of trash cans."

Even fallen twigs can reveal insect sign. Surely you have twigs on the ground in your area? "Neatly severed twigs," as one of Eiseman's book sections is headed, can reveal the presence of a beetle girdler, a pruner, or a borer. While galls might happen to cause a twig to weaken and break, there are various beetles who intentionally weaken a twig: the girdler, after laying her eggs toward the tip, moves toward the tree's trunk and plows a tidy path around the circumference of the twig. When a wind comes along, the twig snaps off cooperatively and the growing larvae in the twig feed on the aged or dying tissue. In other beetle species, it is the larvae themselves who burrow, when they are old enough to begin burrowing, into the twig and chew their way to the surface, creating characteristic sign in the process. All you have to do is look at the end of the fallen twig to see the spiral formed by a hickory spiral borer, or the expertly cut burrow around the perimeter, caused by a different wasp.

The discovery of the day was not the downy woodpecker cruising up and down the hackberry in the corner of a vacant lot—leaving sign in the form of beak marks, itself sign of some tasty beetle under the bark. It was not the adorable pupa of a ladybug, sitting calmly square in the middle of a catalpa leaf, its head tucked under its body and its abdomen folded protectively.

It was the sign on wood by a most unlikely creature.

We had just found some slug slime on a birch leaf. "There's a slug among us," Eiseman said. I did not think of slugs as critters that might want to be on trees. But Eiseman described to me how some slugs eat the film of algae on the bark of a tree, and in scraping their teeth against the bark leave a series of kisses with jagged lips. The resultant mark shows up clearly on light-colored backgrounds, like a birch tree—or on a white propane tank, or an abandoned car covered with weather and detritus.

"It's a feathery pattern, this back-and-forth S-shaped pattern," he was saying, before, "oh, here we go."

On the broad trunk of the tree was a sinuous pattern of spikey footsteps, a series of stamps of a sharpened fern frond. Slug teeth marks.

Eiseman looked entirely satisfied. "I had always suspected it was slugs who were doing it"—leaving this kind of track—"but I couldn't figure out *how*, because I didn't realize slugs had teeth." It took seeing a slug in action to confirm his suspicion.

In truth, slugs do not really have teeth; they have *radula,* a finely toothed kind of tongue that only mollusks have. It allows them to graze, rasping their body against a surface to sop up whatever they are gliding over.

Sign of slug. It was pretty, delicate—even more so for being the unlikely result of a gelatinous, lumbering creature. We gazed admiringly at its path tattooed on the tree. I fumbled through my bag for a camera and snapped a photo of it, surely one of the only extant images of slug sign outside of Eiseman's and other slug enthusiasts' collections.

While we idled down a broad, newly laid sidewalk, hardly a sidewalk ant in its cracks, I began thinking about Eiseman's brain. What was it that allowed him to notice these mystery objects, where most of us see just plain leaves and twig and wall? How was it that lace bugs "jump out at" him while they left me staring blankly at a tree?

The difference between how Eiseman sees and how I see is traceable to a concept popularized in the early twentieth century by Luuk Tinbergen, brother of the Nobel Prize–winning animal behavior researcher Niko, and a noted bird-watcher in his own right. Tinbergen noticed that songbirds did not prey on just any insect that had recently hatched in the vicinity; instead, they tended to prefer one kind of bug—say, a particular species of beetle—at a time. As the numbers of young beetles rose through a season, the birds gorged on these beetlettes, ignoring any other available young insects nearby. Tinbergen suggested that, once the birds found a food they liked, they began to look *just for that food,* ignoring all others. He called this a *search image*: a mental image of a beetle—with its characteristic beetly shape, size, and colors— with which the bird scans her environment.

The concept of a search image has now been widely studied in the animal world and is used to help explain the efficiency many predators have in finding their prey, despite the best efforts of the prey to be unfindable. In the lab, blue jays trained to look for camouflaged moths initially have trouble seeing them—they blend in so well with the speckled bark on which they alight. But after a number of attempts, the birds get preposterously good at finding even the most well-concealed moths. Dogs, skunks, and spiders have been found to have *olfactory* search images: they are more concerned with the smell of their food than its shape, and can find, say, that dry dog food (dogs and skunks) or that particularly yummy mosquito (spider) among a riot of smells in the environment, by searching out its characteristic smell.

Search images are not just used or useful for finding prey or avoiding capture; they are the way we find our car keys, spot our friends in a crowd, and even find patterns that we had never seen before. The neurologist Oliver Sacks writes about a splendid, human example of this phenomenon from his own experience. At a time when Tourette's syndrome was not widely recognized, Sacks saw his first Tourette's patient, exhibiting the tics that define the syndrome. The following day, he says, "I saw three [ticcing] people on the streets of New York and another two the next day. And I thought, 'If my eyes are not deceiving me, this must be a thousand times commoner than it's supposed to be . . . why haven't I noticed this before?'" He had acquired a Tourette-tic search image.

Everyone needs a mechanism to select what, out of all the things in the world, they should both look for and at, and what they should ignore. Having a search image in mind is what makes finding your friend among the crowds of people disembarking trains at Grand Central Terminal possible at all: it is the visual form of the expectation that allows you to find meaning in chaos. At the same time, if you are searching for your friend who you last saw twenty years ago in high school, she may no longer look quite like your search image representation of her. Jakob von Uexküll, the German biologist, wrote about this with his own search for a pitcher of water, which he expected to find at his table at lunch. Though he was assured that the pitcher was in its usual place, he could not see it right in front of his face—for the clay pitcher he had expected had been replaced by a glass pitcher. The "clay pitcher search image" obliterated the perceptual image of the glass pitcher. Von Uexküll recognized this as the same mechanism that led animals to mistake harmless objects as fearsome. He described a jackdaw (a kind of crow) flying above bathers at the beach, fooled into attacking an innocent person carrying his bathing suit over his arm: the jackdaw had a search image for a jackdaw-in-a-cat's-mouth, and the wet, drooping trunks mimicked it. The jackdaw unreflectingly set to attack the feline killer of his brethren. Presumably our German biologist emerged with only minor peck marks.

Eiseman has an *insect sign* search image. He has got galls bumpily imprinted on his mind; bug footprints etched in his brain. And in his eyes: neuroscientists who look at "visual search" find not only expected areas of the brain involved—a layer of the visual cortex called V4, the frontal eye fields (in the frontal cortex), areas in the brainstem and other areas involved in eye movement—but also the retinal ganglion cells in the eye itself. Our visual system has what researchers call inhomogeneous processing; this is a fancy, and slightly unflattering, way of saying that even when we want to, we cannot see everything at once. We see best right in front of us, in the center of vision made crystal clear by the abundance of photoreceptor cells in the center of our eyes, the foveal area of the retina. The periphery of our vision? Not so much. Our eyes simply are not designed to focus on what is to our sides: that is why we have nicely swiveling heads (presumably evolution was not concerned with what was *behind* our heads). Once our eyes are open, we automatically begin scanning the environment, flitting our gaze to and fro in short saccades—quick, automatic hops of our gaze back and forth to move our two degrees of central vision across the fifty or so degrees of our future path. We gaze-hop to scan a scene and we gaze-hop simply to stay looking at the object in front of our noses. You cannot stop saccading (except with anesthesia to the eye), nor would you want to: if you looked steadily ahead without saccading to and fro, the image you were looking at would seem to disappear. After constant stimulation, our sensory receptors get tired and stop firing. The result is that we become inured to constant sensory input: we stop noticing the foul odor in a room (but it is still there for a while, as evinced by the expression of others entering the room after you) or the heat of the steam room air on our skin (though it is still the same hot temperature). Saccades are the eyes' way to avoid having the lion, mouth agape, disappear from our vision while we stand in front of him, frozen in fear.

Saccading and searching are normal behaviors, done every visual moment of every eyes-open day. Search images are for the masters. That is not to say that the masters always know how they use these search images to solve the puzzles before them. Interviews with expert radiologists, satellite image analysts, and fishermen show that though they recognize their own expertise, they often cannot tell you exactly how they identify the hidden malignancy, detect a target from a bird's-eye view, or spot the school of sardines as it surfaces. Me, I felt one step closer to being a gall search master myself—without knowing how.

As our walk wound down, I was reluctant to let Eiseman go. I slowed my pace to get him to talk about the insect sign on a limp plant by the side of a dusty road. It turned out to be a winding trail of one of two known grapeleaf moth miners. Following it, we found sweet purple grapes. We gobbled a handful. A melancholy thought occurred to me. Most people are not going to have an invertebrate tracker on their walks with them, I worried out loud. Eiseman reflected for a moment, and then quoted one of his tracking teachers, Susan Morse: "Half of tracking is knowing where to look, and the other half is looking." If you understand even the most superficial elements of the life histories of different animals—such as what kinds of things they are attracted to—once you start looking, you are going to find them everywhere. If you want to find otters, find a peninsula in a big body of water where they might scent-mark and loiter; if you're looking for rats, try the alleyways behind restaurants, where overflowing bags of trash are left, kitchen floor mats are shaken out, and busboys eat hasty meals on break. Hence the ease at finding gulls around Dumpsters, raccoons sheltered in the holes in a stone wall, and, we discovered, parasitized flies on the bottoms of leaves in Springfield.

A small bit of knowledge goes a long way when thinking about "where to look": "Every kind of mammal has a particular landscape feature or microfeature that it keys in on, where it does its marking behaviors," Eiseman explained. "With insects it's just the same, just smaller: microhabitats." You need only know those habitats. Once you have an eye for those features, whether alley, leaf, or wall, as long as your eyes are open, you are likely to see the animal or the traces it has left. Eiseman described coming across the sign of a palmetto tortoise beetle while on his cross-country insect voyage: "I had seen a picture in a book of this beautiful structure that a palmetto tortoise beetle makes—it's a beetle larva that only feeds on palmetto leaves. It extrudes this long strand of brown segmented excrement [which might only be beautiful to palmetto beetles and Eiseman], this twisted mass of segmented straw. I didn't know what size it would be. My brother and I were walking along a trail in Georgia and I—I wasn't specifically looking for it—I just spotted one out of the corner of my eye; it was that big"—he held his fingertips almost touching—"about eight feet away.... Somehow it jumped out even though it seems physically impossible to see it."

After our walk, I had a bit of the sensibility of a spider: find a corner and build a web to catch insects bopping around. I had a search image for a sinewy trail on bark or leaf that would indicate a leafminer or a barkminer. This intuition is not always desired, I will admit: after our first encounter, I found a dozen motionless, parasitized flies on the undersides of leaves. That is an image I will be happy to remember how to ignore. But once you have an eye for these things, even when you're not looking for them, they just jump out at you. Everything is a sign of something.

"It did seem like the more we just stopped in one spot . . ." I began.

". . . we just started seeing more things," Eiseman, my tour guide to the bugs, finished the thought.

"It matters not where or how far you travel—
the further commonly the worse—
but how much alive you are."

(Henry David Thoreau)

The Animals Among Us

"A spill of spaghetti, cooked and sauced, formed a sunburst at my feet, attended to by a cluster of pigeons."

It was December twenty-first, the winter solstice. The business of being a pedestrian in the city had changed: any mosey that crept into people's summer gait had been replaced by the determined fast stride of the winter walker. It was cold out, and I hunched my shoulders in a futile attempt to warm my ears and bully the chill away. But I was walking slowly enough to scan the tree branches and windowsills and fence tips for squirrels. For December twenty-first is the first day of the mating season for the eastern gray squirrel, apparently. Perhaps I would see some courtship, a typically pell-mell affair in which many males race after a single female squirrel—up tree trunks, along delicate branches, leaping across wide crevasses. It sounded like the rodent version of a great chase film, without the small European cars and tourist-crowded plazas. At the very least, the squirrels should be out and about on this monumental date, engaged in something other than the non-stop nut-collecting and -consuming that has been their occupation for the last months. I knew this because John Hadidian told me so.

He is Senior Scientist in the Wildlife division of the Humane Society and had flown up from Washington, D.C. to meet me. Even to those of us familiar with seeing pigeons and squirrels on our daily walks, looking for "wildlife" in a city may sound oxymoronic. But New York City, the most densely peopled city in the country, is, like all other urban environments, host to a huge population of nonhuman animals. The bears, wolves, and mountain lions that roamed the land that became our city are no longer here (we think). But squirrels, raccoons, bats, deer, fox, coyote, possums, and scores of bird species are. Hadidian and I aimed to see if they were, what is more, on my very block.

Like most animal behavior researchers, Hadidian began his scientific career studying a relatively exotic animal—in his case, the crested black macaque, an Old World monkey you have likely never seen outside of a zoo. Just when he was looking for a job, though, the National Park Service was hiring, trying to get a handle on the raccoon population, which, like the rabies the animals were carrying, was skyrocketing. So Hadidian became, all of a sudden, a rare breed of animal researcher: one who studies the most common, least exotic animals. He began tracking and observing the urban raccoon more than twenty-five years ago, and he never went back to primates.

Happily for me, though, he readily agreed to walk around a city block with this human primate. Also like most animal behavior researchers, Hadidian is full of a kind of animal trivia that comes from long hours observing, reading, and discussing animal habits and quirks. Studying the macaques, Hadidian cataloged their yawning behavior and found that the males not only yawned much more often than the females, but they nearly always yawned in response to thunder. This kind of gem can only come from many, many hours of watching and yawn-counting.

A compact man with a gentle smile, Hadidian stepped out of a cab dressed in two, maybe three layers of sweatshirts, as befits someone whose profession involves standing outside for hours at a time. We were not a minute into our walk before his squirrel trivia came up.

"One thing I'd want to comment on—aside of the fact that there's a squirrel's nest here," he began, gesturing with his head up in the bare branches of a gingko tree. A dense cluster of dried leaves smudged the silhouette of the tree against the sky. I took the bait.

"How do you know it's a squirrel's nest?"

"Just by the way it's built—it's messy—and how it's positioned in the tree. It's a leaves nest, a *drey,* which is not at all cuplike . . ."

. . . and he dove into a veritable natural history of the squirrel. It was in this way that I learned that this very day was the first day of our arboreal squirrel's breeding season, one of two it engages in per year.

Just today! The specificity of the claim was astonishing. Though as city residents we come to expect to see animals out-side . . . *some*where . . . whenever we leave our homes, it is another thing to think of them living through their own datebooks, their own calendars of things-to-do and when to do them. But just as there is a time of year when we uninstall the air conditioner and send it to the basement, or flock to a Florida beach to warm our chilled northern skin, the animals around us are habitual as well.

The mating-season news got my hopes quite up for squirrel sightings. But the wind was whistling through the nest. It looked abandoned: perhaps last season's nest site, housing its handful of hairless squirrelettes for two or three months. No squirrels remained. And Hadidian had moved on, too, back to the topic that the squirrel's nest had interrupted.

"I was going to say that the primary distinction in the city is between night and day."

For urban wildlife, that is. Though we think the city is fundamentally the same place in the nighttime as in the daylight, it is not. It is not just darker, cooler, and quieter; it is teeming with animals. As plentiful as the pigeons, the sparrows, the chipmunks, or the squirrels may seem to be on city streets, what you see outside by day is a fraction of what you would see along the same route at night.

The reason for this is simple: us. "Humans are predictable, in terms of their behavior," Hadidian went on. "We create pulses of traffic: we're going into town, and then we're going home. And long about one thirty, two thirty [in the morning], things really quiet down." At night, we retreat from the streets, pull into our shells, tuck ourselves cozily in bed. And that is just when the animals' city day begins.

It is a logical move for animals. If they are to live around us, they must adapt to our galumphing presence. We are rather noisy, for instance: in an urban environment the ambient din is regularly 50 to 70 decibels, with spikes to 100, a point at which a sound can be both physically painful and destructive to ears. Where Cooper's hawks, a North American bird of prey, have settled around humans, as in New York City, Washington, D.C., and San Diego, the birds have resorted to vocalizing more frequently, ensuring that at least *some* of their calls are heard by other Cooper's hawks. The great tit, a small bird common in the Netherlands, and the song sparrow in the United States both sing at higher frequencies in cities, as most of human-produced sound is at relatively low frequencies. Urban scrub-jays breed earlier (giving them more time to recover from unexpected losses) and forage more efficiently than their country cousins. Some animals have changed themselves with lightning speed. The most famous case comes from the UK at the time when cities became industrialized. With factories belching black smoke, a layer of soot settled on every surface, man-made or natural. Among the population of the small peppered moth—*Biston betularia*—which counted on its coloration to be camouflaged against tree bark, a rapid transformation occurred. Where once the peppered coloration was dominant, suddenly a rare black varietal made up the majority of the population. These black moths were better camouflaged against the soot-coated trees. Birds couldn't spot them, and the little black moths flourished.

There are good reasons for animals to live around us humans. We provide plentiful food resources. We create shelters that easily accommodate small, discreet animal homes. But humans are also, for the most part, predatory, disruptive, and destructive. In our ordinary lives, we eat animals, kill them with our cars, and disturb their trash-can meals and garden-dirt baths. Thus, some animals have become more crepuscular—active at dawn or dusk—to avoid us. And more have become entirely nocturnal, even if the same species in rural areas is out and about in the day.

The first ones out at night are the raccoons.

You might think of raccoons as suburban animals, but if you live in a temperate city with a park, chances are you live quite close to a few hundred of these cat-sized mammals. Raccoons are classic urban adapters. They are generalists: they are so unpicky that they will live anywhere and eat nearly anything. In the city, the raccoon avails himself of the convenient supply of all things edible in our city trash bags, left insecurely tied on the streets twice a week. While a dog or rat might open a bag and scatter its contents, the raccoon tears a small hole, reaches in, feeling around for what he wants, and pulls it out. Hadidian noted that the animals he observed ate almost *anything*—except raw onion.

They are also alarmingly intelligent: "They're what I call the North American primate," Hadidian said. Watched closely, the behavior of *Procyon lotor* is indeed oddly familiar.* They sit upright, grasping food in their front paws—which, with five fingers, look like and function remarkably like human hands. You might catch a raccoon dexterously *finger*ing an item; or gripping, exploring, and fiddling with it. Their reflexes are better than ours—a raccoon can snatch a fly out of the air—but give one a Rubik's cube and he will, like so many humans, turn it methodically and not solve it. Like young persons, raccoons love to play—with their own tail tips or with each other; with a corncob rolled between their front paws; by drumming on the floor with their fists. One raccoon was spotted attempting to tie a bit of straw around his nose. Their facial mask—the familiar glasses of black hair around their eyes—adds to the feeling that they have distinct personalities. Should you be stealthy enough to come upon a sleeping raccoon, you will likely find it in one of two positions: either flat on his back, with his front paws over his eyes; or on his stomach, his head tucked between his front limbs as if frozen in the beginning of a somersault. I observed strikingly raccoonish sleep poses in my own husband and toddler last night.

As a culture, we are decidedly ambivalent about the raccoon. "Criminals!" some cry, surely accusing these masked bandits of more than they are able of being. But raccoon researchers speak of their subjects' "knavery," greed, and curiosity. We seem caught between identifying the raccoon as wild animal or as an urban

---

* *Lotor* is Latin for "washer," alluding to their habit of dipping food in water before eating.

pest. On the one hand, it is cute, costumed and catlike; on the other, it is a disease-carrying scourge. Even a century ago, raccoons were fairly beloved in America. They were popular as pets and were known as mischievous, inquisitive, and quick studies. President Coolidge, sent a raccoon for his Thanksgiving table, promptly decreed her his pet, named her Rebecca, and took her with him on long walks and on whistle-stop train tours. The sight of a crowd of children gathered around the First Lady clutching Rebecca to her chest on the White House lawn for the annual Easter egg roll, an image captured in the newspapers of the time, seems about as unlikely today as one featuring the current president cozying up to a brown rat.

I asked Hadidian to name the most surprising thing he noticed about the social life of his raccoons, the ones he had tracked and radio-collared for decades. "Culturally, these raccoons were a little like lions," he replied. Though thought of as solitary animals, urban raccoons live in groups. The pressures of city life lead to this crowding. They have many different den sites—in sewers, basements, hollow centers of stone walls, and holes of trees. One animal that he tracked even traveled well outside of his home range each fall, to build a den near a beautiful persimmon tree, a huge wildlife lure: "Every animal you can think of is drawn to the persimmon tree," Hadidian said. They notice the smell of the tree's fruit, surely, but even outside of their olfactory range they remember where this special treat is and migrate toward it.

Hadidian stood by the curb, gazing down, it appeared, at the sewer grate. I reluctantly joined him.

"There. Someone is living in there."

Although it was hardly put there to deter wildlife, the city sewer system would seem to be an inauspicious place for an animal. But the sewer, with its curbside drains and pipes running along every street and connecting to every building, is home to innumerable raccoons, rats, and possibly possums (rats willing). Plenty of the raccoons Hadidian tracked made homes in the Washington sewer, which sweeps away the excreta of some of the country's most powerful people.

"A couple of the animals we followed actually gave birth and raised young there," he said.

"Coming out . . . where?"

"Oh, anywhere." He pointed at a small gap between a step leading into a neighborhood bodega and the sidewalk. Bits of debris clogged the opening, which did not look in the least hospitable to living and raising young raccoons.

"A raccoon could easily fit in there, even at a full run."

I tried to imagine the raccoon's tail disappearing under the step. It is nigh impossible to picture a raccoon wanting to, or actually darting into that forlorn space. This is what makes the urban animal so elusive. He is actually attempting to elude us, and our imaginations do not seem to account for animals (aside from pets) in cities. Even our sense of scale is distorted when considering urban wildlife corridors and passageways. Remembering, perhaps, a childhood inability to scale a fence or shimmy through a gate, we find it incredible that urban animals are not thwarted by the seemingly impenetrable stone walls and chain-linked barbed-wire fencing we present to them. But the descriptions of nearly all urban animals include an impressive dimension: the size hole the animal can squeeze into, through, or out of. Raccoons, even as adults, can fit in a four-inch space between grates, flattening themselves and taking advantage of their broad, short skulls. Squirrels fit through a hole the size of a quarter; mice, through dime-sized holes. Look around you on your next walk. See any holes at all? Gaps between stair and building? Between sidewalk and curb? An animal goes there (after you have passed).

Raccoons are not only widespread but also long lived for urban animals. Hadidian followed the first animal he radio-collared for thirteen years. For the time it takes a child born in the city to learn to sit up, to stand, to walk; to say simple words, complex words, to talk, to talk back; to text, to do algebra, to play a tune on the piano—during all that time, he may have been quietly accompanied by a raccoon living a parallel life (with less algebra) outside, within a block of his home.

As I looked around me, seeing no raccoons but all the places they might be—in twelve hours' time—I spied a charming brass lion's head at eye level along a granite wall. One cannot help but notice that it is never a handsome raccoon's head emboldened in brass as a knocker. But raccoons have these leonine ways, and are at least as charismatic (and less predatory on humans, to say the least). If the city were overtaken with lions, instead of raccoons, I wonder if we would feel the same way about them.

We had been walking for blocks, and apart from evidence of squirrels past and raccoon accommodations, the only animals I had seen were ones dressed in puffy black parkas and snow boots. I asked Hadidian if we would have to come out at night in order to see the real wildlife of the city.

"Well, we've heard some house sparrows, saw one starling, saw a big flock of pigeons. . . ."

What? This was news to me. "You should tell me about this!"

I smiled, abashed. Even when looking for animals, I had missed them. All three birds are ubiquitous. Our starlings are famous—not for their great iridescent coloration, or even the peek of bright blue on the beaks of the males, but for their being an ecological disaster. "They were brought over [to the U.S.] by a fellow named Eugene Schieffelin who wanted to bring to North America every bird that was mentioned in Shakespeare," Hadidian added. Starlings make their appearance in *Henry IV*. "Nay, / I'll have a starling shall be taught to speak / Nothing but 'Mortimer'," says Hotspur—evidence that Shakespeare knew of the starlings' ability to mimic speech. Clever birds—so clever, unfortunately, that they wreaked havoc on their new environment. Before they proliferated, according to Hadidian, "most of the birds of the eastern U.S.—maybe thirty-four hundred species" traveled through countryside that became Manhattan.

How had I missed these birds? It had to do with how I was *looking*. Part of what restricts us seeing things is that we have an expectation about what we will see, and we are actually perceptually restricted by that expectation. In a sense, expectation is the lost cousin of attention: both serve to reduce what we need to process of the world "out there." Attention is the more charismatic member, packaged and sold more effectively, but expectation is also a crucial part of what we see. Together they allow us to be functional, reducing the sensory chaos of the world into unbothersome and understandable units.* Though we think of expectation as a cognitive experience, the process actually operates on a single-cell level, and even within the sensory organ. Consider it from, say, the eye's vantage. A stimulus hitting the cells of our retina could be one of many things. The eye is agnostic about what it is: a toy car held on the palm of your hand looks the same to the eye as a real car seen from a distance out the window of a building. But we never confuse the two. It is context (am I holding this car or looking out the window?) that allows us to resolve the ambiguous pattern into "matchbox" or "bona fide." That's expectation's doing.

Attention and expectation also work together to oblige our missing things right in front of our noses. There is a term for this:

---

* It is not a crazy crash of screeches, flashing lights, and possibly predatory or confrontational creatures approaching me: it is a subway car approaching the station.

inattentional blindness. It is the missing of the literal elephant in the room, despite the overturned armchairs, dinner-plate footprints, and piles of dung. Psychologists have cleverly demonstrated our propensity to miss a rather obvious element of a visual scene when attending to another by asking subjects to watch a specially designed short video. In this video, two teams, dressed in white or black shirts, toss around a basketball. The task is to count the number of tosses made by one of the teams. That is the expectation: the viewers expect *there'll be basketball-tossing!* They gear up to see it. Afterward, the subjects are asked for their final tally.* Of course, this is not the actual question of interest to the researchers. That question is this: Did you, attentive subject, notice anything else? Anything unusual? Anything else . . . at all?

Nearly half of all subjects did not. In this case, the elephant in the room is an actual gorilla—well, a person in a gorilla costume—who waltzes right between the players, pounds his chest, and saunters off-screen. Paying attention to the basketball players, we miss a rather salient (and furry) figure among them.

Expectation also allows us to miss bits of the ordinary world, not just the gorillas in our midst. Indeed, it nearly prevents us from seeing lots of things happening around us. In an economic move, rather than try to process everything we see, our eyes stop spending time taking in information from those parts of the environment that hold steady. Staring at your computer screen, or the book in your hand, your eyes quickly stop processing all of the details of the monitor or the corners of the pages in depth. If something changes, sure, the eye darts to it and neurons fire away. If nothing changes, those neurons can go quiet. In this way, expectation suppresses activity in the sensory system. This is usually

---

* When I have played this video in my psychology classes, students feel confident of their final numbers, but most of them count incorrectly, a phenomenon I cannot explain as expectation's responsibility.

not only unproblematic but helpful: by limiting our perception to what is likely, we see what we need to more quickly and reliably. A carriage horse wears blinders to restrict his visual world physically, since carriage drivers long ago learned of the inefficacy of simply asking the horse nicely to *Please focus on what's straight ahead, never minding that cute filly to the side*. People who perform highly unusual and difficult memory feats—memorizing thousands of digits of pi, for instance—may wear goggles or headphones to block distracting sensory information from interfering with the parade of numbers in their heads.

Blinders and goggles are ways of physically restricting what you can, and expect, to see in the world; the brain has its own internal mechanism. By thinking about what you are looking for, or anticipating what you might be looking at, your brain grows biased to see it: biologically, the neuronal processes are primed to spot objects that fit your expectation. The object does not need to be simple: think about a face, and you enhance activity in special brain cells that process faces—leading to seeing the face faster and more clearly than you otherwise would have. This, combined with the "search images" that helped Charley Eiseman find the insect tracks invisible to me, enables us to transform the world: expectation magically sorts the world into things-we-are-looking-for and things-we-are-not.

This phenomenon of expectation was discovered through a simple test called the "cued-target detection task." It is a very boring version of a war-games video game. The player is asked to press a button when he notices a target pop up: some simple thing like a flashing light or a triangle on the screen. On different rounds, there will be different cues to where the target might be: sometimes an honest cue, which appears right where the target will be; sometimes a misleading cue, which appears clear across the screen from the target.

Unsurprisingly, the honest cue helped people respond about twenty-five milliseconds faster to the target than the misleading cue.* But in either case—whether the cue is misleading or not—people simply saw the target faster with a cue, because they knew to expect it. The effect is mediated by various neurotransmitters, which start rallying neurons to fire earlier than would otherwise happen.

And we do not *expect* to see animals in the city. So we for the most part do not. If we notice things faster simply by expecting them, then looking at the world as if it holds "cues" for us just might work. I endeavored to test this theory at once, with urban wildlife in mind. My gaze fell on a well-graffitied wall to my left. It encased a schoolyard, full of young, shin-guarded soccer players, prancing around on Astroturf. The wall seemed hardly worthy of careful examination, but with my heightened keenness for signs of animals, I felt there was *something* there. A small, uneven piece of wire mesh was jammed between and over the bricks. It covered, barely, a small gap where the bricks converged. Hadidian followed my gaze and offered his assessment.

"I think that is intended to prevent someone's access."

A pause, and then, as though answering his own question, he continued: "Yeah, it's probably a rodent barrier. Not a great one. Kind of stuffed in there."

It was not a rat, but a past rat! Very likely, the presence of a surfeit of rats prompted this makeshift protection. The handiwork was, indeed, not impressive. We paused to examine it. The mesh was spiderwebbed across the wall—another piece was right below it, another was a yard to the right. Though there was no sign of the animals it aimed to prevent access to, if anything, these

---

* This is true for monkeys who have been tested in this game, too. And they respond faster than humans in every trial.

protuberances from the wall seemed likely to *draw* a rat's attention to the site. *Hmm,* the passing rat might wonder. *Where to enter this fine-looking den site of a wall? . . . Aha! At the great mesh gates!*

I remembered seeing Hadidian sigh, two blocks before, as we passed a trash can on the sidewalk. Not an unusual trash can—in fact, a rather tidy one, as resident trash cans go here—its lid was just ajar over the yawning can. An "insecure" trash can, he had called it. Almost guaranteed to be visited by the local raccoons that night.

Sure enough, on further examination we saw recently chewed bits of paper peeking out through the mesh on the wall. This was certainly the work of rats, whose ever-growing teeth leave them yearning to gnaw, chew, and pulp whatever they can get their mouths around.

It appeared that we had stumbled across one of the ways to find wildlife—or the traces of wildlife—in the city: look for the traps, barriers, or other munitions set up to deter them or ward them off. As Hadidian and I continued down the street, our attention was drawn upward by a rustling sound. On a flagpole, someone had tied strips of plastic, which whirled spastically in the breeze. Nearby windowsills and protruding ledges were lined with unfriendly spikes to deter animals' loitering—"loafing," as it is called by animal experts. While intended to discourage loafers, the plastic strips seem to attract them: as we watched, three pigeons, *Columbia livia,* landed nearby and made themselves comfortable. Pigeons can often be found at just those places that feature pigeon-scaring tactics. A plastic owl peered out placidly from a fire escape. While conceptually this seems like it would dissuade loafing pigeons—they are potentially prey to the predator owl—pigeons easily learn that an immobile, silent, odorless owl is not to be feared. And, indeed, the owl may be a sign of the location of a nice, stable ledge, with access to the crumb leavings of a nearby resident human. As Hadidian put it, the owl effigies "provide pigeons with something nice to sit on."

Similarly, the positioning of rodent boxes—large, enclosed traps baited with poison and, with their rat-sized openings, intended to lure rats—is itself a bit of urban ethology. The superintendents or residents who put them out presumably place them where they have seen rats in the past, so the location of these boxes forms an unlikely map of the paths of the city rat. On one block, I noticed that the view behind an apartment building extended all the way to the next street south: somewhat rare in New York, a city without alleys. I pointed this out to Hadidian, who said, simply, "Corridor. That's a great animal corridor." That is, it was a potential access route for animals, who would like to travel but prefer to avoid the traffic of the sidewalks and streets. At basement level we saw a string of rodent boxes lined up along the back walls of the buildings open to this ersatz alleyway. This was a rat superhighway.

The boxes spoke not just to the rats' route, but also to their idiosyncrasies. All the boxes were lined up against the building walls because rats are *thigmotaxic*: a splendid word to describe an animal who likes to walk along walls, touching something as it goes. Thigmotaxic, or thigmo*philic*—touch-loving—animals scurry along at the edges of the spaces we make. They feel most comfortable keeping in contact with something as they travel. You might spot the smudges of their body oil left as they hug the walls while moving. Mice are thigmotaxic; so are cockroaches. It is the same phenomenon, worn slightly differently, that causes caterpillars to move in massive processions, one touching (or clambering over) the caterpillar to his fore, who himself touches the caterpillar in front of him, and so on and so on.

This fact, in turn, tells us something about the biology of the animal. Thigmotaxic animals are probably ones who use the presence of a wall to orient themselves or navigate. Their sensory systems are often acute, but proximity to a wall limits the territory they must scan for possible dangers. And it makes use of one of their abilities: for rats, it is their ability to pick up low-frequency sounds—essentially, vibrations—with their vibrissae, or whiskers. These modest, twitching face hairs are actually the rat's best means of discovering what is out there, how far it is, how fast it is moving, and how high it is. More sensitive than human fingertips, whiskers can gauge, say, the size of an opening a rat is ducking into. If their whiskers are damaged, the animals are truly disabled. Researchers have experimentally cut lab rats' whiskers and found these animals to be not just slower to learn how to navigate through mazes but also likely to drown outright if placed in water.

We humans try *not* to touch things on the street, in public, but whiskers want to touch—to get information about the world through contact. So if you are looking for a whiskered animal, you need to envision the places that allow for lots of touching. Squeezed-into spaces. Too-small holes. Leafy areas. Chewed-out corridors. Pipes, gutters. Curbs.

And then we saw one. A Norwegian rat, *Rattus norvegicus,* peeking over the curb edge. Surprisingly large, balanced on his hind legs, his front raised thoughtfully, he had spotted us first. His nose was in the air—*investigating* us—and his tail was down, a long lean curl of stability.

I stood still. I neither wanted him to come closer nor to run away. Though they live near us, rats are wary of our aversion to them, and are quite happy to avoid actual contact with people. The rat bobbed his head, looking a bit maniacally twitchy. Pigeons head-bob, too, though with more soldierly rigor, in rhythm with their footsteps. Both animals do it to see better: with each bob, they get different vantages on what is in front of them, and they can use that information to estimate depth. Standing still, the rat's vision is very blurred, compared to ours, although as befits their habitat they can see better at night than we can. By bobbing, he was getting a gauge on how far away I was in order to estimate when he needed to begin to flee.

We were both silent, though I wondered if he was squeaking over my head, as it were. Rats' primary communication with other rats is along ultrasonic, high-frequency wavelengths above our hearing range: there is a mother-retrieval call by young pups; a "long call," which accompanies pain or social defeat, and, oddly, ejaculation; and a high chirp that has been interpreted as a laugh, emitted during tickling by humans (in the lab) and during play. They also chatter their teeth, an inadvertent communication of stress. They can certainly hear us. Some rats can distinguish different languages. Resident rats in the basement of an apartment building with a building staff speaking a different language than its residents can tell from their speech which group is possibly threatening to their den, and which will ignore them.

This rat must have decided I was unworrisome, for he soon relaxed into a sit and began wiping his face and ears with his forepaws. Rats spend up to half their waking hours preening. The ritual keeps their coats covered with their musk, and keeps the parasites at bay. They begin grooming at their heads and proceed downward, so you can get a sense how far along the rat is in his self-shower by seeing what part of his body he has gotten to cleaning. My rat got no farther: a bicycle rattled by on the street and he dove under a parked car. He was gone—back into the spaces rats inhabit where they can be invisible to us.

An animal behaviorist to the core, Hadidian took an even-handed approach to the animal.

"From a strictly natural history perspective, they're one of the most poorly understood animals out there."

"What is there to understand about them?"

"How big are their home ranges? How much socializing do they do? What's their group structure? . . . We really don't know what the behavioral repertoire of the rat is."

Partly because of this, and partly because humans have failed to think one step ahead of the rats, "contemporary rat control seems to vary little from what was practiced in the Middle Ages," said Hadidian. "The usual consequence of killing rodents . . . is the return, shortly, to the population level that prevailed before, or one slightly higher."

What we do know is that these rats are only in the city because humans are. Their omnipresence tells us about ourselves. Were we to be tidier, neither rats nor raccoons would keep our company. Both are "opportunistic omnivores": they eat anything that is available. What good fortune for such an animal to find us humans, who provide in our trash and in our homes an omnivore's delight. Rats eat edibles—and they eat through lead pipes. They are happy with a small vertebrate meal or an afternoon's snack of nuts and fruits. Indeed, they are particularly interested in sweet, high-protein, and calorie-rich foods. Like us, they will even eat spicy food, after an initial, wise aversion to the stuff.

Conveniently, we even feed the rats outright. It is the city squirrels who are the intended recipients of the bounty handed out by urban animal-feeders. Every neighborhood has one or many individuals who take it upon themselves to regularly provide animals—especially squirrels and birds—with bits of bread, nuts, or seeds, tossing the bounty on the ground as they sit nearby, or spreading it Hansel-and-Gretel-like as they walk. But it is the rats, emerging after the squirrels and humans have denned up for the night, who ultimately reap the benefits of this human behavior.

As a result of their diet and our feeding, they live wherever we live. If you are reading this in a city, it is a good bet there is a rat living less than a quarter-mile from where you are sitting—not passing through, not visiting: setting up a den and playing house. Studies of rats in Baltimore found that most rat activity is limited to a single city block or alleyway. As generations are born and move out of the family nest, rat "neighborhoods" are formed, with an area the size of eleven city blocks containing many related rats. We have created the infrastructure that supports them beautifully. Grid layouts are particularly amenable to rat populations, as the rats use the grids to orient themselves. They can map their entire home range through its different smells: the area scrubbed with detergent, the trail left by people passing with dogs, the area where the smokers stand by a building's side.

For the remainder of our walk, rodent boxes appeared repeatedly in my peripheral vision. I had never seen a rat in one, and I did not then. Rats are wary of new things—*neophobic*—which is at least partly responsible for their ability to elude the many and various attempts to bait and kill them: rats smell a rat in that big, black box. They will sample a new food first, before gulping enough to find it toxic. Later that very night, I spied a rat running to, sniffing, and then veering exactly *around* one. Given the rat's ability to learn to avoid foods from others' breath, this rat may have had an encounter with a less savvy rat earlier in the day.

• • •

We were again alone on the street, all the animals tucked away. While the subterranean landscape is a popular choice for the urban animal, the city also provides a commodious terrain above-ground. I asked Hadidian how the city we were walking through, New York, looked different to him than D.C. or Baltimore, where he monitors urban wildlife. He did not hesitate.

"Well, it's much higher. Everything in Washington is twelve stories or less because they don't want to overwhelm the monumental buildings. What you have here are functional cliffs."

We both looked up.

As if demonstrating his point, a group of pigeons swooped down from its redbrick clifflike perch over Amsterdam Avenue. Just as it seemed they would nearly land on the cab of an eighteen-wheeler going uptown, they curled upward, then settled down and rounded the corner, out of view.

Biologists do not know exactly what the pigeons—or any birds—are doing on these great swooping flock dives. The birds may be in search of food, avoiding a real or imagined predator, or just stretching their wings. In any event, the "flock-swoop," as I think of it, is one of the magnificent natural sights of the city. And it is a sight that repeats itself daily, even hourly, in every sector of every city—in high-rent and low-rent districts, over empty lots and between skyscrapers. Even as I write this, my peripheral vision notices motion: out the great long windows of Columbia University's library the white of the sky highlights a flock of pigeons arcing gracefully south to land on the ledges above the windows.

This kind of bird flock behavior is commonly described in the academic literature as "wheeling and turning," though even to an amateur eye this hardly captures the dynamics of it. A group of thousands of European starlings is an ever-changing, amorphous splotch that pulses and throbs, ceaselessly erasing one shape and proposing another over it. Flocks of dozens of pigeons rollercoaster along invisible corridors ten to thirty feet above the street, and wend along and around a curvy, hilly highway we cannot see.

Biologists and others interested in emergent behavior—behavior of a group that is not under the control of any of its members—have identified a number of features common to all these flock-swoops. They are highly synchronized flight patterns that follow certain reliable rules. Individual birds often prompt the flock to take wing, but there is no leader once the flock is in flight. The flock-swooping can happen at any time, but it is more common at dusk or just before sunset, before the birds roost for the evening. Within the flock, the birds stay at least a wingspan apart from each other, though they pack more densely around the periphery than in the center of the group. The flocks themselves are much longer and wider than they are deep: the birds are spread, not layered. When the group maneuvers, it turns in what are called equal-radius paths. That is, if the flock turns left, it is not the result of each individual bird suddenly turning left. Instead, the birds at the front arc only slightly, and wind up being on the right side of the flock. Those birds at the left side wind up at the leading edge. When it is pigeons gliding, they keep a steep angle to the horizontal, which makes them more stable, especially in wind. No wonder they do so well along the breezy valleys of a skyscrapered city.

Watching the birds soar, pitch, and roll, and feeling happier just observing them, it occurred to me that one of the reasons that it is hard to pinpoint the function of this behavior may be that it is functionless. And the most classic functionless behavior, seen in all mammals and most vertebrates, is play. Might these birds be soaring for the mere pleasure of it, a communal recess run to nowhere in particular?

Continue watching this bird play, and the paths that they travel almost start to become visible. When you imagine the city from the bird's vantage, it really does look like a series of canyons and cliffs. That notion of "functional cliffs" intrigued me, and I pressed Hadidian on it.

"The whole business of cliff ecology is something you can start talking about when you get these structures," he replied, motioning to a few buildings in the vicinity. "Any building will have what we can call 'wind shadows': little places where the wind doesn't hit. It certainly doesn't *scour*, the way it does on most structures or surfaces." The result is that although buildings look like hostile, lifeless zones, the face of a wall can support a whole ecosystem. Natural cliffs, too, have their own microhabitats and microclimates, and they support a huge amount of specialized flora and fauna.

The textbook *cliff* is a tall, steep rock face, with a flat top and maybe a bit of overhanging rock on the top edge. In other words, almost precisely the shape of the classic apartment building, with a vertical face and an eyebrow of cornice at the top. On a natural cliff, there are ten million places for life to bloom. Algae lives on the surface, small plants root in crevices between stones, multiple horizontal ledges collect debris and things that grow in debris— and this then attracts all the animals, invertebrate to vertebrate, that feed on these plants. Similarly, on a building, plenty of opportunistic, specialized plants live in porous stone, in cavities between stones or in broken stone, and at the intersection of brick and marble, or stone and steel. And on the top of the cliff may well be a raptor, perched on a ledge or nesting in a nook.

. . . Or under an air-conditioning unit. Falcons, hawks, and even eagles are again a common sight in the urban sky. They build their aeries in cathedral bell towers; on bridge towers; on, famously, an ornamental stonework ledge on a Fifth Avenue apartment building. Indeed, the animals, plants, and ecology of buildings—man-made cliffs—show "striking similarities" with those of natural cliffs. Cliff animals include mice, various squirrels, the aforementioned raptors, raccoons, porcupines . . . stop me if these sound familiar. Coyotes have been seen to feed and reproduce in cliff sites—and coyotes are among the most recent urban settler. We do not see many cliff-using black bears, lynx, or mountain goats in the city. Well, not yet.

Indeed, some ecologists have even proposed an "urban cliff hypothesis": that the urban rats, mice, bats, pigeons, and plants that are so familiar to us evolved from ancient cliff-dwelling rats, mice, bats, pigeons, and plants. Hominid fossils from *Homo erectus* onward have been found in caves at the base of cliffs. As our ancestors moved from caves and rock shelters to shelters of wood, steel, and stone, the animals may have simply moved with us. Humans still live in "concrete and glass versions of their ancestral cliffs, caves, and talus slopes," Doug Larson, a promoter of this theory, writes. The unlikely habitat of the cliff supported species that had to adapt to their unusual conditions. This adaptiveness turned profitable as the species followed humans, and were flexible enough to dine on our food and live in and on our structures.

The evidence for this hypothesis is multifarious. Pigeons, for example, are well adapted to perch on cliffs or building ledges, as their takeoffs are terrific, explosive affairs, as anyone whose step disturbs a flock of grazing pigeons knows. Their wing muscles are very strong, allowing them to hover and take off nearly vertically, helicopter-like. Rodent remains have been found in cave dwellings dating back tens to hundreds of thousands of years ago. Even the bedbug probably evolved from caves and rocky outcroppings in Africa and Asia, where the nasty things fed on pigeons and bats who lived there; the German cockroach, that ubiquitous city bug, can still be found on the toe of rocky slopes in Africa, where it feeds on fallen cliff detritus. One could even make the case that we build the structures we do *in order to* reproduce clifflike dwell-ings. Often our buildings have lots of "subspaces," which replicate ledges and crevices. We grow plants and trees on terraces—since plant species may thrive in small cliff juttings. We prefer to have our front doors set back and slightly elevated from ground level— just as an entrance to a cliff cave would be. And around us in these urban cliffs is exactly the biodiversity that we look for in nature.

As we rounded the final corner on our walk, a group of loaf-ing pigeons, startled by a passing bike, lofted upward. Until that moment I had not realized what was so odd about our urban-wildlife tour. In part, it had held more *traces* of wildlife than actual wildlife. But more than that, even those animals we saw were remarkably quiet. Mute, even: any sounds made by birds in flight were largely lost among the sounds of the city. When these pigeons took off, though, we heard their wings slapping the air and their bodies. Until then, they were silent-movie stars, padding along not twenty feet from us in complete silence. Pigeons are typically far from silent. Males coo as they woo, generating a large round warm noise while they puff their chests, spread their tail feathers, and try to look mate-worthy. When eating, pigeons ham-mer their beaks against the ground, messily spraying food around them. Their long nails scrape the ground audibly as they walk. But our pigeons stepped lightly, cooed psychically, and muffled their pecking. And we had only to look around us to see other stars of this spontaneous silent film: above our heads, dried and curled leaves noiselessly rustled on a towering oak; to our right, apparently weightless squirrels leapt from a stone wall to a tree trunk. All make sound, and all were close enough to be heard, but we were not bothered by not hearing them.

And just as in silent films, without sound the scene we saw was suspended in time, the action having no clear beginning or clear end. I watched a dog across the street venture forward, unhurried, noiseless. It felt like a little peek at infinity.

I asked Hadidian if he had any predictions about what the next animal to move into the big cities might be.

He smiled and was silent for a minute. When he spoke, he began slowly, almost cautiously, then quickly built into an outpouring of tumbling sentences.

"The real question is what animals will truly come to adapt to cities and accept the urban environment for the opportunities it presents, and it certainly does present a lot of opportunities— food, shelter . . . I'm sure you know about the phenomenon called the Heat Island effect?" (I did not.)* Hadidian continued all the same. "So an animal could subsist in a more northerly latitude than the species might usually be found." Thus we see the mockingbird, a warmth-loving bird, in the Northeast; the beaver and Canada geese are, as we all know, so well adapted to human presence that they are considered "problems."

"I guess it depends on the city. I mean, twenty years ago people didn't think that javelina would be colonizing Tucson, Arizona."

"What is that?"

"A peccary? The wild pig."

"They are in Tucson?"

"Yeah."

"Seriously?"

"Yeah."

"On the street?"

* I have since learned: the mean temperature of a city with a million residents can be up to 5.4 degrees warmer than the suburb outside the city—up to 22 degrees warmer on some evenings.

"Well not by day, but yes. They're in backyards. They come to water." Wild pigs, in search of a good drink in the desert, have lived in Tucson, a city of half a million people, for twenty years. In some cities of Germany, wild boar—feral hogs—are common sights on the streets. A wild boar in New York City would surprise me, I have got to admit.

"Wouldn't coyotes have surprised you?" Hadidian reminded me of New York's alarmed, overblown reaction to the arrival of a handful of coyotes, *Canis latrans,* in the city parks over the last few years. Some Chicagoans are surprised to learn that there is a well-established group of coyotes living in the city proper. Night dwellers, the animals may grow up, mate, reproduce, and die unseen by the human nine-to-fivers. "It's eye-opening to realize. They shelter in, like, shrubs by the post office." Hadidian pointed to a few bushes packed into a small space beside the sidewalk. "You could have a coyote (nesting) in a place like this. People would walk by all day long, never look, never see it."

I hung back behind Hadidian to take a closer look. No coyote. As far as I could tell.

When I grew up in the foothills of Colorado, canids around our house were not so surprising. But then again, in my early childhood we never saw elk, a five-hundred-pound animal which is now common enough in Boulder that the animal has its own street signs. The city of Bristol, England, has foxes like we have stray cats. When Hadidian began studying urban wildlife twenty-five years ago, even deer were not around.

My question was unanswered. Maybe there is no profit in predicting the next urban animal. Maybe we just have to wait for it, and keep an eye out. But if you are interested in hurrying up the process, take a cue from Hadidian's raccoon tale. Plant a persimmon tree in your city and see what shows up.

> "We must always say what we see,
> but above all and more difficult,
> we must always see what we see."
>
> *(Le Corbusier)*

A Nice Place (to Walk)

"Moving aside to let someone pass, I was nearly seated in a small alcove along a building—perhaps a place to sit, but it was lined with spikes. I did not sit there."

I was late to meet Fred Kent. Google Maps pinpointed his office as being at Twenty-fourth and Broadway but I arrived there and it was not. I chastised myself, remembering the convoluted mathematics that figuring out the cross street for a Broadway address in New York City takes. Surely I should not have expected the ever-seeing but uncaring Google Maps to be up to it.

Until recently, the NYC street address algorithm was printed in the front of those print-age relics, phone books, alongside numbers for the local emergency room, the FBI office, and instructions on how to perform the Heimlich maneuver. This seemed apt, for the algorithm answered an urgent need: the translation of an arbitrary number to its location in space. For Broadway, one needed

139

to take the building number, drop the final digit, divide by two, and then subtract either 29, 25, or 31 from that figure, depending on the initial address. The pleasure of completing this calculation was reliable, and each figuring brought forth in my head an image of the intersection that was my now-known destination. Knowing the calculus for any given street was a marker that one was a true Manhattanite, just as the realization that on side streets the odd-numbered addresses were on the north marked one as a sufficiently long-term resident to have had a couple of odds and evens among one's past apartments.

Today, phone books appear more often in buildings' recycling bins—still encased in plastic wrap—than by a telephone, and one emotionlessly asks Google Maps to bring up a bird's-eye view of a building's location. Well, on this day it failed me, and I found myself a mile uptown of the Project for Public Spaces, where I was to meet its president, Kent.

I emailed an apology, fruitlessly phoned, then briefly jogged, and finally taxied to the correct address downtown. When I burst in, the office was still but for the sound of computer keypads being tickled in the distance. I spotted Fred Kent chatting amiably with someone across the room. He waved off my apology. "Time doesn't matter," he calmly welcomed me.

What does matter to Fred Kent is space: how urban space is used or not used; usable or inhospitable. Kent founded PPS thirty-five years ago after working with the urban sociologist William "Holly" Whyte, a masterful observer of the behavior of people in cities. In the 1970s, Whyte and a posse of young volunteers set out to determine how the design of the city—in particular, New York City—worked or failed to work for urban dwellers. His group placed cameras atop buildings and light posts (quite unusual for the time), set out with clipboards and observation sheets, and *watched.** They watched where people sat and how they negotiated walking by one another. They noted who loitered, who flirted. They captured the dynamics of bus-stop queuing; they even recorded a day in the life of a trash can on Lexington Avenue. Though I admit to being curious about that trash can's day, I was walking with Kent to try to see, through his eyes, the theater of the sidewalk, played out by the people who find themselves on it.

Despite leading PPS for four decades, Kent is more public than presidential in his bearing. His height forces the individual of average altitude to strain to look him in the eyes, but he wears a perpetual almost-grin that puts one at ease. On the day we met, he was pleasantly rumpled, in a way that bespoke attention to things more important than whether one's shirt is properly creased. Unlike the majority of New Yorkers who do their best to avoid looking like tourists, Kent carried a camera with him and began searching for places to point it as soon as we stepped out the door.

He immediately found something. We were barely a half block into our walk before I had to maneuver around a vendor's huge food cart. Kent stopped outright—not to begrudge it, but to admire it. Just as the food cart is an adjunct to the city sidewalk, this cart seemed to have its own adjuncts: protrusions, displays, and containers that widened its girth. Kent snapped a picture.

"This is not just a little cart . . . that's the Cadillac of carts," he

---

* By contrast, there are now thousands of surveillance cameras in Manhattan set to constantly monitor the behavior of persons in their view. In some areas of downtown, there are nearly as many cameras per acre as there are *residents* per acre in Denver, the city nearest to where I grew up. But it is an open question whether anyone watches the video they record. While many have bemoaned the lack of privacy that cameras seem to impose, I find myself tickled that all of my walks undertaken for this project were recorded and registered in the aggregate of superintendents', police, and store owners' tapes.

said admiringly, later adding, "The vendors add a lot [to the city], because they tend to slow you down."

Before I could protest—after all, weren't vendors a nuisance at every moment except when you wanted a salty pretzel?— Kent segued to his next assessment: "Oh, that's a bad window." I followed his gaze to a modest shop window featuring clothing designs set back from the street. "It's too recessed and it should really be farther forward—so you spend a little more time there."

We were on one of my least-favorite blocks: Broadway in the Village. To someone who enjoys walking in the city, this street made me second-guess my hobby. Its sidewalks are constantly busy with slow-moving pedestrians clutching recent purchases and looking at the storefronts, up in the air, and anywhere but where they are going. The storefronts that attract their attention are ubiquitous and cluttered—to my eye, visually messy. I must have furrowed my brow at Kent, because he smiled and set to explaining himself by gesturing to a crowd of loiterers outside the clothes shop's entrance.

"See this? People stand right at the entranceway, right at the traffic flow, so then you slow down even more."

I looked at the folks checking their phones and leaning against the building's wall, adopting the poses of the unhurried and idle. There were enough of them that they had begun to crowd the sidewalk, and both pedestrians and people entering the store were obliged to slalom around them. And then I realized what Kent saw.

"You view slowing down as *positive*," I offered.

Kent answered without hesitation: "Sure, yup. Yes! It's *social*; it's kind of getting a sense of something. That's what a city is."

To Kent, the density of shops on Broadway was ideal. A good urban experience, in the Whyte spirit, was one that encourages us to slow down and loiter. I tend to see a surfeit of slow walkers and loiterers as hindering my progress on a rushed morning. These same people were viewed by Kent as essential constituents of the urban landscape.

Already, on that block of Broadway with Fred Kent, I was starkly reminded of the very simple truth that there are many ways to look at the same event. So, too, might we look at pedestrians not just with tolerance, or with acknowledgment of their role in making the city rich, but also as impressive collaborators in an unlikely sidewalk dance. As Kent and I stopped at a corner, a large group of people clustered around us, all of us waiting to cross the street. Car traffic steadily puttered past. The light turned and both our side and the opposite sidewalk exhaled large groups of people onto the street. Kent lit up: "It's a platoon!"

A *platoon,* to researchers in the field of pedestrian movement analysis, is a large collection of bunched-up, unaffiliated walkers. Fifth Avenue in Midtown serves as the prototypic platoon generator: the walking signals running up and down the avenue are not synchronized to allow the normal walker to make the light for block after block; they are synced for car traffic. Given the pace the average person walks in the city—well south of two meters a second—pedestrians get stopped at nearly every light.* Once the light turns, two large platoons set forth toward each other—and toward what is called a "likely conflict."

It is not that cities have not studied or planned for pedestrian

---

* Six and one half feet per second is the high end of comfortable fast walking: it is around 4.5 miles an hour, or, in New York City, ninety blocks an hour, an incredibly brisk pace. More people walk around five feet per second. This holds for the average healthy adult, though, not for the very old or very young. (On my walk with my son, we might have managed five feet per minute.) Until recently, the recommended time allotted for pedestrian travel across a street on the walk sign was based on the assumption that people can cover four feet every second. Even this conservative estimation almost certainly excludes most disabled and elderly walkers, whose pace leaves them barely halfway across the street by the time the light turns. With the latest walk-signal revision, they have been granted an extra couple of seconds.

movement. Indeed, I spent a happy afternoon with a book that details just what we can expect to find on our sidewalks. The charming *Highway Capacity Manual (HCM)* is a product of the Transportation Research Board (TRB), one of the private, acronymed national advisory committees trying to analyze, assess, and model all elements of contemporary civilized life. Charged with describing not just highway activity, but that of the pedestrians and others who might affect how those thoroughfares run, the *HCM* characterizes six stages of sidewalk traffic. Their description essentially ranges from "fancy-free walking" to "feeling oppressed in a crowd." At one end, "level A," movement is open and unimpeded. You have whole blocks of sidewalk to yourself—at least 130 square feet. You can, the manual cheers, "basically move in (your) desired path" without having to alter your course for anyone. At level B we take the leap into "impeded": there are others in sight, and you may need to choose a side of the sidewalk, but you can still walk at whatever speed you want. Then comes level C, constrained: though you are walking normally, you are not alone. If some of the other pedestrians are walking toward you, unspecified "minor conflicts" might occur. D, from constrained to crowded: some of these others are in groups, and you can no longer walk at the speed you want or pass people with ease. At this point you are down to only a paltry 15 square feet for yourself. This is the highest "tolerable" flow rate for the design of pedestrian walkways. Congested, level E: there are what could only be described as *a whole lot of people*. Everyone slows. You might even have to slow to a shuffle. Don't bother trying to forge a perpendicular path to a group this size. By F you are packed in tight. Your speed is probably down to less than a foot a second. If you shuffle, you're glad for it. Essentially, you are waiting in a queue, and a queue in which contact is frequent and unavoidable. There is, in the lingo, *high jam density*.

A Nice Place (to Walk)

Back on Broadway, our own south-walking platoon weaved smoothly through the north-walking platoon, some forty persons strong, with nary a bang, a bump, or a jostle, defying the *HCM* odds.

"We don't bump people," Kent shouted over the crowd to me. He was reporting our experience at that moment—we were indeed unbumped—but he was also reporting what urban sociologists have discovered by eavesdropping on walker behavior. They were impressed: urban pedestrian behavior is quick and fluid—all the more impressive for being largely unconscious. Together we are doing a cooperative dance, a kind of pedestrian jig, without even knowing we are dancing.

When we walk in a heavily trafficked city, we adapt to being but a wee fish in a big pond by subtly adjusting our behavior in parallel with those around us. Fish happen to be a good model for our behavior: research on fish "traffic" management has led to the formulation of the few simple rules they follow to avoid congestion while moving together with hundreds or thousands of other fish. The same rules explain the remarkable synchrony of behavior in flocks of birds, as John Hadidian and I saw, as well as swarms of locusts and army ants, and mass migrations of wildebeest, whales, and turtles. Schools and herds execute impressively sharp turns; flocks gracefully swoop, soar, roll; and all groups pulse effortlessly around obstacles. Millions of army ants move together across the forest floor foraging for food, but their paths are never marked by the crowd-stopping congestion you see on a typical interstate highway at ten minutes past five in the evening. These group behaviors are especially impressive when we remember that some of these animals are exceedingly simple neurologically—insects, for instance, have no brain to speak of. While birds are much bigger brained, bigness-of-brain does not actually seem necessary for the behavior. Instead, all of these animals rely on three simple rules. The rules are these:

First, *Avoid bumping into others (while staying comfortably close)*. What counts as "comfortably close"—an animal's "personal" space—will vary by species; what is similar for all animals is that if you follow only this one rule, it forces you to attend and react to the behavior of those in your vicinity. And that is the essence of what is called swarm intelligence: everyone must make movements that are sensitive to everyone else. The second rule: *Follow whoever is in front of you.* "Whoever" need not know where she is going: she may herself be following another. And so on and so on, until you reach the very head of the pack. Even there, the animal at the leading edge is neither leader nor sovereign. In flocks and schools, the role of leader is constantly changing hands. For only a moment will she determine the group's direction. The final rule: *Keep up with those next to you.* Everyone must speed or slow with attention to those around them. This seems like an impossible calculation, until you realize how little effort you have to pay to walk next to someone else down the street, never once considering how you will be able to keep at the same pace.

These rules of "avoidance," "alignment," and "attraction"—keeping apart while staying together—are sufficient to explain all herd, school, flock, and swarm behavior. Artificial intelligence scientists have created animations of mindless "boids" programmed with just these rules: their behavior matches that of swooping sparrows and swarming ants.

And big-brained-and-busy human pedestrians. Sidewalk walkers follow the same rules. We try to avoid bumping, like other animals, though we do want to stay more or less together. We tend to follow others, and this leads us to form natural walking routes that become well peopled with people. While we do not settle exactly in someone else's slipstream like fish do, we *hover,* preferring to look over the shoulder of the person in front of us instead of ducking right behind him. On a sidewalk, this tendency sets up ever-widening-and-narrowing channels of walkers headed in the same direction.

One element Kent and I encountered that the swarm management teams do not is the simple fact of *other* swarms: there are always people coming the other way. Here the urban pedestrian has a special skill.

"It's interesting how people from the suburbs get on subways," Kent mused. "They come in as though they're SUVs," and they are immediately distinctive from the "native" walkers. They barge ahead, but this is not the way to smooth traffic flow, and crowds of visitors then clog a route or entrance. "*We,* who know the city, can kind of . . ."—and here Kent mimed a small movement out of the way of an oncoming walker.

He was doing the "step and slide." If sidewalk traffic is dense and collision seems imminent, we pull this two-step pedestrian-dance move. While striding forward, the walker turns ever-so-slightly to the side, leading with his shoulder instead of his nose to turn the step into a side-step. We twist our torsos, pull in our bellies, and generally avoid all but the mildest brushes of other people (and if we do brush against someone else, we keep our hands close to our body and our faces turned away from one another).

This commonplace maneuver was identified after researchers watched untold hours of people walking past one another. Some of the more daring researchers also studied it by doing the walking themselves. They set out onto ever-busy Forty-second Street between Fifth and Sixth Avenues in Midtown Manhattan and walked back and forth, acting naturally but for intentionally *not* step-sliding out of anyone's path. The people they inevitably knocked into clearly felt that the researchers had committed a small pedestrian violation by not doing their part to avoid the collision. In the seventies, when some of this research was done, the most common result was a mild imprecation or an indignant,

Whatsa matter—ya blind? Even without knowing exactly what the rules are in order to avoid bumping each other, we sense at once when someone else is not following those rules.

Urban pedestrians make other small adjustments to others near us. When crossing paths with another walker, one party slows his pace just enough—maybe only for a fifth of a second—to enable both to keep the direction of their route unaltered. If someone behind us approaches quickly, we slide slightly to the left or right to give them space to pass. As Kent and I saw on the street, sometimes these accommodation behaviors are less subtle. Walking aside each other and approaching us on a part of a narrowed sidewalk was a couple holding hands. Expecting some full-body contact with them, I braced myself and continued forward. Unprompted, the male of the couple swung his partner in front of him, dancelike, to pass us single-file. Another man walking alone behind them stepped lightly into a tree pit to avoid us, leaving an imprint of his shoe in the dirt.

Even those who stop right in the middle of a sidewalk are accommodated. Whyte's cameras noticed that people in the city (not just tourists) tended to stop to chat smack in the center of the flow of pedestrian traffic. People in the kind of conversation that obliges one to slow to a full stop—greeting a long-unseen friend, doing the final rounds of good-byes, or responding to someone's surprising or serious comment by stopping outright—wound up squarely in others' way. Oddly, the "others"—the walkers inconvenienced—navigated smoothly around them, shoals of fish opening and closing around a jutting reef. Perhaps the cameras were too distant to catch any imprecation muttered under their breath. More likely, the urban pedestrian, moving toward his destination, simply steers around stoppers as he would nonhuman obstacles: no one chastises the lamppost for being in his way.

One reason all of our step-sliding, pedestrian-jigging works is that we are regularly *looking*—ahead and at each other. We do not just look to see who is there; we constantly, steadily look to calculate how we need to move relative to those around us. We regularly turn our heads back and forth, to the left and right, surreptitiously peeking at who is behind us or to our sides. When our heads face forward, we survey the scene ahead of us. Our eyes make small saccades. Within a long oval projecting forward from our feet to about four sidewalk squares ahead, we quickly note the direction and pace of anyone headed our way. We also glance at others' faces, which tell us if they are likewise looking forward into their own long ovals (and whether they are reacting to something surprising or alarming that might be behind us). There is *information* in the angle of others' eyes and the turn of their head. Most of the time, people are looking where they are going: gazing straight ahead. But they begin actually *inclining* toward their destination when it is in sight. Should someone seem to peer over to the doorway of the building down the block, more likely than not, he will walk there directly. Or just follow his head: we all make anticipatory head movements when we are going to turn a corner. Our heads lead our bodies by eight degrees and as much as seven steps, as though all in a hurry to get around the bend. Watch a walker's head and you can predict his path down to a single step. We learn this without anyone teaching us, and without knowing we know it.

The importance of this "looking" in the success of the dance comes into play with the relatively new species of pedestrian on the street: phone talkers. Their conversational habits change the dynamic of the flowing shoal. No longer is each fish aware, in a deep, old-brain way, of where everyone is around him. The phone talkers are no longer even using their fish brains: they have turned all their attention to engaging with the person on the phone. They block out their sense of someone walking too close; they fail to look into their walking ovals and step-slide out of the way. They no longer follow the rules that make walking on a crowded sidewalk go smoothly: they do not align themselves (they swerve); they do not avoid (they bump); and they do not slip behind and between others (they blunder). They stop minding the social convention to stay to the right, and weave across lanes of traffic. Texters are as bad or worse: they fail to even move their heads before turning, since they are slumped over to monitor their texting thumbs. I fantasize that the phone talker's route, if reconstructed and synchronized with their conversation, would reveal the organization of the chat: straightforward questions-and-answers matching straight, forward walking; sidetracking and topic-changing marked by weaving and divergent walking.

Notably, not *all* of our crowd behavior mirrors the animal swarms. Mormon crickets and desert locusts seem to cooperate marvelously, march-stepping in the same direction in caravans miles long. But they are not just cooperative; they are also cannibalistic. Cooperative, streaming swarm movement can also be generated, it turns out, if you are trying to eat the animal in front of you while avoiding being eaten by the animal behind you. Thus the double-takes seen when a foot race comes through a neighborhood not expecting it: whether the racers are running *together* or *away* from one another is not obvious from the simple fact of their speedy running.

Some desert locusts also have a gregarious side, which is useful in swarming. And there is a neuropsychological mechanism that may explain what prompts the lowly locust to seek company. Their gregarious behavior correlates with a huge increase in the amount of serotonin in the central nervous system. In humans, serotonin is involved in many behaviors, including moving in a group. Some of the most common contemporary antidepressants modulate the action of serotonin by increasing the amount of it lying around in our brains. One could speculate that a rise in serotonin also allows us to be sensitive to—and, for some of us, to feel rewarded by—moving smoothly in a swarm of our own species.

Emerging from our platoon on the next corner, I looked over at Kent. His head was just turning to look across at the other, westerly side of the street. I took that as a request. With a small adjustment of my path we crossed the street together without exchanging a word.

I should note: we crossed the street—but not at its corner. Every good New Yorker makes herself known in foreign cities by doing what we just spontaneously did: we jaywalked, crossing the street in its middle. As we were crossing, I looked up into the cab of a truck turning onto the street, aimed right at us. In response, the driver chose not to hit us and slowed to a stop.

A couple of classic street-scene events had just occurred: one historical, one psychological. Historically, we continued the proud urban tradition of walking wheresoever we pleased. *Jaywalking* was first used a century ago to describe the behavior of a pedestrian unaccustomed and naive (a *jay* being a silly person) about how to walk safely in a city. It was among many terms of mild opprobrium used about bad walkers. A *New York Times* article from 1924 includes "the veerers who come up sharply in the wind and give no signal," "the runners who dash to a goal and then dash back again," "the retroactive, moving crabwise," "left ends and butters," "the plodder," and "those who flee and turn swiftly" among those who deserved equal blame for the chaos of the streets and sidewalks at the time. "Jay driver," though suggested by many jaywalkers who saw the speedy driving of the new auto menace on the streets as the real hazard, never caught on.

Jaywalking is a civic traffic violation, but I happily do it. I rationalize my behavior by noting that crossing the street against the traffic light makes me pay more attention to what I am doing, rather than mindlessly following the traffic signals. And that is the psychological component: sharing attention. Kent agreed: "You're actually safer because you're making judgments based on eye contact."

Our jaywalking during this walk might have been the most eye contact I would make on the street all day, in fact. In the city, eye contact is carefully wielded, as I saw when my son stared at a destitute man limping toward us. Moving along a sidewalk on a summer's day, full to D-crowd levels, eye contact is fleeting and reserved for estimating others' walking paths. To stare—to look continuously into the eyes of someone else—is laden with meaning. Between passersby, the intent can be provocative or salacious: *I hate you* or *I want you*. But it also may be, as it is between driver and walker, path-directing. By holding someone's gaze, you actually control his movement to some extent, obliging him to move around you. One psychologist I walked with described a quasi-mind-control game she used to play with unsuspecting fellow bus riders. She would try to "seat" people on the bus by making eye contact. "Nobody likes to be looked at, so they keep walking" as long as they noticed her looking at them. If, then, she turned away, "that's when they sat." The rule against maintaining eye contact with strangers makes any eye contact powerful. Conversely, in a context where eye contact is supposed to be made, one person can, in theory, "move" the other by looking just to his left—forcing him to adjust himself until he can make eye contact again. I tell my undergraduate students to test this out with their professors, looking just to the right of the lecturer. Often, their gaze unconsciously inclines her (or me, as the case may be) to move more and more to her left to get back within her class's line of sight.

Some research suggests that the very presence of signs, traffic lights, crosswalks, and raised curbs, all intended to make walking safer for the pedestrian in a car-filled city, actually make it less safe. In the Netherlands, the traffic engineer Hans Monderman came up with the idea of a "naked street," empty of all these safety accoutrements. His idea was that by forcing us to look at each other—walker to walker, walker to driver, driver to driver— we could use eye contact to negotiate our routes. A few cities are attempting to enact this planning idea; at a main intersection in one Dutch city, Drachten, through which pass tens of thousands of cars, bikes, and walkers a day, traffic moves slowly and perfectly smoothly.

When we arrived across the street, my gaze left others' faces and, as is often the case, it went to what was underneath our feet. I asked Kent how much he thought about what was underfoot.

"Designers think it's very important," he hedged. I knew a geologist who did, too.

"From your perspective . . ."

"It's not. This is what's important," he said, motioning at a wall. It was a long, uniform wall of one of the ubiquitous branch banks in the city. Kent frowned.

"People walk faster by banks: there's nothing to do in a bank. Banks used to have a ballroom on the second floor in small towns, so that people would come and get familiar with a bank, and associate it with pleasure. But a bank has become more like a place you just go to the bathroom."

I reflected on the last time I associated visiting a bank with pleasure. A ballroom featuring, say, a pianist playing Gershwin would surely improve my impression of the mushrooming banks in my neighborhood.

Kent and I (quickly) walked by. We headed west on a long street that used to be industrial, then artists' residences, and now was full of the commerce of handbags, designer clothes, and technology. My gaze stayed down. Something sparkled underfoot: the sidewalk was studded with small glass domes, lit up from underneath. These, Kent explained, were remnants of the street's industrial past. The only natural light workers in the basement of these buildings got was through these small sidewalk domes. With the advent of incandescent light, the roles were reversed, and they brought artificial light from the basement aboveground.

These domes are rare now, the sidewalk equivalent of finding an early-twentieth-century copper penny in your pocketbook.* We only noticed them because we were looking down at the ground. Funny, that: we were out to take a walk and see what was around us; what was underfoot should not have reached our consciousness. It turns out, though, that walkers of all ages spend a lot of time looking at the ground a step ahead of their toes. A recent study reported just how much time. The researchers sent pedestrians out to take a walk while fitted with a device tracking their eye movements as they walked along a level, unremarkable sidewalk. The walkers spent nearly one-third of the walk fixated

---

* Until the 1980s, the "copper" penny was around 95 percent copper and 5 percent other metals; not since the nineteenth century has the penny been fully copper. Pennies currently produced are mostly zinc, a less expensive metal, though the cost of production of one penny is, as of this writing, 2.41 pennies.

at the near or far path—just as much time as they spent looking at the objects around them.

If the research is accurate, we might expect we would know a whole lot about our sidewalks. But I would guess that if I stopped a random pedestrian and queried him about the sidewalk, I would get a description along the lines of, *It looks like a sidewalk*—gray concrete, poured and leveled, divided into squares, hmm, that's about it. The sidewalk seems uninteresting and ahistorical, but this is borne of perceived familiarity. Sometimes we see least the things we see most.

Our use of the sidewalk—as a walking path—is now so entrenched that I cannot imagine it any other way, but unobstructed mobility was not always the point of sidewalks. They were public spaces. There has always been panhandling, wareselling, soliciting, and loitering going on among the walking. Once automobiles began encroaching, the mixed use of public space—horses following egg sellers abreast newspaperboys and people idling, convening, and chatting—was sorted into its constituent parts. The street belonged to cars. The sidewalks were for the people, but "Street Departments" were formed to inspect them and regulate their use.

Though sidewalks date back four thousand years, their popularity waxed and waned. In the nineteenth century, the sidewalk began its latest climb: 876 linear feet of it in Paris in 1822 swelled to 161 miles by 1847. At the same time, sidewalks began to be intentionally separated from the road by posts or by egg-shaped stones placed beside the route. These markers actually created a new location: the curb, or the gutter. It was not just a politically charged area (destination for unsavory loiterers) but also where dogs could be led to pee (and, in the wee hours, one might find more upright urinaters). Until last century, many sidewalks were still made of wood or gravel. Adjacent property owners were responsible for paying for and tending the paths. But there was little restriction on the position of their buildings or doorways, so the sidewalks in front of them were often irregular enough to require stairs to connect neighboring lots.

Now we walk on concrete, for the most part, set in slabs and drawn into squares or rectangles as it sets to dry. It is layered over a waterproof membrane and compacted sands. There are other options: stone slabs, cobblestones, bricks, even monolithic asphalt laid in a continuous sheet. But concrete is cheap, reflects light instead of getting warm with the sun, and it feels solid—not settling awkwardly like bricks or becoming slippery like stone. It does not, I am sorry to say, go down to the center of the earth: to stand on a sidewalk is not necessarily as secure as we imagine. City sidewalks are often hollow underneath, just covers for basement spaces that extend out from the building. Concrete also lasts for many decades, during which time dropped gum and splattered soda collect the dust of the city and darken.

I admired a particularly well darkened corner of the sidewalk, in front of a corner tobacco and magazine shop. Those blotches may go back eighty years, I thought, mildly disgusted.

At this point in our walk, nearly midday, the street was increasingly crowded with the sort of pedestrian activity that brought a smile to Kent's face: loitering, chatting, socializing. General liveliness. I navigated around another vendor's cart that was reducing the walkable sidewalk space by half. This is the sort of thing that the early sidewalk ordinances regulated against: in New York City at the turn of the twentieth century, there was even a municipal Bureau of Incumbrances tasked to remove the barrels of dead fish, bales of merchandise, pots of flowers, and squatters or loiterers in order to provide smooth thorough-faring. I suspected that Kent would be pleased that the Bureau was eventually dismantled. But "incumbrances" turn out to be facilitators in some ways. On another day, in a public lecture hall not far from where we were walking, I asked Iain Couzin, a mathematical biologist who studies "collective behavior" in animals at Princeton University, how the crowd of people in the auditorium should proceed smoothly out the exit doors, or proceed down a busy sidewalk so as to minimize congestion. To answer, he invoked fluid dynamics, describing the motion of fluids and gases, as well as the motion of people:

"It's counterintuitive, but putting in a barrier can actually increase flow," he said. As long as it is visible, a bar or a pole in an exit door, or an obstruction in the path—just a little off of center—makes movement through the door or down the path run more smoothly. This paradox is related to the "packing problem": "if you're trying to pack all these things in [to a small space], putting this thing off center and people having to avoid that breaks the symmetry, and then you get oscillating flows [through the space], which is much more effective."

If a corridor is narrow, the crowd (or fluid or gas) oscillates going to and fro. It self-organizes. At some level, it does what these walks were doing: making me notice something new. In that way, an obstacle can aid movement, instead of stopping it altogether.

Kent himself suddenly stopped. We had worked our way around the block in a labyrinth path that led us back to his office before I had expected it to. Despite all our slowing down, we finished the walk quickly. Back up in his offices, he saw me admiring the open feeling of the space, dotted with colorful chairs, and slyly quoted Whyte, "Please, just a nice place to sit." A person's experience in the urban environment, Whyte thought, had a lot to do with whether there was "a little something" they could control—like a chair not just to sit in, but that could be adjusted to their liking. His videotapes of people sitting in chairs in public spaces showed lunchtime workers reliably making small adjustments to their chairs before sitting.* One of Whyte's realizations was that people could feel very comfortable in a fundamentally noisy, public environment, if they just had a nice place to sit.

With that, Kent sat down and wished me well. Out I walked, slowly, to a totally changed, crowded, social street.

---

* More than one thousand lightweight chairs now dot the block-long Bryant Park in Midtown Manhattan, and nearly all of them are regularly warmed by Manhattan behinds. Kent's PPS contributed to the park's renovation in the early nineties; it is a wildly successful public space.

"What is life but a form of motion and a journey through a foreign world? Moreover locomotion—the privilege of animals—is perhaps the key to intelligence."

(George Santayana)

The Suggestiveness of Thumb-nails

"An older gentleman was resting in the median. . . . As he resumed, he teetered, and I swung widely around him so as to not knock him off course."

Before concocting the character of supersleuth Sherlock Holmes, Sir Arthur Conan Doyle was a doctor in training. Fans of his writing will see many allusions to his medical interest in the pages of his books, but the biggest allusion comes in the form of the behatted Holmes himself, modeled on one of his medical-school professors, Dr. Joseph Bell. Bell was a member of an increasingly disappearing class: doctors who are able to make diagnoses simply by looking carefully at the patient in front of them—before taking a single blood test, ordering an X-ray, or even placing a hand on the patient. For the cast of one's skin, the smell of one's breath, one's posture and step are all diagnostic, in the language of medicine, of the condition which brings the patient to the doctor's gaze. To his students, Bell would exhort that they learn "the features of a disease or injury . . . as precisely as you know the features, the gait, the tricks of manner of your most intimate friend." One's friend can be identified in an instant amid a crowd, but so, he suggested, can a disease, if you know what you are looking for.

Doyle was stunned when Bell was able to identify a man's profession after a glance—by noticing a hobble and a worn area on the inside knee of his trousers (where a cobbler typically held a smooth, heavy lapstone for hammering leather). Sherlock Holmes was bequeathed this genius for minutiae—a genius for observation more than one of learning. I wondered if this practice would persist among doctors today, well schooled in hospitals typically well equipped. I have been a patient in a few hospital rooms where the heart-rate monitor by my bed was given more studious attention than my own heart in my chest. Are there still practicing doctors who attempt to interpret their patients' conditions through observation—of the seeming trifles that reveal things about ourselves—as much as through instruments? According to Doyle, Bell often spoke of the particular importance of the "infinitely little" detail: the visible traces on ourselves and others that we don't bother to notice. I set out to find a Sherlock Holmes of my own.

I found Dr. Bennett Lorber. He agreed to walk with me in his hometown of Philadelphia, a city I knew but had quit after college. Lorber is a professor at Temple University School of Medicine and, at the time, was the president-elect of the College of Physicians of Philadelphia, the country's oldest medical organization; we were to meet in its dark-paneled lobby. The college is home to the Mütter Museum, an astonishing repository of medical history ephemera. As I waited, I browsed through the museum display cases, one of which held the recently arrived slices of Einstein's brain. I considered whether being donated to a museum of medical grotesques was enviable or dreadful.

Lorber is also a practicing doctor. On our walk, I was asking him to, essentially, diagnose on the fly. Simply by being outside on the street, people are inadvertently revealing their life histories in their bodies, in their steps, in the hunch of their shoulders or set of their jaw.

Waiting for Lorber, I couldn't help but feel a little trepidation: What characteristic tic would I display? What would the flush of my cheeks disclose? What was I revealing with my pupils, my teeth, or the grip of my handshake that I may not know myself? I thought of Sherlock Holmes gently chiding his assistant Watson for his pitiful skill at noticing obvious details: "I can never bring you to realize the importance of sleeves, the suggestiveness of thumb-nails, or the great issues that may hang from a boot-lace." I tugged at my sleeve, straightening it, and peered down at my shoes: laceless. Whew. Glancing at my own thumbnail, I noticed it was ridged somewhat. Each thumb's nail had a tiny downturn, a kind of keratin pothole. My brow furrowed: What could this mean? Low iron? Liver disease? Imminent collapse? With my thumbs, I Googled "nail abnormalities" on my iPhone. Thousands of hits. Among the first, this news: "Superficial nail problems are caused by proximal matrix disruption, while deeper nail abnormalities are caused by distal matrix disruption." Uh-oh—a disrupted matrix? I felt wary of any medical news that used not one but two words I did not understand.

The appearance of a slender, be-suited man at the front desk in the lobby distracted me: that must be Lorber. Feeling proud of my detective work (he was the best-dressed man in the room, and it was the precise time we were to meet), I quickly forgot about my bumpy thumbnails and approached him.

Lorber greeted me with a gentle smile and a look of calm

exhaustion. He seemed to exhale deeply as he turned toward me and shook my hand (without commenting on my grip). He had just been lecturing on microbiology and art, the convergence of his professional and personal interests. We sat down on one of the dark wooden benches in the lobby for a few moments of repose before we began our walk. Lorber specializes in diagnosing and studying anaerobic infections, but I had come to walk with him because of his side interest in the physical exam. Like many professors, Lorber serves as preceptor to medical students who are learning clinical techniques. He demonstrates how to take a history and how to do a physical exam—and he clearly delights in it, for it gives him the opportunity to undo some of the damage done by years of pre-med memorization, and teach the students to see the patient in front of them again.

He described being influenced by his father, a metalworker who was also an artisan and draftsman, and who bequeathed to his children the visual awareness he had: "We'd go someplace, and when we would leave, [his father] would ask us to draw a floor plan—where was the piano, where was the window. *He* knew. Once we did that a few times we started really paying attention."

Years later, as an adult, Lorber turned these early visual lessons into a similar test he devised for his medical students. Leading a group of students into a patient's room, he allows them introductions and a look, and then he says, *Everybody turn around and look at the wall.*

"And then I'll say to one of them, 'Tell me *one* thing about Mrs. Johnson that you learned. A single thing. Anything.' And they usually say, 'She has an IV.' That's the most consistent answer. And I'll say 'Right, she does. Where is it? Is it in her arm? Her right arm? Her left arm? Is it in her neck?' And they very often can't tell you that. And then I turn to the second person—and they always say, 'I was going to say she has an IV.'"

Then Lorber proceeds to rattle off the details he has noted: the patient has a bible on her nightstand and one on her lap; there are photographs on the wall and chair and notes beginning "Dear Granny," and so forth. So he knows she is a religious woman, has lots of adoring grandchildren . . . and suddenly a picture of this patient starts emerging from behind the IV. The next time Lorber's students enter a patient's room, he reported, they look intently at the patient and all around her—and they start seeing things they otherwise would have missed.

We had seated ourselves to give him a breather, but Lorber was clearly not a man who rests for long. Before I knew it we were up and he was giving me a tour behind the velvet ropes of the college building. Between the grand classroom spaces, ancient medical libraries, artwork, and medical paraphernalia, there were various examples of a kind of art reality. For here was a Thomas Eakins portrait of an ophthalmologist, one Dr. William Thomson—and in front of the oil painting lay the ophthalmoscope that the subject holds in the portrait. Up a grand staircase, between us and a large photograph of a late-nineteenth-century surgeon performing a dissection before a large audience of eager students, was his very dissection table, a huge marble slab with a large webbed drain in its belly.

We, too, were about to be artwork embodied, springing forth out of this building, which stands as a kind of museum to medical investigation, and doing our own medical investigating on the street. While we would not be palpating anyone's thyroid or percussing their spleens, those simply walking toward us would be presenting themselves for brief inspection. Moving through space, we reveal the ways we are functioning poorly: stiffness in a gait; an asymmetry to the swinging of our arms; a tendency to look overly closely when listening; a lugubriousness in carriage and expression.

Indeed, we were not yet ten yards out of the building before we saw a couple of men approaching. The investigation had begun. I took a quick survey of our surroundings. December already, it was late in the season to be as warm as it was. It had been raining. Philadelphia is already the color of rain, and she wore the damp comfortably. Yellow gingko leaves decorated stone-slab stairs and sidewalk squares. While talking, Lorber and I stole looks at the men approaching us. I began my discovery: What could be wrong? *Coats?* Check. *Raingear?* Nope—but it was not raining this moment. *Um. Hmm. Have all their body parts?* Seems so.

I had come to the end of my diagnostic tether: I had nothing. Lorber, though: "That gentleman needs his hip replaced."

That's all Lorber said, but as soon as he said it, I saw the limp on the fellow on our right. As my vision awakened, the limp seemed to get more pronounced by the step. A huge limp! All I had noticed was a puffy jacket.

Gait is like the poker player's tell: revealing of all faults. We can think of walking as a kind of controlled falling, accelerating toward the center of a circle with our legs as radii and the journey of our hipbones drawing an arc on the circle that is ours alone.* Despite the large range of body types among members of the species *Homo sapiens,* it is as easy as identifying features on a face to identify a normal gait. Researchers have quantified the order, duration, and phases of what are called "interactions between two multi-segmented lower limbs and the total body mass"—i.e., between your legs and you.

This is how it goes. You are standing. (Congratulations on that, by the way. Bipedalism is fairly rare among animals, and causes all sorts of organizational and balance issues for our bodies, which we spend our lives fine-tuning. Infants might take a

---

* Speedwalkers define a much less hilly arc: their acceleration is directed more toward going forward and less toward falling down.

full year from their birth to be upright without support, recapitu-
lating in that year what it took our species millions of years to do.
By fourteen months old, toddlers are taking approximately two
thousand steps an hour. They are also falling—*ka-boom!*—about
fifteen times an hour.) To begin walking, you lurch forward, nose
first. You are aloft! One foot has begun to lift and swing, your
weight shifts to the other leg, and you are already off-balance,
both from front to back and from side to side. Your lightening
foot rises from the knee, which itself requires the hip to lift. Your
pelvis pivots back. If your abdominal muscles do not kick in right
there, you begin to feel it in the muscles that are stronger: your
lower back, your rear end. The toes of your raised foot are pointed
down, but must lift, too, climbing above the plane of the foot and
raising high, so as to send their blunt friend the heel toward the
ground. Already the toes of the other foot are feeling the pressure
of the motion, of holding your body's weight, and begin to clench
to encourage that foot's readiness. Your heel strikes the ground,
the rest of the foot slapping down after it, your knee flexed to
absorb the shock. You rock from the outer edge of your foot forward and toward the inward edge, knee wobbling over the center
line of the foot. And you are in what orthopedists will call a *stance,*
with a foot on the ground. Actually, two feet. During walking, of
course, we are no horses: we never have both feet off the ground.
That is "running." During walking, the stride time with a foot in
the air is *shorter* than the stride time with both feet on the ground.
No wonder we don't get anywhere fast while walking: we're half
standing still.*

One foot swung, the other races to keep up. Ideally, the second
does the exact same thing as the first.

---

* According to those who have spent preposterously long periods looking at gaits, the
number is actually more than half: each step is divided into 62 percent stance (contact
with ground) and only 38 percent swing (no contact with ground).

But that exact same thing almost never happens, and this is why gait analysis is such a ripe place to see an internal disorder manifest externally. Gait can go wrong in many characteristic ways. An asymmetric gait can reveal a spiraling host of one-sided troubles. The whole gait pattern—one "step"—is diagnostic, too. Someone who seems to waddle might do so because of a muscular disease: unable to stabilize his pelvic muscles, a person will tilt his entire pelvis with each step. Some hyperkinetic gaits, legs twitchy and restless, can indicate a problem in the basal ganglia of the brain. A hurried gait, along with shaking or tremors, might be a symptom of Parkinson's disease. If, on taking a step, the toes drag or the knee is lifted overly high to avoid dragging the toes, damage to the peroneal nerve could be indicated.

This last one I knew myself. Much to my chagrin, midway through taking these walks I incurred a back accident. Hoisting my young son into the backpack carrier we used when we needed to get someplace farther than a toddler's walking endurance, I felt a tweak. A few days later, I learned that "tweak" wasn't a bad description of what had happened: the disk between two vertebrae (L5/S1, for those of you with back injuries who collect the alphanumeric jargon) had herniated. My sciatic nerve was pinched, and with that, pain shot spastically and electrically through my left leg. A week, various steroids, and even more various narcotics mitigated the pain. But I was left with a compressed nerve, which takes weeks, months, maybe years to recover. In the meantime, various muscles, including those of my left foot and my left glute were not being innervated: they were numb and nearly useless. I spent a lot of time gazing at my foot, willing the toes to flex. They looked like perfectly good toes. They would bend if I pushed them manually, but they were cold to the touch: the muscles were deeply asleep, covered in pillows, blinds drawn and earplugs in.

Walking was an awkward, slow affair. The muscles assigned

to lift the toes and push the foot—and thus the body they carry—over and forward were not working. Nor was the muscle responsible for lifting the leg. So, using muscles in my back, I essentially threw my leg forward each step, then pivoted over it.

My gait had become, in the parlance of physical therapists, "disorderly." I learned about the other disorderly gaits after I had my own. Eventually, I had surgery on my back to relieve the compression on the nerve; six weeks later, I found myself barefoot and in shorts, walking down a long hallway in a physical therapist's office. At the end of the hallway was Evan Johnson. He sat with perfect posture on a low stool and studied me walking. The "gait test," a classic, simple test of function, is widely used among physical therapists, and is surprisingly good at revealing disorder. It is also refreshingly low-key: you walk off, then you turn around and walk back.

Having looked at the innards of my spinal cord, excising a slice of my wayward disk, and sewing me up, my neurosurgeon (to whom I am forever thankful for doing those three things so well) had given me this diagnosis: "You could get full recovery" of the use of my leg, he said. "Or not. I can't tell." *Really? My neurosurgeon can't tell?* This was incredible and depressing news.

I was coming to accept that the prognosis for recovery from a nerve root injury is decidedly uncertain. But after seeing me walk off-and-back, Johnson popped up from his stool. "You'll be running again," he told me. "With time," he added.

He was right. I went through intensive rehabilitative therapy. It was so successful that, one day six months later as Johnson and I went out to take a walk from his office, neither of us even commented on the fact that I was walking with no apparent limp. Walking again represented that most desirable of conditions: ordinariness.

Johnson is tall and his smile is wide, neither feature revealing that he used to be a professional dancer. It was an injury while lifting another dancer that prompted him to seek his own care, and ultimately to earn a doctorate in physical therapy. Now he is the director of physical therapy at the Spine Center, a neurologic division of Columbia University Medical Center. He met me for a walk on a Friday before a long weekend, and the city was filled with people trying to get out of it. A rain had just scoured the air and pedestrians reveled in their shirtsleeves and coatlessness.

We looked left: people walking; we looked right: people walking. All seeming to be unwittingly submitting themselves for the gait test. I confessed to Johnson straightaway that I already felt there were two kinds of gaits: unremarkable and lame. People either seemed to get along fine or they had a limp, a weakness, or were afflicted with youth or age. It was not clear to me that there would be more that we could see.

Johnson spent the next ninety minutes disabusing me of that notion. Three steps into our walk, he had found his first subject.

". . . If you look at this woman while she's walking, she's carrying a very heavy bag"—on her right shoulder—"and her body is listed all the way over to the left as she negotiates her heels, her arm is swinging on the left to give her momentum. Notice her shoulder height on the right? Rather than have it relax and pull on her neck, she actually activates her upper trapezius and hikes the whole side of her body up . . . there's a good chance the scalene muscles on that side are going to be tight."

The woman was wearing high-heeled boots, a short dress, and looked like a very ordinary urban walker. But on closer inspection, it did appear as though her right side, holding the bag, was frozen in an uncomfortable position. And her left arm swung excessively to and fro, conducting an orchestra at her toes.

"She's holding on for dear life. A potential patient," he added.

I wondered if everyone begins to appear to be a potential

patient when you are a physical therapist. As she swung away from us, I asked Johnson what the most common disorder he saw on the street was.

"One thing you see a lot is the habitual stooped posture, a forward head with a big kyphosis, especially in older individuals. Many wind up with stenotic spines, and when they lean forward, they actually create room for the tissues and the nerves in the back and it brings relief." Two seconds later, his exhibit materialized. "There, that individual . . ."

A tall, large man in a suit, his hair gray and thinning, was stepping off our sidewalk into the street. His neck brought his head forward rather than up, and his back was hunched, just as Johnson had said. The front of his suit hung lower than the back. I thought aloud how hard he must be to tailor.

"Indeed! That follows from his body: can you see how his hands are facing backwards, how the palms are facing you? That's a product of internal rotation of the shoulders. As he stoops, the back becomes rounded, the head goes forward, and the shoulders, too. And so does the front of his suit.

"It's basically our succumbing to gravity. It takes less musculature work to hang on the ligaments. Over time the ligaments yield; even the bones deform. If you have osteoporosis and the bones are soft, the vertebrae of the spine start to wedge to support that"—actually reshaping themselves so they are smaller in front and larger in back.

We were not just seeing a man crossing a street; we were seeing vertebrae in the process of wedging.

One minute later, clothing again served to accentuate a disorder in the making:

"Look at the pants," he said, of a heavyset man. Okay, I did: the pants were blue. Also, they were so long that they gathered in rolls above the man's shoes.

Johnson patiently unpacked what he saw: "So look at how the cuffs are, and the shoes. The cuffs are bunched up more on the outside of the leg than the inside, and on the shoes you can see uneven wear where it looks like it's worn more on the outside than the inside. If you look at the way he walks, his knee is valgus—it's basically a moment where your knees come together and your feet go out. It effectively shortens your leg, particularly on the outside, while your inside becomes effectively longer. So your pelvis moves somewhat differently, and you end up wearing your shoes unevenly."

From disorderly cuffs and worn shoes, the astute gait observer can infer structural problems. Maybe his arch tends to drop, or maybe the ball of his hip is turned slightly forward in the socket of the pelvis. Over time, and after millions of steps, a subtle anatomical variation turns into an acquired deformity.

What had seemed like "unremarkable" gaits were looking more remarkable. Johnson and I moved onto the edge of the sidewalk and paused. A nearby subway unloaded a phalanx of walkers onto the sidewalk, and walkers hurried to make a short light across the street. This particular intersection frequently came up in discussions in his clinic, he said, because the street was extrawide and the walk signal was extrashort. Many patients cannot make it across the street without hurrying or breaking into a run. Every gait disorder was accentuated under the stress.

Looking out onto the corner and the sidewalk, Johnson's

assessments were rapid fire: "She hyperextends her knees, using the inert tissues—the ligament and the calcus—to absorb the shock. Her knees rotate in, see? She's a likely knee-injury candidate, hip injury candidate." He added, "She would not be a good candidate to be a runner."

Another: "If you look at that individual"—an older woman with thinning hair, an extralong jacket, and a defeated air—"she's waddling. Every time she steps on her right leg she leans way to the right and her left hip drops: that's called a Trendelenburg sign. It's weakness of the glute medius muscle and muscles of the side of the hip."

Followed by: "He's very thin"—an older man with a black hat, looking fragile—"and he's bowlegged on the right leg, which means it's taking a lot of weight on the inside of the right knee, and he's not bending the knee, he's landing on it, keeping it stiff. So he has a painful knee joint. He lacks muscle definition: that leads to a lack of control on that limb. His foot slaps down, and comes way inside the knee, where the heel lands. This contributes to his weaving back and forth, too."

Johnson found lots of so-called gait "faults," but he was also admiring of the people we saw: more than anything, one becomes aware of how many different but successful ways there are to propel oneself around one's day. Nor is every odd gait a pathology. A Hasidic man in too-large shoes flopped by us, prompting Johnson to remember a recent patient: ". . . an Orthodox gentleman who had a gait that was contributing to pain in his back: a tear of his annulus or his disk in his back, which is worse when you're leaning forward. So we worked a lot on posture, to get him into a more upright posture. But he refused to do it. He explained to me that it wasn't the posture of a humble man."

It was a revelation that gait might reveal religion. Or profession: a middle-aged man passed by balancing a ladder by one rung over his left shoulder. "His gait speaks to the fact that he's walked with ladders like that quite a bit."

It is no surprise that "balancing a ladder" indicates that one might be "a person whose work employs ladders." But we could also see roughly how long he had been so employed. Because despite balancing an unwieldy object on one shoulder, it looked as though if we were able to surreptitiously slide that ladder off of him, his gait would change not a whit. Were he inefficient in his gait when hoisting ladders, an injury would have had him retired long ago. In the same way, a furniture mover who can strap five boxes of books onto his back and head off down the street like a normal—if slow-moving—walker is one who knows what he is doing. Hire that man. He has found a walk that is efficient and low in stress, and he is unlikely to be injured moving your dictionaries.

Efficient was how Johnson defined the perfect gait. This is a word that comes up in dog-show judging, too, in which each entrant's gait is examined, usually at a trot. Many of the breed standards for gait are a version of Johnson's definition: "tireless and totally efficient" (malamute); "balanced, harmonious, sure, powerful, and unhindered" (rottweiler). Sometimes the descriptions range into the more lyrical: the "steady motion of a well-lubricated machine" (German shepherd); "true, precise, and not slurring" (Irish water spaniel); even "a perfect balance between power and elegance" (Rhodesian ridgeback). Despite the preponderance of potential patients among the pedestrians passing us, Johnson pointed out plenty of balanced, precise—*perfect*—walking. On a hilly street, two men, diametrically opposed in style, approached us going downhill. One man was heavyset, wearing a loose cotton jumpsuit and cradling a sports drink in one hand. His whitening dreadlocks were pulled into a cap. The other was slim and shorn, wearing a shiny gray suit and a bright pink shirt. The first walked loosely and evenly, his knees bending to comfortably absorb each step, his pelvis rotating and his arms swinging smoothly. The gray suit was perfectly aligned in his steps: his ears over his shoulders, his shoulders over his hips.

Each, Johnson said, was a version of the ideal walker: their gaits had few asymmetries, were smooth and loose, and wasted no energy doing anything but going forward. From an evolutionary perspective, efficiency is the key. Our ancestors may have been easily outrun by any potential predator—we are not a particularly fast species—but we have endurance: those proto-humans who could keep running won their lives. And they could do that if their gait was efficient.

The gray suit lapel flapped in the breeze as its wearer jaywalked a diagonal across the middle of the street. The man in the jumpsuit ducked under a scaffolding. Neither was felled by predators on this day.

In Philadelphia, Lorber and I turned left onto Chestnut Street. Occasional raindrops were becoming less occasional. I had been back in this city exactly one day and was struck by how it was at once familiar and unfamiliar. Against a backdrop of urban design, shops, and citizens on the whole quite similar to those of my current city, the differences stood out as bas-relief. The sidewalks were narrower, befitting a place slightly older than my neighborhood. Buildings were on the whole shorter, allowing me to feel towering at five feet nine. The urban horizon was farther away: from some streets I could see to the next street, or to the next neighborhood, quite unlike the blindered, cavernous view one gets on a New York City street. Alleys interrupted long blocks, providing peeks onto the backsides of businesses. Peering down one alley, I wondered what kind of superhighway this was for one of John Hadidian's urban species.

I also recognized what I thought of as a "Philadelphia look": people with features reminiscent of my now-deceased grandmother, Johanna, who lived here for all of her eighty-six years. I can remember meeting her in a darkened restaurant on Chestnut Street for clam chowder. We sat in a hushed booth with velvet pillows, and she crumbled soda crackers into her soup bowl. And now I seemed to see people who resembled her, in the softness of her skin, the shape of her eyes, the pride in her walk. I could almost hear the jangles of the bracelets she wore on her arm. I asked Lorber, also a native of this city, if he knew this "look." He responded with a blank expression. Apparently the look was simply a nostalgic concoction of my own head.

We picked up our pace as the rain did, and began discussing the kind of shelter we might soon seek.

"That woman," Lorber interjected, his voice not changing tone from the previous sentence, "may have a genetic disorder."

"What?" My mind was still attending to the rain and my eyes were still looking at awnings.

"On the XY chromosome. The way her ears were set low, her short stature, and what was called 'webbing' under the face, that's indication of this disorder."

I looked behind us. There had been a woman; on reflection, I had indeed noticed that someone had walked by. Now she was retreating and soon disappeared around the corner from which we had come. She was broad and brunette. That was all I had noticed. Lorber, meantime, had seen a genetic deformity on her twenty-third chromosome.

I was amazed. In a vague, theoretical sense, I of course knew that we all wear our genes on our faces, bodies, and sleeves. My blue-eyedness is not a function of anything that I have done over my life: it was preordained once the sperm hit the egg. Still, eye colors seem categorically different from the kind of global diagnosis that Lorber was willing and able to make. This deformity would not only have physical ramifications, but behavioral ones. Seeing that woman's face, he was also seeing her probable behavior.

Lorber was confident but appropriately circumspect about his on-the-fly diagnosis. After all, he was not able to use some of the most useful and overlooked elements of an introduction to a new patient: simply hearing the patient tell her own history, revealing details classified as "non-contributory," such as her profession, family life, and daily habits. Symptoms need a backstory.

Lorber himself likes to shake a patient's hand. He was hesitant to say just what it was that a handshake told him, but I got the impression that it was simply a way to open a conversation with touch, something both professional and personal. I made a note to shake his hand with conviction at our walk's end.

Nor were we close enough to the people walking by to really experience their bodies. Now, this may seem like a fine thing indeed, as to be close to a person is to smell that person, and often the smell of strangers' bodies can be repugnant. The smell of (quite a lot of) perfume used to cover the smell of bodies can be even more execrable. But by not getting close, we miss a fair amount of information. Lorber talked with a nostalgia usually reserved for childhood pancake Sundays and Aunt Léonie's madeleine cookies about how doctors used to smell a sample of suspect skin cells with their eyes closed, something few do anymore. When Lorber sees a patient who has had diseased tissue aspirated by another doctor, he always phones that doctor and asks them how the tissue *smelled*. What we might call bad breath is itself revealing of systemic or specific illness. There might be fishy, ammonia-like, musty, or bloody notes in bad breath—each indicating a different diagnosis. Lorber has written about a trio of his patients for whom their "putrid" breath—before pain in breathing, a cough, or fever appeared—was the only or first sign that they were harboring an anaerobic lung infection.

I clamped my mouth shut involuntarily.

Bodies do not only smell; they hum and whirr when everything is running smoothly, and especially when it is not. The nineteenth-century French physician René Laënnec made a catalog of the sounds one might hear in a person's body, were one permitted to lean in close enough. Laënnec curled a piece of paper upon itself to listen to his female patients' bodies, as to bend over a woman could be impracticable, if she was buxom, and was in any event indecorous. His simple paper cylinder later evolved into the stethoscope. Simply the muffled thuds of the heart's valves snapping shut and the rhythmic wash of blood rushing away from the heart speak volumes about a person's health. There is plenty of literature about how the *lub* (closing of the mitrial/tricuspid valves from atria to ventricles) or the *dub* (closing of the aortic and pulmonary valves as the heart pushes blood out) can vary with health. When you slip on a blood pressure cuff in addition, someone listening through a stethoscope can hear the difference between the pressure of the flow of blood through your arteries when the heart is contracting and when it is relaxing. One imagines that with another simple tool, doctors may be able to hear the hoofsteps of our mortality approaching.

Laënnec was especially interested in the sounds of disease. The list of sounds he heard through his paper tube reads like poetry. Of the various rattles from the bronchi, he heard pneumonia coming on as the sound of raw salt being gently heated in a pan. A pulmonary catarrh was so exactly like a pigeon's cooing that he might check under the bed for uninvited avian guests. With an obstructed bronchi, he heard "the chirp of a small bird and the slick squeal made when layers of oiled marble slabs were pulled brusquely apart." A cough like "a fly buzzing in a porcelain vase" might indicate lung disease. Other unfortunate illnesses made their presence known sonorously, through "sighing of the wind through a keyhole," "the murmur" from a toneless bellows, a pin "striking a porcelain cup," the sound of a spun top. Lorber and I stood under an awning, listening to the rain. Thinking about such purring, cooing, whistling, sawing, hissing, and crackling happening within me made me feel oddly musical as I sneezed.

As Lorber and I surveyed the street scene, each person who approached us became a demonstration of something new. The game of finding out what, exactly, they were presenting was a great one. My own version of the game was less medically informed, of course, and was instead imbued with the bravado of someone too new to a field to realize how little she knows. I was less able to identify specific problems than to locate potential subjects of interest. Bus stops were minefields for this kind of medical lens on the passersby. We saw an older woman standing just apart from the other people waiting and wearing layers of ragged clothes with brand-new shoes. I am not sure what her health was like, but I could take a pretty good stab at the rest of her circumstance.

A young man waiting near her caught my eye. He was pacing, his head bent under a sweatshirt hood; his left hand held a phone to the side of his head. His gait was odd. It was as if his torso and hip were rigid as he moved, not fluidly rotating as they do in a comfortable stride. His toes were pointed outward. I pointed out my find to Lorber, who gently informed me that I had diagnosed a fashion statement. The fellow had his pants pulled down excessively, in the manner of lots of young men about his age—leading to a stiff swagger necessary to keep the pants from dropping to his ankles.

I looked for someone else whose gait might be based on their actual biology. There was a middle-aged man delicately crossing the street. Lorber was on it.

"I would guess that he has a disorder in his back, a spinal stenosis, which restricts the movement of his legs, and there is some atrophying of the muscles."

Sure enough, looking more closely as the man crept across the street, that seemed to be precisely the case: the man's trunk was solid, but his legs looked like they were dangling. He was not striding, but shuffling.

"It looks like he's not actually using his legs," I offered.

"Yes. He's not *propelling* himself . . . he's pushing his center of mass from side to side, using his legs as leverage."

Across the street the pedestrian traffic was suddenly heavier—to D levels. A bus stop up ahead might have disgorged its commuters. A tall raincoat hurried a small raincoat along, all but their connected hands hidden under waterproof clothing. I thought about what it was like to be a young person dragged through an adult's days. Walking with my son had already made me less likely to drag him anyplace, and instead to follow his lead (read: we have become experienced sidewalk loiterers).

Perhaps to have true empathy for one's patients, one must know how to *become* a child, or a middle-aged woman, or a man with spinal stenosis and an anaerobic lung infection.

There is a likely neural explanation for the empathy those practitioners of medicine like Lorber and Johnson have, and it has just recently been discovered. In the early 1990s, an Italian researcher named Giacomo Rizzolatti and his colleagues were looking at monkey brains. In particular, they were recording, using single-neuron microelectrodes of brain activity of awake and alert macaque monkeys, which neurons in an area of premotor cortex called F5 fired when the monkey reached for a peanut. They were able to find particular neurons that were active for the reaching and nut-grasping. One day, Rizzolatti noticed something unusual. The brainwave recorder was turned on as an experimenter set up the apparatus, placing a nut in front of the monkey. The machine captured evidence of those same neurons firing even as the monkey was sitting still, watching the preliminaries to the trial. The neurons were active just as the *experimenter* reached for the peanut; the monkey's arm was by his side, unmoved. In other words, the monkey's neurons fired both when *doing* an act and when *seeing it done* by others.

This was remarkable: the individual neurons had been implicated in specific behaviors *and* the neurons fired at two very particular times. Let us reflect again on the scene. Macaque monkeys are beautiful, small-faced creatures with overhanging brows that give them extra expression. On that day, one monkey, forced to sit in a small chamber with his head immobilized and his skull cut open to record from his brain, watched a human in a lab coat come into his room and mess with some peanuts on a platform. The monkey's brain, whatever else was going on, also registered two things: that that person was another *individual*—and that he was doing just what the monkey himself would soon be doing.

This result has since been replicated and refined, and we now know that these "mirror neurons"—cells that fire at doing something and seeing it done—are found in various areas of the brain, in humans as well as monkeys. Two such areas are the insula and the amygdala, a part of the limbic system involved in feeling emotion and perceiving emotion in others' faces, tone, and words. These mirror neurons may be part of our ability to match our behavior to others'—and, indeed, to cringe when we see someone twist his ankle and fall in pain; to be infected by a smile or laugh of a friend; or to feel real fear when in a darkened room watching actors play out a contrived horror scene on a film screen. These cells may be part of our ability to learn, as infants, how to toss a ball, tie a shoe, or turn a doorknob by merely watching someone else do it. And they may be what allows for the empathy that, for most people, comes along with seeing others' behavior and emotions.

Without the benefit of seeing inside their brains, I can make a pretty good guess that Lorber and Johnson's mirror neuron systems are heightened to notice even more aspects of others' physique and movement that map to their own bodies, because of their experience with the variety of ailments typical to their professions. In one research study looking at brain activity of expert dancers, ballerinas were asked to watch ballet dancers perform. Their mirror neuron systems went wild: they could feel all the moves the dancers were enacting. When nondancers watched, their brains showed evidence of mirror neuron activity, but it was much more modest. When capoeiristas, whose dance forms overlap in many ways with ballet, watched the ballet, their mirror neuron systems also fired wildly, though somewhat less than in the ballerinas themselves. Likewise, ballerinas watching capoeira had less activity than the experts in that dance, but both had more than the nondancers. Expertise matters, but it builds on something we all share: a propensity to feel others' movements in our own bodies.

Lorber and I had toured around a long square block and were headed back to the college. Fewer people passed by, and for a moment we fell into the silence of those who have finished their dinners and are gazing at their cleaned plates admiringly. Then Lorber brightened.

"Like that?"

"Yes!"

I was pleased. I knew just what he meant: a woman with the Philadelphia Look had passed us. Just as he was sharpening my attention, I had tickled his awake. I cannot tell you exactly what Lorber saw, but somehow he extrapolated from a few examples and came to identify an instance of what I was beginning to think was an imaginary category. Those who study facial proportions might tell us that we could map this look. "Anthropometric" research uses facial landmarks to measure distances and altitudes and angles, then compares the proportions of one measurement to another. Instead of the eyes, nose, and mouth, there are less obvious markers: the lowest browline point, the bridge and tip-top of the nose, the outer edge of the eye, the place where a jowl would hang if you had jowls, the outer edge of the mouth, the most concave point of the chin, and so forth. Researchers use this to get an average measurement—the "average" face—and to mark divergence from it in anomalous faces. Perhaps different "looks" might differ from the average look in similar ways. The typical six-year-old has an eye opening about one third as tall as it is wide, a mandible height half its width. To us he just *looks* six—but his look can be measured.

As we reached the college, I shook Lorber's hand—strongly, I hoped, though I feared my hand was just cold and clammy. Certainly my thumbnails did not catch his attention . . . or did they? A smile flickered on Lorber's face and he turned and jogged up the steps.

On walking back to my hotel I found that I was looking much more deliberately at passersby—as though they were still presenting themselves for inspection. In short order, I found that this encouraged people to look that way back at me (or simply look at my looking). Ack! Had I already forgotten the lesson from my son, staring too hard? I ceded to the rules of human interaction and looked away.

Some of what both Lorber and Johnson had seen was hardly visible to me, but none of it was invisible. While I had a vague sense of *Hmm, something's amiss . . . ,* they could diagnose. It is not only the diagnosis that I valued; it is the way that knowledge orients their looking—an ability to "see what they see," as it were. I felt I had looked behind the curtain—and there, instead of a small man pretending to be a great wizard, I found a great wizard, expert at simply using his eyes.

SENSORY CITY:

Things That Hum, Smell, or Vibrate

"Look, with all your eyes, look!"

(Jules Verne)

Seeing; Not Seeing

"A breeze lured me from down the street and I reflexively pursued it."

Begin taking a series of walks around the block and, if ironic twists tend to befall you, soon enough you may find yourself unable to walk. This was what happened to this walker. A few weeks after herniating the disk in my back, I found that I could not push myself forward with my left leg. That is how it felt: I could use my leg *at all,* but I was not using it *at all well*.

My sciatic nerve was not on speaking terms with my left foot. I was frustrated that I could not run (a minor obsession) or pick up my son (a necessity), but I was alarmed to have a temporary disability: I could not walk normally. I was lucky: I could still walk, in an "ish" sort of way. Walking was an awkward, slow affair. Even after I had back surgery, I was still not walking well: my foot was paralyzed and I was forced to swing my leg around to the side instead of propelling it forward.

The street changed for me during those months, as it certainly changes for anyone who is temporarily or permanently injured, or suffers the ultimate injury of simply aging. I had no balance on my left side, so to maneuver I had to plant my right foot. This meant that small adjustments—stepping back to make room for someone on an elevator; moving slightly to the side to let someone pass on a narrowed sidewalk—were impossible for me to do quickly, and even with time were laborious and graceless.

I became aware of the little movements that we do naturally when we see people approaching us on a path. I had learned from Fred Kent (and Whyte by implication) about the pedestrian side-walk dance. Though interaction with your fellow pedestrians feels as though it begins when they come within handshake distance, you are each adjusting your path and stride to the other well before that. In *theory*. Now I saw it in practice. Without the nerves relaying messages to the muscles to make that adjustment, a walker becomes a blundering target. I made more personal, tactile contact with people in those months than I had over the decade of my urban residency.

I was very much in the throes of this handicap when I met Arlene Gordon. The day was still with heat. Along the sidewalks, air conditioners gurgled and thrummed with an unseen number of chilled apartment dwellers sealed away behind their windows. Park benches sat lonely. I could almost hear the "grass grow and the squirrel's heart beat."

I turned a corner onto a broad street unshaded from the sun. A generator was sputtering nearby; a siren dopplered across the horizon, the toenails of a small dog being dragged out for his constitutional scraped the concrete, other sounds melted into the air. Hoses snaked the sidewalk and emptied themselves into tree pits smelling of moist dirt. At the third building on the left side of the street, inset more deeply than its neighbors, I approached the doors. They sighed open for me. I passed through the marble-floored lobby, pulled myself up a few stairs, weaved over to the elevators, fingered their engraved buttons, entered, and emerged after six beeps. On that, the seventh floor, I turned left and heard someone call my name: "Alexandra?"

Gordon stood in the doorway across the hall. Tall, smiling, with perfectly white well-coiffed hair, she held the door open with one hand and held out the other. Her fingers were directed slightly to my left, but as I greeted her, she looked me straight in the eyes. Highlighted by her shocking blue shirt, Gordon's eyes shone an iridescent blue-green. She led me into a compact, tidy apartment. The blinds were drawn and there was a low light on. A bookcase held a television, neat lines of hardbacks, and shelves and shelves of treasured objects: delicate porcelain boxes; figurative objects; tiny stone sculptures of seals, elephants, birds.

As I moved to examine these tchotchkes, Gordon spoke up: "Pick up anything; I'll tell you about the trip."

I placed one of the objects in her palms. She grasped it gently, gazing down at her hands. Her fingers quickly worked over its surface. As she dislodged a lid she said, "Oh, this is one of my little boxes. Let's see what this is . . . this has a picture on the cover . . . flowers . . . I'm sure I got this in China. I've been to China twice—actually three times if you count Hong Kong."

Over the last forty or so years Gordon has traveled the world, often with friends. She once took a three-week cruise up the North Atlantic, around Iceland and Greenland. On each trip, she gathered mementos, these souvenirs, which she calls her "pictures." On this summer's day, she had just returned from a visit to Storm King, an open-air art museum north of the city whose large-scale sculptures and site-specific pieces are scattered across a few hundred acres of manicured landscape.

"Storm King!" she smiled to tell the story. "I was absolutely flabbergasted when I got there because I was there many years ago. And nothing fit my memory of it."

This flabbergastery, her many trips, and the souvenirs there-from might seem unremarkable were it not for the fact that for the last forty-two years Gordon has been blind.

Her memory of Storm King was a creative one—not con-cocted, but also not experienced entirely through her own senses. It was formed partially from the descriptions provided by her companions. Gordon experiences most trips through those she travels with. She prompts them to describe what they see, and not just the spectacles but also the ordinary details of every eyeful come alive for them both.

"I've traveled with friends all these years," she offered. "Each one has said how much more *they* see because they're walking with me."

Her memory of Storm King was also the memory formed by experiencing the world with all her nonvisual senses. She might have captured the smell of the air, the way sound bounces off lawn and metal and into open sky, the scale of the space as felt by the amount of time spent traveling from one artwork to another.

I grappled with this while sitting in her cool, dusky apart-ment, Gordon three feet away, bolt upright and facing me. When speaking, her eyes seemed to find mine, then traveled someplace up and to her left, just as they might in a seeing person. Indeed, she was the model of conversational eye contact.* When listening,

* In normal conversation people gaze at each other only about a third of the time, with the listener looking at the speaker about twice as much as the reverse. When speaking, we mostly look not at the person we are talking to, but anywhere else—up to the sky, at our hands, out toward an indefinite segment of air. Many utterances begin with a brief look, then a turn away. (If you are speaking and you want a moment to hold someone's attention before they blast in with their thoughts, look away. Your eyes are signaling that you have got the floor.) We can pass the conversational baton with gaze, too, by

she stared calmly in my direction, her eyes locked onto mine. We chatted about her family and she pointed to a space over my left shoulder, roughly to the wall behind a wide couch. Following her point, I saw what she cannot herself see: two photographs that she nonetheless described perfectly. Her son, now grown, took them, ten minutes apart. They showed a natural jetty in the north Atlantic covered by waves and then bared as the tide receded. Light played on the water in just the way that Gordon said it did.

I had come to meet and walk with Gordon exactly because she is blind. After a handful of city walks I realized that what many of them were missing was any experience other than a visual experience. This was not terribly surprising. After all, humans are visual creatures. Our eyes have prime positioning on our faces. We have trichromatic vision, which is sufficient to paint a Technicolor, million-colored landscape of the world. Our brains' visual areas, with hundreds of millions of neurons designed to make sense of what we see, takes up a full fifth of each of our cortices. The resplendent scene our eyes carry to us is entrancing. As a result, we humans generally do not bother paying attention to much other than the visual. What we wear, where we live, where we visit, even whom we love is based in large part on appearance—visual appearance.

But the world around us is not entirely or even mostly defined by its light-reflective qualities. What of the odors of the molecules making up every object, and those loosened odors wafting in the space around us? Or the perturbations of air that we can hear as

---

turning and looking at our partner in conversation when we are finished speaking. Just by using eye contact, it is taught in improvisational theater, you can wordlessly establish a relationship between two actors, marking higher status or dominance, for instance, by holding eye contact while speaking.

sound—and the frequencies higher or lower than we can hear? I imagined that someone who has lost her sense of sight could lead me, however superficially, into the invisible block that I miss with my wide open eyes.

The notion that the blind might use their other senses better than the sighted is not fanciful conjecture. Born of necessity, and supported by a nervous system that is much more adaptable than scientists thought even a few decades ago, the blind simply use their other senses to see. Often, people blind from birth get around so smoothly in a seeing world that it is hard to tell from their movement that they cannot see where they are going.

Gordon went blind half a lifetime ago, when she was in her forties, after years of deteriorating vision and unsuccessful surgical interventions. At the time, coincidentally, she was working in the city at a facility that helps the visually impaired manage and negotiate the world. As a social worker and advocate for her blind clients, she knew about and had access to the best technologies for aiding herself. But going blind in adulthood is a slightly different prospect than hereditary or early-childhood blindness. In all groups whose blindness is due to problems in the eyes, the visual cortex remains intact: ready to interpret what we see, but suddenly getting no visitors, no information from the optic nerve. Waiting for the flood through a door that never opens, it eventually starts to get some noise from the side doors: the other sensory organs, or even other cortical areas. Rather than turn off, the area becomes busier than ever.

The result is striking. Though blindness is hardly trivial, the brain of a baby born without the ability to see can undergo significant reorganization, enabling the developing child to depend on other cues to entirely replace vision. Scientists first learned this, as well as most of our knowledge about our brains, not from examining our own brains, but from peering at monkey brains. The monkeys did not submit to this voluntarily, of course: the content of the words you are about to read come from the poignant sacrifice of enough monkeys to type that Shakespearean play after all. A monkey's brain is similar enough to ours that scientists find it informative about human brains, but different enough that the same scientists are willing to sacrifice a monkey life for that bit of information.

The similarities are many. First, our brains are shaped much the same: each resembles an overstuffed dumpling, a generous half-sphere with an extra dollop (the cerebellum, which controls movement, and thus is a crucially important dollop) on the back. In the early twentieth century a German neurologist named Brodmann made a map of the primate cortex, the outer layer of the brain, identifying dozens of distinctive areas whose cells essentially do different things. There are visual areas; smelling areas; hearing areas; areas that register when you are being tickled in your belly; areas that coordinate your reaching for a cup. What Brodmann effectively demonstrated with this mapping was that the brain does not serve as a general-purpose depository for sensation: when our eyes spy the horizontal line of a knife blade held over our thumb, that event registers in one specific area of the brain; the pain we feel when the blade slices into our thumb involves another area. What was stunning about Brodmann's work, and the reason that the areas of the brain he identified still carry his name, is that he was able to create a map showing the shape and approximate location of each area in *every* brain. The "visual area" of your brain is going to match up, more or less, to mine (the "more or less" is important, too, of course, in making you *you* and me *me*). Were we skilled at such things, and if neurons regenerated like succulent roots (which they do not), we could each lop off this portion of our brains and we could swap. It appears that the role of the cells of the brain are designated in the genome. All else being equal, twins are born with the same brain.* Later, as their lives unfold and their experiences diverge somewhat, their brains develop differently—as, indeed, does every brain. But no one's brain reorganizes itself so much that it is not recognizable with Brodmann's map.

Except. The brains of those who have prolonged sensory deprivation are different. What research on these people or other animals reveals is the *plasticity* of the brain: its ability to fundamentally reorganize itself, most especially (and in some ways exclusively) early in life.

This plasticity is rooted in the way the brain represents information about the world. Per Brodmann, something seen with the eyes gets sent to a very particular part of the brain: the occipital cortex, also called the visual area. When we perceive an object, and when we later remember perceiving that object, there are cells in that visual area that fire, generating electrical connections with other cells that light up fMRI machines and our imaginations. This is how the brain represents our experience, present and past.

Now, say you have been looking at many examples of a certain kind of object—to make it simple, let's imagine you are employed to look for errant blue marbles at a green-marble production facility. Your occipital cortex will reflect this experience: it will change its very structure in a way that reflects that you have seen many green marbles, and it will react with a heightened interest and attention to the blues. This is a simplification of what happens in natural, real-world settings all the time. Our brains are changed by experience—in a way directly related to the details of that experience. If we have enough experience doing an action,

---

* All else is never *exactly* equal: even the same genome will be expressed differently given the slightest difference in environmental exposure, which every twin has from the time he is in the womb.

viewing a scene, or smelling an odor to become an "expert" in a field, then our brains are functionally—and visibly—different from nonexperts. So Charley Eiseman's brain is insect changed; Paul Shaw's is full of lettering; Sidney Horenstein sees rocks as we see faces. Examine the brain of a professional cellist (should such a brain make itself available to you), and you will find traces of her expertise in the gross anatomy of the organ. Not only will her auditory cortex be more developed—and larger—than that of someone who had not spent her life pursuing music, the traces are even more specific. In the somatosensory cortex, the part of the brain that receives tactile input from our bodies, there are individual, identifiable groups of neurons that receive input from each finger. In other words, there are "first finger" cells, cells committed to the "second finger," and so on. The somatosensory representation of the cellist has many more cells in the areas that map to the fingers of the left hand. Why? The expert cellist is a prodigious user of her left fingers to not only create, automatically and without reflection, the correct note on demand, but to do so with just the right pressure and vibrato to make it musical.

The brain is especially plastic early in life. Ordinarily, each baby's occipital cortex represents largely visual information but also receives some input from the other senses. What if that baby cannot see? There is not yet a change in the brain that can make him see if his eyes do not function. But many studies have confirmed that if there is no input from the eyes, the neurons of the visual area begin to reorganize themselves. Rather than dying off, more and more neurons start to fire upon receiving sensory information from the ears, from the nose, from the mouth or the skin. This neural plasticity can involve changes in the structures of neurons, the neurons' firing rates, or the connections between them. The result is that the blind baby grows up to be extra-attuned to his other senses.

This is the principle of plasticity of the brain: especially when we are young, our brains change depending upon what we are exposed to. Even in adults, the brain is always changing: the simple fact of learning something means that neural changes have occurred—if not as radically as in youth. A child who, in his first years of life, is unfortunate enough to lose an entire cerebral hemisphere, a half of a brain, due to tumor or other problem, will develop relatively *normally*. The other hemisphere simply takes over all the responsibilities of the lost one. By adulthood, though, a sudden loss of half a brain would mean the loss of impossibly many critical abilities, knowledge, and experience—and would be devastating. If it were the left hemisphere, for instance, the ability to understand language, use words, or write would likely be entirely wiped out, and the other hemisphere could not muster the forces to re-create them.

The baby born blind is (relatively) lucky: her brain will reorganize. With adults, the process is less dramatic. But even those who lose their vision as adults often pick up a heightened sensory ability or two. After he became blind as an adult, James Thurber continued to draw his famous long-faced hound dog, moving the pencil in a characteristic way between his fingers that let him trace its head without seeing what he was producing. He also had visual hallucinations: his visual system continued to think it was seeing something (including a blue Hoover vacuum, dancing brown spots and melting purple spots, and a couple of eight balls). All these images could well have informed his own whimsical writing and drawing.

Some blind people notice smells more vividly. Sacks writes of a doctor who became hyper-sensitive to the odors that we carry around with us. That would include body odor, certainly, but also the fragrances of the lotions or soaps or detergents that cling to us; and, for this doctor, even the odor we emit when anxious or unhappy. The doctor felt that through smell he perceived others' emotions more clearly than he had as a seeing person. This perceptual acuity is not just the realm of olfactory prodigies: with training, or simply attention, even the sighted can detect these smells. Might Gordon smell the lotion I spread on my face or the shampoo I lathered into my hair? Would people be olfactory curiosities or olfactorily offensive?

If she was vexed by the varieties of cosmetic scents we encountered in the elevator, Gordon did not let on. In fact, she told me she was sure she had *not* developed superhuman sensory powers with her blindness. Instead, she said, she simply used her senses better than she had before. But she belied this in the next breath. ". . . And a number of years later I also realized how much kinesthetic memory meant."

We were heading outside. I hesitated on the stairs, trying to step out of the way of other residents in the entryway while staying close to Gordon, but she moved with confidence, freed of this visual clutter. Gordon was using a cane, and it promotes and expands a kinesthetic image of the world. Kinesthesia is one of our senses—one that works within our bodies, mapping where our limbs are in space. Sensory receptors on muscles and joints give feedback to the brain, mostly without our thinking about it. Kinesthetic memory is, thus, muscle memory. It is what was at work for me when I got on a bike after a dozen years of not being on bikes, or when my fingers roughly knew their way around that Chopin waltz I long ago could play on the piano. Though you often are not consciously aware of your kinesthetic ability, it is always with you. Should you find it easier to show someone where an object is, or demonstrate how to do something, rather than tell him, your kinesthetic ability is trumping even your linguistic ability.

At Gordon's previous home, she explained, she navigated

the kitchen while cooking—or found a coordinated outfit in her well-organized closet—using this sense, her body's sense of how it should move within the space of the kitchen or closet. Thus the reliability of everything being in the same place was crucial to her. After her kitchen was remodeled, shifting the placement of appliances and commonly used items, Gordon spent years reaching for the dish towel in the place where it used to hang. Her magnificent new top-of-the-line oven was functionally useless to Gordon: its interior was so cavernous that she would lose track of where the casserole was inside. In the old oven, it fit perfectly, and she knew the width and depth of that warm dark space.

When a compressed nerve led to some loss of feeling in her left hand, she became more aware, too, of how she used touch in her closet, "to feel the fabric, to know whether I was hitting a knit, or a silk, or a cotton." Nonetheless, despite a reduced sense of touch, on the day we met, her clothes were impeccably coordinated. Even the color of her cane matched her outfit.

The cane was a long fiberglass number with a single colored stripe and a round ball at its tip. Gordon tentatively tapped the ground about two steps in front of her. She held my arm lightly and lingered a half step behind me. That way, "if we get to the edge of a cliff," she suggested, "you'll fall—but I won't." I accepted this deal.

As we progressed, I noticed that Gordon angled her head ever-so-slightly to the side, her ear leading her as much as her eyes. She was listening—for the cane, where it touched the world a step ahead of her. Cane work, as using a cane for navigation is called, is still a common skill taught to the visually impaired or blind. Though seeing-eye dogs get all the press, the "long cane" remains the most popular companion of the blind. Typically, users move the cane so that it traces a low arc in front of the body, touching down before the foot that is next to step forward. Approaching more troublesome spots—doorways, curbs—the cane might be swept lightly across the ground. Variant techniques, learned through much practice, are employed for ascending stairs, descending stairs, and walking along a continuous wall.

As we slowly made our way down the street together, I saw how much holding a cane serves as a signal for others: it fairly shouts out that this person is to be navigated around. With my relatively inconspicuous injury temporarily hobbling me, I appreciated the usefulness of the neon sign signaling that this person must be treated differently. (I can imagine not wanting different treatment, too, but on a city sidewalk it seems salutary.) For the most part, pedestrians walking toward us abandoned the sidewalk jockeying game wherein two approaching people try to yield as little as possible to each other.

But the real utility of the cane is in what it conveys to its holder about the space she is approaching. It carries tactile information about the surface underfoot, whether grass or concrete, smooth or rocky. It locates holes, gradients, obstructions, even errant distracted texters (although rarely fast enough to avoid collision). But more than that, it conveys information via sound. The cane is the fiberglass version of an echolocating little brown bat: it sends out a sound—a tap—which then bounces around the environment. Listening, Gordon, with her ear trained to the bounced sound, could discriminate the sounds of the space not just underfoot, but above her head and to her side.

Dolphins and bats naturally echolocate, sending out high-frequency sounds and listening for the sounds to bounce back at them. The frequency of the reflected sound paints a picture of the objects in their environment. Amazingly, these animals do this in real time, using it to make their way with the speed of, well, dolphins and bats: incredibly fast. Humans, sighted or not, also have some ability to learn to do a kind of rudimentary echolocation, using mechanical clickers, but we do not spend a lot of time flexing that muscle. Often, blind persons do. In some, this sensitivity is accompanied by an ability to hear the echoes of clicking sounds they produce themselves. With this skill, some can fluidly ride bikes and skateboard.

I became aware of Gordon's auditory acuity as we walked along her street. A classic Upper West Side street in New York City, it houses various towering apartment buildings. One barely notices the difference among them from street level: the bottom floors are often lined with a similar limestone. Any characteristic brickwork, cornice, or grotesques on the building face needed distance to be appreciated. Along this stony monolith to our side, Gordon suddenly spoke up:

"Are we under an awning?"

We were not. Each of the buildings we were passing had an awning projecting over the sidewalk. It is in its shade that the building's residents can wait for a taxi when it rains, or simply relax in the quasi-private transition from the city streets to home. But Gordon and I were not under an awning. We were, however, fast closing in on one.

"We're about two feet from it," I said, a little disappointed that she had gotten it wrong.

A moment later, we moved under it. With the warmth of the sun blocked temporarily from grilling our skin, even I, sighted and unobservant, could notice the change. The shade spoke relief for my arms and head.

"I sensed it," Gordon said with satisfaction. "There was a big difference in the sound."

Oh. *Oh!* The sound. The clap of her tapping cane bounced off and hit the underside of the awning, coming back at us muted, clipped. I could suddenly feel the closeness of the awning overhead, the way it broadened the sounds of our footfalls. A doorman chatting with a tenant in a low tone was perfectly intelligible. This public space felt private, protected from the sounds of the city.

Three short steps later, we were out from under the awning's shading reach, and noises again flew away into the open air. I asked Gordon if she could tell we had emerged. She took another step.

"*Now* we're out."

The awning Gordon perceived, I realized, was wider on either side than the awning I could see. This "sound" awning projected a good two or three feet more on both left and right: that was where the sound from the cane tap began to change. Gordon could see the awning. Hers was just a broader umbrella.

A professor of religion named John Hull, who lost vision in one of his eyes during his teens and in the other eye in his midlife, describes in his memoir how rain colors the landscape for him. With its "tapping" on everything in sight, it "throws a coloured blanket over previously invisible things," Hull writes. "Instead of an intermittent and thus fragmented world, the steadily falling rain . . . presents the fullness of an entire situation all at once." The lawn, the hill, the fence, the path, the bush are articulated by the pitter-patter of rain. Distances, variation, height, material, and curves all appear in splashes and drips.

This is how the cane does its canely magic. Gordon described to me what she was hearing of the landscape from its echo off her cane tap. She heard when an alleyway appeared between buildings lining our route. She heard the height of buildings and noticed when we had arrived in front of a school (quieted in summertime) set back more deeply from the street. Inside her building, she told me, she uses the sound of the floors that present themselves when the elevator doors open to identify whether she has arrived at the basement gym or the penthouse. "In a carpeted room," she added, "I'll sometimes get lost. Because I can't hear sounds." A tap on the carpet bounces exactly nowhere.

In Gordon's case, using the cane has changed her brain. Beyond "personal space," the space around us that we discourage most other bodies from entering into, our brains are also alert to "peripersonal space," the bubble of space outlined by and directly surrounding our bodies. The bubble extends to right about where our limbs can extend—so it is larger for people with longer arms, piano-player fingers, or legs up to there. Neuroscientists discovered cells in the brains of monkeys and humans that are specialized to fire to sounds, touch, and sights in this near space. Even with normal fingers and limbs, if you have ever sensed someone sneaking up behind you as you sat engaged in a book or a meal, you were experiencing your own peripersonal space. For even the sneakiest of persons creates small noises of movement and breath, emits ample odor, warms the air, and, with his body, changes the way sounds bounce around your head. We can feel his presence.

Wonderfully, our brain extends that bubble when we extend ourselves. Wear a top hat for a day and you will soon stop knocking it on low doorway lintels; after using chopsticks regularly, the brain begins to consider them extensions of your fingers. The brain of a baseball player experiences his bat as a continuation of his hands; the trumpeter's trumpet is an adjunct of herself. And a blind person experienced with using a cane has the athletes' and musicians' skill with it.

Your top-hat or chopstick bubble, though, lasts only as long as you wear the hat or eat your meal. The brain is plastic, and can creatively adapt to a new situation, but it changes right back when it no longer needs to be creative. In one study, researchers who blindfolded willing subjects for five days used fMRIs to show that the subjects' visual centers (their occipital cortices) had begun to fire at non-visual stimulation, such as when feeling the bumps of Braille. A day after removing the blindfolds, their brains morphed back into their ordinary, non-Braille-reading shapes. The authors speculate that connections in the brain that already exist but lie dormant are simply unmasked with visual deprivation. In blind people, they suggest, these connections are what are exploited, temporarily and then indefinitely, to help them take advantage of that visual real estate.

For an expert cane user, the broader sense of peripersonal space is permanent, too. The space around the cane tip is as thoroughly experienced by her brain as the space around a sighted person's hand is to him. She will be able to react as quickly to a sound from or touch to the cane tip as sighted people do to something near their heads or hands.

After a short way, Gordon let go of my arm, mindful of my promise that I would not let her wander off a cliff or into traffic. Immediately, her cane found a bulky concrete planter, which she probed, identified, and negotiated around. Clear of any obvious obstacles, Gordon nonetheless began veering very definitely to her left. And to her left was a fourteen-story prewar building made, I could see at a glance, of the kind of stone that is extremely unlikely to give if you walk into it.

So here I committed a cardinal walking-with-the-blind sin: I tried to guide her. I reached out, about to grab Gordon's arm to prevent this inevitable progress into the wall. Barely restraining myself, I managed to plainly offer, "Um, you're swerving to your left quite a bit. You've about a quarter of the sidewalk left before . . ."

Gordon was unfazed. "If I go too far, I'll hit the building. But I know where I am."

I couldn't be convinced. ". . . And now you're pretty close to hitting the side of the building . . ."

She stopped and seemed to look at me steadily, then resumed walking. True to her word, she went ahead and banged right into the building with her cane. Gordon's cane tapped a quick pattern on the wall and sidewalk, a perfunctory petting of an unbeloved animal. Then she smoothly righted herself, turning just enough to take a path parallel to the building's line.

Gordon had deliberately veered, I realized, in order to get a reference point. Out of the sea of the middle of the sidewalk, she headed for something tangible that could give her her bearings.

I was at least in good company in my overweening desire to help her avoid bodily injury. People grab her all the time as she approaches buildings, Gordon said. But they, and I, were simply not seeing how *she* was seeing the space. She was aiming to run into the building, not trying to avoid it.

"It's not an obstacle at all, is it?" I asked. "It's something you're using to navigate the space."

"Exactly." Gordon smiled, continuing on a perfectly parallel course.

I had watched her do something similar earlier as we left her apartment building together. Rather than merge into the flow of pedestrians walking to and fro along the sidewalk, Gordon cut straight across them until she hit something tangible—a lamppost—at the far side of the sidewalk. Heading into an undefined space, she had begun to define it by locating its breadth and its edge.

Even without a visual sense of it, she was essentially drawing a map of the space. Sighted people, blindfolded, do something similar. Left alone in a room, people tend to explore first by making loops out and back—and then they try to find a wall. Having found one, the blindfolded will follow it, then tentatively cut across to the opposite wall. After only ten minutes of this wall-bouncing, they are quite good at describing the shape and size of the room.

Essentially, Gordon and the blindfolded are developing what psychologists call cognitive maps: representations in their head of the space of their environment. This is something we all do, even under ordinary, non-blindfolded circumstances. Arriving at a new scene, we first compare what we see (or hear or feel) to the various stored representations of previously constructed maps of environments we have been in. If there is a match, we can proceed to ignore what we see—save anything novel or unusual that pops up—and wander into it with confidence. Thus we do not find ourselves truly examining a familiar environment every time we step into it. Stumble out your front door in the morning, and you can count on that stored map to guide you, blearily and barely awake, through the streets to your car or subway station. You already know which block has the fewest missing sidewalk stones, where the potholes are, on which side the sun is low and direct. Blindness does not stop this process of developing a cognitive map; it simply obliges map-making through non-visual means. For Gordon, that meant wayfinding by locating the edges of her path first. Once a location was familiar, she could use her stored map of the environment to walk through it without "looking" in her path-veering way.

• • •

It would be a mistake to think that all that a cane user experiences is the information borne through the cane, though. After a half block of supervising Gordon's left-veering and straightening behavior (never once needing me to help her), I saw an interesting scene ahead. It was the end of the block. Would Gordon see it?

The corner building was another grand old prewar apartment house—tall, well bricked, and shade lending. The moment we stepped past its corner, Gordon stopped.

"Are we at the end of the block?"

I grinned. "Right!" I assumed that she had heard her way to that conclusion. The street intersected with a larger boulevard, full of car and truck activity and its accompanying horns and hubbub. But I was wrong.

"I could feel it."

"Feel it?"

"The breeze."

Indeed, there was a subtle but noticeable current of air traveling along with the traffic, going north to south. City dwellers grow familiar with the superficial appearance of the buildings on their regular walks to and from their home and work, but there is another, unseen architecture that is nearly as consistent: the winds. Though winds change with weather, the shapes of large structures like buildings act on those winds in reliable ways. Urban microclimates are created largely by the changes in airflow induced by the man-made environment. In a city like this one, full of right angles between streets, a turned corner almost always brings with it a change in the flow of air. Though the direction and temperature of the air might vary by hour or day, the contrasting orthogonal airflow is more reliable than the particulars of street or sidewalk activity.

The urban windscape manifests a Who's Who of physics phenomena, involving forces and flows described by the Bernoulli principle, the Venturi effect, turbulence, and the properties of eddies and vortices. Streets lined by tall buildings become wind tunnels, through which the air being blown around in a large, wide-open area accelerates dramatically as it gets pushed into the small canyon of the street (the Venturi effect). Thus, winds over the rivers flanking Manhattan Island speed down side streets on land. No one who lives along one of these side streets needs to be told that the wind plasters the face and requires a whole-body lean to push through.* This occurs whether the streets are lined with particularly tall buildings or not, but in the former case, the winds blow faster for farther. Tall buildings create other wind effects: winds that hit high on a building rush down its face, sometimes creating enough pressure to make passage in and out of the doorway difficult. Sheer glass towers can pull air not just down, but also up from below (the Bernoulli principle)—as well as lift any skirts being worn in the vicinity. The edges of buildings have their own wind phenomena: circling eddies of air appear as air travels around the building's corner, snatching hats off approaching heads. Combine enough of these forces, and a vortex may appear, an independent whirlwind which lifts fallen leaves, discarded plastic bags, and city debris in its path down the street.

Gordon and I turned left, and I watched as people took a wide berth around us. With her cane and me riding sidecar with a microphone, no one could miss us. I wondered how she fared when there was not someone walking along with her. In particular, thinking back to my walk with Kent, I asked her, what about the cell-phone users?

Walking-while-talking (on phones) or texting is now commonplace, as is decrying the activity (unless you are doing it your-

---

* This is especially so along Manhattan's westerly edge, as much of the country's weather pattern flows west to east.

self). The decriers can be a sympathetic lot. When Oliver Sacks lost peripheral vision on one side, the West Village outside his home became suddenly unnavigable. In particular, he bemoans the hazards presented by people rushing hither and yon, "so preoccupied with cell phones and text messaging that they themselves are functionally deaf and blind." For people like Sacks, the behavior of people not considerate enough to look out for others makes the sidewalk a perilous, stressful place.

The trouble with cell phones on the street is that, though "talking on the phone" and "walking" do not seem cognitively complex, each requires attention. Even before there were retail mobile phones, there were studies using them to test distraction. A 1969 study asked subjects to listen to sentences on phones while driving to see if this distraction impaired their judgment and increased the mistakes they made (it did, on both counts: including mistakes in judging if that gap up ahead was big enough to fit one's car through). The reams of subsequent research on how cell-phone use impairs driving ability has led to bans in most states on doing these activities simultaneously—and to the subsequent upsurge in hands-free headset use (solving only part of the problem).

It is understandable that cell-phone use is problematic when doing something requiring concentration, such as driving at breakneck speeds down an interstate highway. But even walking down the street requires concentration, albeit of a more unconscious sort. Simply by having open eyes, pedestrians notice changes in the environment: a handcart being pulled across the sidewalk, an approaching carriage, a wayward long-leashed dog. Without consciously intending to, we make small adjustments. My walk on Broadway with Kent had been a testament to the success of this in keeping us, as most people, from colliding.

With Gordon, I became more attentive to the violations of the pedestrian rules. I noticed that people tended to slow down when using their phones. Rather than a benefit, this could be a menace, as the pace of pedestrian traffic is usually instinctively adjusted by pedestrians considering each other's pace and route. I saw examples of cell-phone walkers weaving, violating the time-honored stay-to-the-right street rules. Most critically, they were not *checking*: they did not look up. Walkers typically acknowledge each other with eye contact, enforcing the social rule of at least attempting to mind other people's paths. Cell-phone talkers are less likely to notice others, let alone acknowledge them. Nor do they notice something unusual at their feet, or even see a unicycling clown with a red nose and purple jumpsuit on their route (as one study tested). The pedestrian dance of Fifth Avenue is replaced by the herky-jerky stop-and-go dance practiced by poor dancers—and by pedestrians who suddenly find someone directly in front of them. With their eyes focused not on the street, but on the conversation in their ears, the skill we have developed in navigating pedestrian traffic is wasted.

So how did Gordon feel about these cell-phone users? They were always a hazard, she agreed, describing a number of full-body collisions because of distracted walkers. As she spoke, a young woman on a cell phone was gaining on us from behind. Her laughter was punctuated by periods of silence presumably filled by the person chatting into her ear. Gordon stopped. She often slowed to a stop herself when she wanted to make a point. The cell-phone laugher passed us.

"But one thing I will tell you. They make it easier to hear people."

For a noisy species, human pedestrians can be awfully silent. Walking with Gordon, I began to notice the numbers of sneakered, light-footed walkers almost stealthy in their passage by us. There are, to be sure, a number of people who give away their presence in their manners or clothing. There are the flip-flopped, the high-heeled, and those whose boots or hard-heeled shoes gently clip-clopped. There are the key jinglers, the pocket changed; the package burdened, the wheely suitcased; the panters, the grunters, the hummers, whistlers, and singers. You hear the foot scrapers and scuffers coming; and you can smell the perfumed or smoking brushing by. You hear the suspiration of a bag strapped across and banging against the body. The corduroyed.

Apart from these people projecting their path ahead of themselves, most people are remarkably quiet: the electric cars of pedestrian traffic. So people on cell phones may be a nuisance, but to the visually impaired, they are also beacons, sending out information about where they are (and what they are doing). To Gordon, they served to identify at least some of the presence in the otherwise unknown space around her. She appreciated their uncivil loudness.

They also were giving Gordon something I might not have heard (or, at least, attended to): details about themselves, conveyed in their voices. A voice carries a large amount of information about the speaker—from the person's sex to his size, ethnicity to age, even level of fitness (we can all hear the habits of the cigarette smoker or the physique of the obese in their voices). Voices carry emotional information, too, from disgust to sadness to surprise, even when speaking words that have nothing to do with emotional state. Most of us are quite good at naturally distinguishing emotions in vocal sounds. Potentially, the blind could be even better, although they are not always. With this in mind, the Belgian Federal Police force recently hired a few blind officers especially attuned to analyzing voices, especially on wiretap recordings. These officers are masterful at distinguishing accents and identifying what kind of room a speaker is in—things normal listeners can hear but do not attend to.

I cleared my throat, probably in an Alexandra-typical way,

and, telling Gordon something she likely knew, announced that we were at the corner. Gordon was already turning it. She began reminiscing about the building we were passing. As a young girl, she lived in this same neighborhood, less than a block away. "I remember when [the corner building] was being built." Her cane began tapping faster. "It has a gorgeous roof garden, overlooking the river." High above our heads, trees that would have been saplings when Gordon last saw them rustled and murmured.

A huge wind hit us as we turned the final corner back to her home. Gordon stopped in her tracks and stopped reminiscing. "That [wind] would be hard for the blind," she said, clearly thinking about "the blind" as though the category did not include her. The white noise of the breeze drowned out all the little sounds that are such a large part of Gordon's vision of her environment. But as she resumed walking, she continued to talk about her memory of the "new" building that had gone up on the corner. Gordon described the windows and the long, deep garden—and I gazed right at it, into her memory.

In front of her building she turned to shake my hand. "Nice to see you," she said. And then, as if noticing my smile in response, she added: "There's someone in my building who asked me, 'How come you use that word, "see?" How can you say "I see it"?' Well, I do see it. I said, 'see' has many definitions."

"Sound comes to us; noise we come upon."
(Hillel Schwartz)

The Sound of Parallel Parking

". . . the only sound was the hum of air conditioners . . ."

What was the first sound heard? The Canadian composer R. Murray Schafer, who wrote about the natural soundscape, answered his own question: *It was the caress of the waters.* As a species, our ancestors rose from the seas. We developed ears even earlier than we developed the ability to breathe on land. As individuals, the first sound heard by each one of us was watery again: we all began hearing the world filtered through the splashes of amniotic fluids. A fetus twenty weeks grown in her mother's belly has only enough sensory equipment to hear relatively low-frequency sounds, around 500 Hz or below.* It is speculated that the developing ear, with its first few nerve fibers grown, can fire only up to a few hundred impulses per second, so that defines what the

---

* *Hertz* (Hz) is the standard measure to describe the pitch at which we hear a sound. Sound is simply a wave of pressure moving through space; the number of hertz indicates the number of those waves per second. The higher the hertz, the higher the sound we hear.

211

growing baby hears (not a lot). Still, it is enough to capture her mother's voice, important for her survival and development, as well as the sounds of the placenta, the gurgle of intestines, and the coursing of Mama's blood around the womb. Later in the fetus's development, more nerve cells will begin to fire together at rates representing a wide variety of frequencies, from 20 to 20,000 Hz. Before birth, as well as after, these young ears will hear sounds from speech to birdsong, from the rumble of distant thunder to the high hum of fluorescent lights.

As I headed out onto the street with Scott Lehrer, a sound designer for theater and a sound engineer for everything from vocal recordings to museum installations, the first sound heard was a bus idling loudly by the curb. This was not entirely unexpected. We were in the city, after all, and any urban dweller grows accustomed to being barraged by an unwelcome clamor. In this case, the sound seemed designed for our consideration. Which is not to say *well designed*. The engine made a bubbling, roiling sound—noisy, slightly interfering with sidewalk conversation. We would be happy when it, or we, moved away: the cumulative effect of the sound was to make me feel increasingly uneasy. I wondered aloud if anyone could think of a way to like that sound.

Lehrer could.

"If you were just listening to it *for itself,* it could be a soothing sound, I think: it's a steady-state sound. And actually, if I recorded that sound and brought it into the studio, dropping down the pitch four octaves, you'd end up having this deep low repetitive sound, like a kettle drum."

The idle was just percussion, Lehrer was suggesting; just rhythm. Without knowing the sound came from a tourist bus; without seeing the bus's girth, overly large for a city street; without smelling the bus's diesel spewings, the bus sound was just a waveform moving through the air. At a "steady state," meaning the shape of the wave is somewhat predictable, constant—and made up of low frequencies, below 500 Hz. In other words, it was hitting us with tennis-ball-sized packages of air pressure at a rate of a couple of hundred a second. "Constancy" distinguishes it from the varied, changeable sounds that usually attract our attention. And it was a loud sound, but not overly so in a city full of sounds.

I welcomed the idling sound-ball–throwing bus because today we were walking to hear what we could hear. My time with Arlene Gordon had gotten me interested in listening. Most of my walks had focused on attending to the blocks visually. While some sounds have slipped through to my attention, I was struck by how unimodal I had become, trolling for the new thing to see and ignoring anything that I could not detect with my eyes (or nose). The human ear is open all the time; it has no lid to naturally refresh the auditory scene. Even holding our hands over our ears in the way children do, elbows akimbo and face a-grimace, many sounds get in. But while our ears are always open, we only half attend to sounds they carry, given the racket coming from within our own heads.

To walk and listen. To some extent, this would be an exercise in paying close enough attention to name what we hear. Simply giving a name to a sound can change the experience of it: when we see the thing that clatters or moans or sighs, we hear it differently. Naming, though, is not the exclusive reason for listening. Indeed, at times naming a sound aborts the experience of hearing altogether, shutting us off from continued listening and exploring the nature of the sound. *Oh, that's just a downy woodpecker rat-a-tat-tatting.* (*Now we can move on.*) Satisfied with our identification, we shift from attending to the downy ruckus to ruminating on dinner plans. So, too, goes the safari phenomenon: looking out over a savanna, patient observers will finally see a majestic creature appearing . . . then another . . . then a herd. The first thing we tend to ask is, what is that? To identify it—to name it—gets us no closer to understanding the creatures we have spotted, but it is often taken as a stand-in for that understanding. So named, the animals move on, and we move on to the next animal on our lists.

To be sure, it is difficult to describe a sound without invoking its name or source. "What's that funny sound?" my young son asks me about almost everything. I tell him, "It's a jackhammer," or "It's coming from that pipe." I default to an answer about the content of the sound. But another answer might be, "It's a *wocka-wocka-rattle-tattle*" or "It's a *fffsssstttsss*." With his unbiased ear and lack of vocal inhibition, my son will blow and toot a surprisingly accurate echo of what we are hearing. I am hopelessly bad at mimicking sounds with my own voice. I suspect my son will soon be just as bad: rare is the children's book that does not teach him that the dog says *bow wow* and the pig *oink oink*. This does not resemble what comes out of any dog or pig I know.*

So on this walk with Lehrer I was also aiming to listen to the sounds in and of themselves, to hear beyond their names. This is easiest to do as a tourist in a new environment, when even ordinary sounds are slightly off: the siren screams in discrete descending tones (as in the UK) rather than rending the air with a continuous ascending and descending peal (as in the United States); the telephone rings with a different ring. In an old city, a tourist hears the rumble of wheels over cobblestones that the native does not and notices sound bouncing differently between walls more tightly constructed than in spacious American cities.

---

* And what of giraffes? One might get the idea from children's literature that giraffes are silent. Not only do they whimper and grunt, but giraffes also emit an infrasonic, low-frequency sound when they "neck stretch," reaching the neck back over the body, and when tossing their heads up and down.

THE SOUND OF PARALLEL PARKING

• • •

I met Lehrer while he was working, on assignment tracking a sound. In a creative turn, he was looking for the sound in a palace of visual art: the Metropolitan Museum of Art, on the Upper East Side. His project was to find a sound to fit into a documentary film about a museum show in Vancouver. As he described it, one sequence taken of the museum's atrium was unaccompanied by realistic "museum atrium" sound. Lehrer was now in search of that sound, based on an appreciation of what the atrium *should* sound like, given its size, height of ceilings, construction of floors, and density of structures and persons. I shadowed him as he moved through the Met, quickly scanning each room before judging it useless—a central room that served as passage to other exhibits was "too busy"; a fountain in a large, atrium-like room was disqualified because "the water is pretty specific"—or promising. In the latter cases, after surveying the scene, Lehrer stood out of the way, spoke a description of the room into a small audio recorder, and then stood quietly recording the room. To all who passed he would have looked like a man in reverential contemplation of a distant sculpture.

When Lehrer had gathered an audio-recorderful of atrium sounds, we left the museum. That was when we encountered the bus. We crossed the avenue and left it behind. On a side street on the Upper East Side, we were wrapped in relative quiet surprisingly quickly. It was an early spring day, and the streets were full of the humanity that emerges after a winter's sleep. But in this part of the city the humanity is remarkably peaceable and hushed. I worried that we would only hear the rustle of expensive silk undergarments from this neighborhood.

The morning had seen rain but the afternoon had forgotten it. Trees were in hopeful bloom; children ran up and down the steps in front of the museum. Their gleeful shouts grew faint. We heard birds cheeping above our heads; our footsteps were again audible. Lehrer paused and looked back out at the street. "It's dry now, but did you hear the sound of the tires earlier?"

I had not.

"Tires actually stick to the pavement more because of the water" when it rains, he said. "You can actually hear the sound of rubber on water; it's different than rubber on pavement."

I felt for a moment like someone who just discovered she had ears. How had I never heard this sound? It was not just the sound of water splashing; it was not just the sound of wetness; it was the sound of tire rolling over water. I had not heard it! A barreling taxi, its tires probably making the regular old rubber-on-pavement sound, broke through my reverie as its driver rode his horn. Another car horn responded with equal outrage. I smiled: *there* was the noisy city I knew.

Utter noise: this is the familiar acoustic impression left by a city. Even standing side-by-side, two city dwellers attempting conversation must make an effort to be heard; a mumble would disappear into a passing truck's braking sigh, or the white noise of street traffic. The landscape of the city is filled with broadband sound drawing from a wide range of frequencies. While we may be able to attend to particular sounds, our experience is of a clamorous, unintelligible din—what has been called a lo-fi soundscape.

What makes that "noise" and not just neutral "sound" is another question. The avant-garde composer John Cage famously declared that "music is sounds," and thus appropriated ordinary sounds to be his music. In one of his compositions, the orchestra is silent for four minutes and thirty-three seconds; whatever sounds come in through the window of the concert hall or emerge from the increasingly restless and puzzled audience constitute his music. Still, if Cage was right, it need not follow that all sounds are music(al). Any sound we do not like we call *noise,* thereby introducing a subjective assessment to the din. That subjectivity is always there in talking about noise. Despite the precision of his science, the early physiologist Hermann von Helmholtz characterized "noises" as sounds "tumbled about in confusion," bothering mind and matter alike. Others invoke simply "interruptedness" as the character feature that makes a sound into noise.

The relativity of noise is reassuring to me. It seems more likely I could find something charming in the soundscape of the city if its noisiness depends as much on my psychology as on the sounds themselves. It is certainly the case, for instance, that one's experience of urban sounds changes with exposure. To the visitor, the city is just noisy; over time, one does not hear less, but one may attend to the details of it less.*

There is one sound that city dwellers seem to agree on as noisy, though. Lehrer and I did not have to wait long for it to come to us. As we walked along the quiet side street, the ultimate in interruptedness, a motorcycle with souped-up exhaust pipes came racing down the avenue we had just crossed. It might have been in our sights for two seconds at most, but the disruption was enormous. We had to stop talking. People walking by us stopped talking. I could almost swear that the birds stopped their chirping, the buses their rumbly idling, and our footsteps their echoing.

Some of the motorcycle's noise is just its *loudness,* clearly: less than a half block from the cycle, we were probably hit with 100 decibels or more. Decibels are the subjective experience of the

---

* Alas, sometimes one hears less, too: not only does hearing loss occur naturally with age (by this writing I have lost ability to hear the top 6,000 or so hertz of my original hearing range), but it occurs with exposure to any sound at all—even at non–Spinal Tap levels.

intensity of a sound.* Zero decibels marks the threshold for hearing a sound—and in a modern city, there is never a moment of zero decibel silence. We mostly reside in the 60–80 decibel range, which includes sounds from normal conversation across the dinner table, vacuum cleaners, and traffic noise. Once a sound gets to 85 decibels, it begins to damage the mechanism of our ears irreparably. The reason lies in the mechanism itself.

Cilia, tiny hair cells that stand upright in the cochlea, sway and jiggle when the vibration of air—the rush of air that is sound—wends its way into the inner ear. So stimulated, the cilia trigger nerves to fire, translating that vibration into electrical signals that give us the experience of hearing something. If those vibrations are strong enough, the hair cells bend deeply under their force. Air pressure can mow, crush, or sever the hairs until they are splayed, fused, floppy, or fractured—an earful of well-trodden grass. Bent and damaged enough because of exposure to loud sounds for prolonged periods, the hair cells do not grow back; the ears lose their neural downiness. The world becomes progressively quieter for the person attached to those ears, until there are no sounds, no music, no noise.

Cities are crowded with sources of sound regularly approaching this threshold of hearing loss. There are biological reasons for why we are so afflicted: our ears are designed to let in the frequencies at which we speak—from a few hundred to a few thousand hertz. Enormous numbers of man-made sounds occur in those same frequencies. We often find high pure tones the most irritating: the screech of a subway turning a tight corner or braking, at 3,000 or 4,000 hertz, or the sound of fingernails on a chalkboard, between 2,000 and 4,000 hertz. These sounds clobber us because

---

* Named for Alexander Graham Bell (his second *l* lost to history) for his role in sending sounds across telephonic wires to waiting ears.

of the shape of the human ear, which allows high frequencies to find their way efficiently to the cochlea. The very design of the ear amplifies these vibrations for waiting hair cells. But it is not just our ears that find the sound distressing; it is our brains. If we know that we are hearing what we have already deemed an "annoying sound," our bodies react to it as though it is: we have a sympathetic nervous system response, usually reserved for final exams, suddenly appearing lions, and the sight of our beloved. We sweat, and then we notice that we are sweating, and we sweat some more.

As Lehrer and I walked down the street in the wake of the motorcycle's roar, I noticed myself curling my hair around my left ear to expose it for better listening to what he had to say. This was perfunctory: our hearing is exceedingly sensitive, whether covered with uncurled hair or not. As Lehrer spoke, sound energy was heading down the winding caverns of my outer ear and being conducted through slender bones, making a membrane vibrate and those tiny hair cells dance. The force required to move our dancing ear hairs is so minimal that it would disrupt the tiniest mosquito not at all.

Unlike our other senses, in listening, the normally functioning ear actually makes its own noise, something called otoacoustic emissions. Though we do not generally hear these sounds ourselves, they are suggested to be sufficiently distinctive that they could be used as aural signatures to identify individuals. I inclined slightly toward Lehrer and listened for his. Nothing. Instead, a familiar sound, that of a compact, dense object making quick contact with a softer solid mass—*thwack!*—banged in our canals.

We both turned to our right, detecting the direction of the sound at once, coming from beyond a chain-link fence. A boy was throwing a softball with an older man in a mostly empty schoolyard. Water puddled along the corners of a basketball court; a set of bleachers sat unused. I reflexively grabbed the chain-link as though it would help me hear better while I peered through it. Sounds of a school playground: is there anything more evocative of childhood? The bounce of different kinds of balls on the court or in hand, the shrill cries of children hopping or running or dodging one another or in hot pursuit, the slap of a jump rope on asphalt, the rattle of a ball off a backboard. In the corner of the yard was a set of playground equipment and, whether I saw them or not, I thought of swings—impossibly squeaky swings, standard-issue rubber seats, bowed by the heavy bodies of children, tracing wide arcs. I have not only sat in uncountable swings, but I now sit my son in the city's playground swings on a regular basis, controlling the pace of the squeaking by pushing him faster or slower.

Just seeing the playground called forth a memory (*my own son swinging*) and evoked a clear feeling (*how magnificent this little boy is*) that nearly replaced my perception of the sight and sounds right in front of me. Awakened was the memory of the weight of his body as I pushed him, of looking at his cold hands gripping the chain in winter, of wondering how high is too high; and even of my own childhood, wondering what it would be like to jump off a swing and then, one day, after watching other kids do it hundreds of times, letting go, feeling the slice of space that formed between me and the seat, and then falling. It was nothing like my anticipation. It was like being lifted up by a benevolent soft hand.

I closed my eyes and half-shook my head to return to the present. To pay attention to one's sound memories is to open the door to a closet bursting at the hinges: something is stuffed just inside, on the edge of falling out and into your consciousness. In the present, Lehrer was talking. And I quickly returned my focus to his voice, for he was talking about squeaking sneakers.

"*That* is one of the keynote sounds of the schoolyard," he said, referring to Schafer's idea of those elements of a soundscape that may not be consciously attended to but are characteristic of a space. The ball-tossing boy was wearing orange high-tops, and I tried to match his foot movements to the squeaking I was hearing. It was a basketbally sound. So basketbally, in fact, Lehrer said, that televised pro basketball places microphones on the court itself to pick up the sound of the squeaks. "They know that's an exciting sound, hearing all those basketball sneakers maneuvering." The rambunction!

I wondered if the engineers ever ramped up the sound for greater effect.

"Oh, absolutely!" said the sound engineer.

We lingered a while by the schoolyard. Two teenage boys entered from stage right and headed for the basketball court stage left. One leapt up, his hand extended for the rim, the other added the twang of a dribbled basketball to the space. It hit us like the smell of a ripe melon in our faces. I asked Lehrer why the sounds were so crisp and ringing here. It would not be a good place to hold a chamber music concert, but it was full of bright, loud sounds.

"It's all pretty simple physics," he claimed. All sound travels at the same speed, around eleven hundred feet per second. So if one takes into account the distance from the sound source to the surrounding surfaces, and looks at what those surfaces are made of, the result is a decent approximation of what the listener will experience. In this space, with three brick walls and an asphalt surface underfoot, "It's very reverberant." The softball tossers were close to the back wall; the basketballers were near a side wall. Their proximity to the walls reinforced the sounds they were making. "If you listen," Lehrer said, "you can hear the early echoes, when the sound really snaps. . . . You won't hear the echo off that [first] wall as being a separate sound; it just reinforces the original sound, making it sound louder." For the other walls, another eighty feet away, we estimated, it would take seventy milliseconds for the sound to reach it and come back to our ears, making a second sound—"which is perceptible: it sounds like *TIH-ka*."

The reason we could not distinguish the sounds of the basketball or the softball from their first, early echoes is that the near walls were less than twenty or so feet away. The human ear does not have the acuity to distinguish similar sounds made less than forty milliseconds—less than 1/20th of a second—apart. The sounds blur together, making a single larger sound cloud. Lehrer takes advantage of this auditory phenomenon in his live-sound work when he needs to control the "articulation" or the intelligibility of the sound system: if he uses a speaker in a theater to amplify the sound from the stage, it had better be set up so that the audience hears the sound from the speaker synchronized with the sound onstage. Given the way our ears work, though, there is room for error—about forty (or less) milliseconds' worth—which means that a speaker can be set about fifty feet away and few people will hear the sound as echoing.

The amount of reverberation of sound in a space like this schoolyard is what Lehrer called the "wetness" of the space. This space was pretty wet. (And full of puddles, too, by coincidence.) Wetness is something a sound engineer can manipulate in a recording, turning it up or down for effect. Deep inside the museum a half an hour earlier we had walked through small rooms with carpets on the floors and weavings on the walls: these were "dry" rooms. The driest rooms are studios, acoustically "dead" rooms with minimal reverberation, which allows the sound mixer to control the sound effects himself, rather than leaving it to the room to define the sound. The wetness of a room, and the kinds of early reflections and echoes one hears, are, Lehrer said, "what makes rooms sound like 'rooms' to us—why a bathroom sounds different from a living room, sounds different than the kitchen."

It has to do with the size of the space, the distance to the walls, the objects within, and the surfaces of those objects.

Despite my familiarity with rooms, this was a kind of noise I had never listened for. Nonetheless, I could at once assent that yes, it seemed likely there was a definitive bathroomlike sound—hence, all the singing that goes on in bathrooms but not in dining rooms. Of course, we do think about these sounds when they are dissonant with what we see. Should a kitchen scene in a movie have a "bathroom sound" to it, the audience might notice something is off. Sound engineers compile and keep catalogs of specific room sounds, each with the right set of reflections and reverberations and frequency content. "I have my 'bathroom preset,'" Lehrer said, "and we plant the actor's voice"—recorded not in the bathroom but in a dry room in a studio somewhere—"into that reverb unit. What comes back is something that gives you the sense that the person is in the bathroom."

I vowed to listen for my office sound when I returned home. I wondered if it made a sound without me in it.

Lehrer and I reluctantly turned from the schoolyard and headed down the street. Passing under a low scaffolding, I remembered Gordon hearing the sound of the enlarged awning with her probing cane. Lehrer heard the change, too. We paused and smiled with the assumption of shared recognition at a clutch of tourists walking in the other direction. They did not appear to understand why these crazy people were giddy at the scaffolding. As we approached an avenue, the air became thicker with sounds: people moving and chattering, birds overhead, eighteen-wheelers and buses roaring downtown. A metal pipe dropped somewhere and banged three bangs before settling.

Among the rumbles and crashes, crowd noises and traffic, I felt impressed that I could hear and understand every word that Lehrer was saying—and he, I. Psychological science names this the "cocktail party" effect: the ability, demonstrated most characteristically when at a noisy party, to distinguish what the attractive person in front of you is saying from the general din of the room. We do this terrifically well, as a species. Even better, if someone three conversations to our right happens to mention something of interest to us—such as our name, or the name of someone we know—we are often able to tune right over to that conversation, like a perfectly smooth radio dial.

How we do this is still somewhat of a mystery, but one clue comes from "auditory restoration," or, less jargonly, perceptual filling-in. You have almost certainly experienced this phenomenon without knowing it. When you are listening to, say, a friend talking, it is rarely in a perfectly quiet environment. Regularly, other sounds are louder than and intrude on the speech sounds coming out of your friend's mouth. We only notice this when the noises drown out all speech; most of the time, noise might mask what the person is saying, but we do not miss a beat. Our brains spontaneously fill in the gap, constructing the sound that was missed. We do not even have the experience of missing it, so smooth is the filling-in.

If you are skeptical, consider the visual blind spot, which prompts the visual analogue of our auditory restorative process. By "blind spot," I do not mean the metaphoric blind spots we all have for the elephants right in front of us. I mean the hole in our visual field created by the anatomy of the eye. The retina, at the back of the eye, is slathered with photoreceptors that convert light to electrical signals. There are so many that any light that hits our eyes will inevitably hit one of these receptor sites; with our eyes open and daytime in front of us, we spontaneously and immediately create an image of a full, dynamic visual scene. But. Just one thing. Right in the middle of the retina there is a small hole. In a strange design twist, this hole is the necessary exit route for the nerve cells from the eye: the tunnel through which the optic nerve, ushering all the visual information that has hit the retina into the brain, leaves the eye. Where there is a hole, though, to let the wiring through, there are no receptors. So any light that hits that part of the retina is not noticed by our eyes or our brains. We *should* see a small black hole in front of us every time we open our eyes. We do not see that hole, however, because our brains, clever tissues, swoop in to pick up the slack. Our brains *fill in* the hole with what it expects to be there. We are constantly, fluidly making up what we see.

Given our ability to "see" things our eyes do not see, it should not be surprising that we "hear" things our ears do not hear. Still, this feat of auditory filling and sorting is nothing compared to that accomplished by other animals. Take bats. For most species of bats, which, though not blind, evolved to navigate by echolocating, tuning in to a conversation on a noisy street would be child's play. Echolocating bats *see* the world by *hearing* it, and they hear it by emitting high-frequency calls from their nose or mouth and then listening for the sounds to bounce back to them, all while maneuvering at high speeds. The intensity and the speed at which the sounds come back allow bats to construct a picture of their environment on the fly. Their sound vision is acute: it enables them to catch their prey—usually insects themselves working hard to avoid detection—on the wing.* It allows them to distinguish soft objects from hard; note whether an object is far, near, or very near; even distinguish between types of trees. New York City's little brown bats must successfully discriminate the broad-leafed London plane from the maples and oaks. Even more incredibly, all this parsing and organizing of the sounds of the world happens

---

* Among the many reasons to appreciate bats, this one stands out: bats are the primary responsible parties for our not being eaten alive every day by mosquitos.

while dodging branches and swooping in on prey. Bats need to adjust their picture of their environment as they move, and they do this by instantaneously changing the rate, pitch, and loudness of their calls according to what they are hearing. Then they are faced with a further challenge: as social animals, bats are always around other bats—all calling and flying themselves. Sometimes thousands of them flit about together in a small space. How they distinguish the sounds of other bats calling from their own echoes, and from the warnings and solicitations that are a normal part of bats' communication with one another, still puzzles researchers. It does appear that once in a while their strategy is just to go quiet.

Lehrer and I took that approach for a moment, too. We paused at the next corner and stopped talking, better to listen.

Our ears were alert to every sound. Cars came and went; pedestrians arrived and retreated. I collected these sounds like beach pebbles, warmed in my hands and pocketed. The jangle of a dog's tags; the scrape of his toenails on concrete; the leaked trickle of music from between a passerby's earbuds and her ears; the rumble of a subway underfoot. Trucks roared by; buses whined. In the lull between the pulses of vehicles, birds tweeted over one another in short sharp descending tones. Then a small sound drama: a man in a jumpsuit dragged a heavy vinyl bag up onto the curb in front of us; the weight of the bag could be seen in the man's cant and heard in its low rasp on the sidewalk. A moment later, an empty mover's dolly was rolled by, attempting to catch up with the jumpsuit. It nearly swiped a third man sweeping trash into a plastic dustpan, which folded up with a *thwack*.

Lehrer looked pleased. "A lot of stuff just happened sonically! Think of all the elements going on in those little events," he said, motioning at the space where the dragger, dolly, and sweeper had passed. "It was a symphony!"

Out of nothing, a symphony. As someone subjected to the noise of the city day and night, I was getting the sense that Lehrer's ability to turn bag-dragging into symphony was a shrewd adaptation. I was witnessing his psychological ability to turn the same noise I heard into music. Surely it is not only Cage who has a monopoly on this kind of transmogrification. Should we be able to do so on command, we would certainly be the better for it. We have not just emotional reactions to music, but physical reactions to sound. In Homer's telling, choral singing kept the plague at bay. Roman writers claimed that a short flute piece could relieve gout discomfort. And David's harp was famously used to loosen the grip of King Saul's mental illness. For myself, just a few chords played by Art Tatum will calm me right down. Of natural sounds, those that are "self-similar" are more likable: the sound of water running; the susurration of a breeze in the canopy of a tree. These sounds share something with fractals: we hear them as the same when played at different speeds or different loudnesses. Something about them resonates deeply in us.

Our intersection was providing the typical voices of the city environment, with its trucks and buses, street preachers and loud talkers, high heels and ring tones. At times, people have tried to make inventories of all the noises of the city—a taxonomy of the bright or dull, simple or complex, brief or enduring sounds that fall around them on waiting ears. It seems an impossible task. We do not have enough attention to notice every sound, or words with which to mark them. Even the buzz of our own bodies working— the thrumming of our hearts, the click of our joints—eludes our attention. To hear this, we need to go into an anechoic chamber. In these strange spaces, all external sound is muted. One can hear only the swoosh of blood circulating, the lapping click of the heart-beat, and the muscles of the lungs stretching with each inhalation.

In the city, residents become inadvertent experts on urban sounds. I know the difference, I realized, between the sound made by a shuttle bus and a city bus; I can recognize the acoustic signature of alternate-side-of-the-street parking days; I can tell from the language spoken around me whether I am on Broadway or a block away, on Amsterdam Avenue. Those who regularly walk in the forest may come to know each tree by its characteristic sound, be it a sob and moan (fir), whistle (holly), hiss (ash), or rustle (beech). In the forest, my ears are blunt instruments. In the city, they are well tuned. Sure, in the country one might be able to count the number of cricket chirps in order to determine the temperature outside.* But in the city, I know within seconds of waking up whether it is a weekday or a weekend by the sounds of the street alone. If a garbage truck is groaning, weekday; if the distant sounds of the highway are turned down a notch, weekend.

At our corner, a car backed slowly into a parking spot parallel to the curb. Its tire, turning, caught the edge of the sidewalk. A splendid rubbing-squealing-yawning-pull of rubber fibers and concrete filled my ears. This was a sound not just of a city but also of a particular moment in this city's life. The sound of parallel parking, of cars fitting into a crowded space, of two synthetic objects struggling to keep their integrity—this noise may disappear from the city in time. Either the design of urban environments, the rules of parking, the mode of transport, or the material of tires or sidewalks will change enough so that at some point the sound becomes rare. Then, if it is lucky, it will live on as a sound effect in period movies about the early twenty-first century, added to the pages of the Catalog of Lost Sounds among the rings of telephones and cash registers, the muffled flash-powder burst of an old camera, and the catch of the latch of an ancient refrigerator door as it closes.

---

* I have read, but not heard, that their pulsing rate quadruples with each degree centigrade the mercury rises.

Lehrer was speaking. "You feel it?" he asked. Under our feet, a train rumbled again. I could hear the subway, if I listened for it, but the sound was low enough that we felt it more than heard it. "Sound is a physical thing, you know—you reach a certain low frequency where you actually start feeling sound as well as hearing it. We can feel that bus." He nodded over to a bus cruising down the street. "That bus is shaking us."

It was true! A large tour bus ripped the air with the sound of its engine and the press of its tires, but I was surprised to find that it also jostled us with bursts of air. Lehrer pointed out another sound: *Ka-PLUMP!* A car struck a manhole cover ill-placed over its hole in the street; again, we heard it, but I also *felt* it. There is a tactile side to sound. More so than with vision, we can experience the physical agent (sound waves) in two ways at once. Once light becomes "ultraviolet" and invisible to us, we can feel it, but it is the feeling of our tissues slowly burning.* With sound, the overlap is less painful and more common: in low frequencies, the sense of hearing morphs into the sense of touch. The subway's rumble was almost tangible in the soles of our feet and our stomachs.

This fact has been used to great effect in insidious ways. In some cities, police sirens have been changed from their familiar—and ignorable—lullaby to a low-frequency bass boom that can be felt in your body almost before your ears. Audible sounds have been used in warfare: the U.S. government currently uses a so-called non-lethal acoustical device, which sends out low-frequency sounds in a very specific range to control crowds or as a warning.

There are other cross-modal components to listening. It is

---

* Ultraviolet light is visible to many other animals. Plenty of bees and birds, for example, use the reflection of ultraviolet light to find food (reflected off a bull's-eye around the stamen in the center of a flower) or a good mate (whose feathers may reflect more UV light if the animal is healthy).

visual, for one thing. Close your eyes, and your hearing is more focused. This is not because we need to shut off one sense in order to use the other. On the contrary, vision changes hearing. Though we hear with our ears, we often turn our heads to confirm with our eyes what the sound is. This practice seems ridiculous—who listens with her eyes?—except that it is so sensible. Straining to hear the person you are talking to on a subway platform, you would do just as well to stare intently at his mouth as you would to turn your ear toward him. Seeing what he is saying—through reading lips and monitoring expression—is sometimes as good as actually hearing it. Should you feel unpracticed at this skill, think again. You have been watching people speak all your life, and unconsciously training yourself to hear visually. Similarly, we may only be satisfied with our guess at the source of a sound after finding it with our eyes. The strident car alarm heard out your apartment window changes character when you discover which car is spouting it (and it thereby becomes more hectoring, usually).

Movie makers take advantage of our hearing with our eyes, Lehrer told me. In capturing a street scene like one we were gazing at, the foleys, in charge of sound, do not try to record it all. Instead, "they look for someone that people might want to visually focus on"—and capture the sounds, say, of just that one person's footsteps.

"And we can't hear the other people?"

"No."

"You don't have to get the other people?" I was impressed.

"Not really. You should watch that sometime on a film and see how often you see three or four people walking and you only hear one person's footsteps."

The sound has created a visual focus, and it is untroubling that we cannot hear the rest. I remembered the mute pigeons from my walk with John Hadidian; in their quietness, the birds now seemed suited to film. It changed my perception to imagine the noise we were hearing as in some way cinematic. The introduction of sound to films swung the expressive emphasis from what was seen to what was heard. Sure, film is a visual experience, but sound is used dramatically and effectively to heighten that experience. And at times, sounds can allow us to see something that is not even there. A dog barking off-screen is enough to invoke the image of a fenced-in, menacing guard dog, a stranger passing by, or an unseen intruder or disturbance. Viewers of science-fiction films know that automatic doors make a satisfying *pssht* sound, so directors can take advantage of its familiarity: to show a door opening, one need only film static shots of a door closed and opened, and overlay them later with the added sound effect.

Of course, one of the things that is not sound track–like about the sounds of the city is that the heard sounds are all functional, not emotional. Rather than inflecting what is happening with swooning violins, or punctuating a scene with comic, melodramatic, or rhythmic sounds, we just hear the sounds things make and the noises people utter. Our steps are rarely synchronized with a beat, or our emotions with a tune.

What would it be like to walk through a city with your own expressive sound track, in which a mugger arrives with menacing music, or the sight of a loved one is decorated with a swell of violins? I suspect this is one of the pleasures of walking while listening to music through headphones, or with earbuds burrowed into the inner ear. Certainly the activity distracts the walker enough from the actual experience of being on the street that he can become an annoyance to others, as his social sense is reduced to almost nothing, much like Fred Kent's cell-phone talkers. Others become merely characters in the great movie unfolding in three dimensions to the sound track coming through his earbuds. He moves through the film weightlessly, undisturbed, with nobody breathing down his neck and interrupting his flow. He stops experiencing what is actually happening outside; he is merely an observer, watching it happen, even while moving through it. It is almost as if, if he reached out to touch the person walking astride him, his hand would fall through their arm, it being but an illusion projected on the mesmerizing screen of his creation.

From our corner we were treated to a spitter's throat-clearing, mouth-contorting expurgation, so phlegmy we reflexively recoiled even at our safe distance—as though we were at risk of tasting it ourselves. Hearing can invoke memories that are emotional—as the nostalgia of the swings—or visual or tactile. To hear a regular, tonal beeping in the city is to imagine a truck's rear lights on and to nearly picture it creeping backward. Much of what I was finding to be distinctive about the sounds on this urban walk was the non-sound sight or feeling associated with them: the back strain felt in the man struggling with his dragged load; the feeling of popped gum in my mouth and on my lips on hearing a girl casually snap her gum as she passed.

The ears feel connected to the entire body. Music taps our fingers and feet and, if we are so inclined, our hips. The pleasure of a lover's voice is felt in our viscera and stands the hairs of our neck's nape on end. Or, as on this walk, we can feel nostalgic, empathetic, disgusted, or exhausted by what we hear. Hamlet's father was killed by the herb henbane poured into his ear—and no wonder, because the ear was thought to connect to all internal points, to course "swift as quicksilver . . . through / The natural gates and alleys of the body." Even the sound of the click of heels from a woman walking by felt empathically translated into myself, and I could feel what it is like to teeter on those high-heeled perches.

Daily, we are exposed to sounds that affect our bodies in ways we might not know. Low-frequency sounds are the source: waves coming too infrequently for our ears to make much of them but slipping into us quicksilver-like. Low enough, and we call it *infrasound,* as though if humans cannot hear it, it is not a true sound. Of course there are plenty of familiar animals who make a living using infrasounds—elephants, for instance. A bull might stomp a message that travels ten kilometers along the ground, as infrasounds are resilient to weakening as they travel over space and time. Lots of man-made objects inadvertently produce infrasound. These noises are omnipresent and damaging.

Ventilation fans moving stale air out of large office buildings, thrumming along at a few hertz, are doing a service, but they have also been implicated in thrombosis. Their low-note hums not only get into our bodies' gates and alleys but also might vibrate in rhythm with the heart, amplifying and thus disturbing normal circulation of blood. Sounds traveling at 7 hertz, including wind sounds, have been implicated in headaches and nausea, as they vibrate in time with the alpha waves of the brain. Loud sounds can cause the heart to seize or skip a beat. For whales, Navy sonar signals interrupt their communication and damage the tissue of their ears.

Sounds are also contagious, whether they are emitted by a living thing or a simulacrum. The sound of someone breathing heavily in a movie can affect your own breathing rate. A commercial jingle is successful if it lands in your head and stays there, replaying itself unceasingly. You may not want a Coke or a mattress or a pizza right this second, but the suggestion has wormed its way into your subconscious in case you grow thirsty or sleepy or hungry. And the contagion of sounds has a biological component: if a predator growled at our ancestor's ancestors tens of thousands of years ago, his insides likely vibrated to this growl, and he hightailed it away from the scene. Today, if my son, recently an infant, cries, I feel it viscerally. I can locate no anatomical mother-button he is pushing, but I react as though there were one. It is as if he cries at a frequency that makes my interiors rumble—and I hightail it toward him.*

I can tolerate the sounds of my son's cries, but the sounds of other people's cries, as well as most sounds shared in a city, have made generations of urban dwellers first cringe, then fume, and then, finally, form Quiet Leagues, Anti-Noise Campaigns, and Noise Abatement Commissions. As early as 500 BC there were complaints about the noises of animals working (elephants trumpeting, horses whinnying) and men playing (gongs, drums, or just making merry). By the seventeenth century in London, the complaints began to find their organized center. These afflicted urbanites were subjected to not just babies but also street criers hawking their baskets, beans, bells, cabbage, eggs, or flowers to anyone within earshot. Chimney sweeps, chair menders, and tinkers hollered notice of their services; dogs yelped, roosters awakened, and street musicians added musical insult to auditory injury. Parliamentary action was taken against the musicians and their "devious and hurtful" sounds. By the turn of the twentieth century, New York City had joined the din against the din. The din itself had changed: no longer was the urban soundscape full of noisome animal sounds; machines had overtaken them. The polemics against noise cited the incredible cacophony of engines revving, honkers honking, pneumatic drills, pile drivers, and wheezing trucks. This was on top of the people playing piano poorly inside and saxophone poorly outside. All the singing, crying, rattling, whistling, thudding, slamming, ringing, rasping, and alarming was bad for health and for habitation.

By the time Lehrer and I finally left our position on the corner,

---

* Indeed, some research using fMRIs found that two areas—the amygdala and the ventral prefrontal cortex—in the brains of parents grow more active at the sound of an infant crying. Not so nonparents, whose brains showed a bigger response to laughter than to crying.

my ears were well nourished, stuffed full. I had almost stopped listening to the city, and that may be why, when Lehrer was saying, ". . . like that siren we heard over there," I was struck. I had heard no siren. How I could have missed one of the noisiest features of the urban soundscape is beyond me. What Lehrer was describing partially explained it, though: the way the city sounds simply is not the sum total of the sounds in it: "You know, we can't really record that [siren sound] because if you recorded the siren so far away all this other, closer noise happens," crowding the sonic scene. "If you record the siren closer, you get a clearly defined sound. But then if you just take that and put it into your soundscape when you're making an environment, it sounds wrong."

In the real world, the sound is reverberating in a particular way based on the structures it is passing; the sound arriving at listening ears is changed depending on what lies between the ears and the siren. The pitch and loudness may seem steady, but they are changeable, and they are different if the listener is a block or three away. The Doppler effect will be different based on not just the speed of the ambulance bearing the siren, but on the direction of your movement relative to that ambulance. Viewed this way, every moment of listening in a city is unique, a sonic landscape painted for the moment and then washed away.

Even temperature changes our perception of sound. It is not our ears that are changed, nor the sounds themselves (for the most part), but that different temperatures control how far and where sounds will travel. Perhaps you have a memory, held in your body as much as in your head, of being outside in the wilderness, in a wide open area, the sun beating down on you—and experiencing an intense silence. Or, relatedly, on a clear night outside, hearing distinctly what is going on in a tent three campsites away. Lehrer's siren carriers farther on the city's coldest days, when fingers are balled up in mittens and footsteps clop loudly on sidewalks.

We can turn to the sound-making habits of animals to explain what is happening here. Natural selection naturally selects the animals who send signals to their potential mates that can be most clearly received: so, in many cases, evolution favors those who intuitively know how to best send a sound signal through a medium— say, air or water. Not all air (or water) is alike: often it forms a kind of layer cake, in which each layer is at a different temperature or a different pressure. For instance, as you dive deeper into the ocean, the pressure steadily increases: the greater depths have a much higher pressure than the shallower waters. On land, each night the earth cools, and in the morning the radiated heat makes the ground cooler than the sky: here, the lowest layers are cooler than the higher layers. We can think of the layers as having certain "sound speeds"—speeds at which sound can travel.* It turns out that sound travels more slowly in warmer air (or lower pressure) and faster in cooler air (or higher pressure). If the sound is traveling along a cool layer and there is a warm layer above it, the sound will spread into it and diffuse. On the other hand, if the sound is moving through a warm layer and there is a cool layer nearby, it will continue to travel along that warm layer, which now channels the sound farther before it weakens and fades away.

This is why you will hear the most birds singing at dusk and dawn. After a cold night, when the earth is chilled, the ground layer is cool and the layers above the treetops are warmer: a tem-

---

* Sound is always the same kind of stuff: compression waves propagating through a medium, causing particles to hand off the vibration to their neighbors. We hear these waves as pitched higher or lower, or as being more or less intense—but they can also travel faster or slower. Counterintuitively, while sound moves at around 1,100 feet per second in the air, it races along at somewhere on the order of 5,000 feet per second in water. Though water is denser than air, which slows down the passing of the waves through the water molecules, it is also stiffer than air, which speeds up the sound. Sound passes through solids, which are stiffer still, at fifteen times the rate as through water.

perature inversion from the ordinary arrangement of the ground feeling warmer than the air. A bird singing at dawn can send his tuneful song traveling much farther along the treetops than it otherwise would. This is good news for singing birds, who are hoping to reach as many other bird ears, especially of the female variety, as possible. Likewise, few birds sit around on the ground calling to one another in the middle of a sunny day, and temperature is again the cause. In a warm layer of sound, their calls get scattered every which way. The message they are sending to the bird a skip and a jump away may not even reach them, the sound disappearing into the ether.

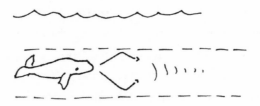

Similarly, there is a fine whale radio channel in the ocean—in a layer of ocean. The layer sits at about a thousand meters below sea level in the North Atlantic, where the pressure is not yet too great and the temperature is not too cool. This allows for long-distance sending of sound signals, on the order of miles, channeling the sound horizontally to distant whales' waiting ears. Some twenty hertz sounds made by fin whales, who live in deep water often under ice fields, are speculated to travel for hundreds of miles. Though these whales are highly social, they are also often quite well dispersed, and make these low-frequency sounds to keep in contact with one another. Their calls could travel even farther but for interference from other sounds made by other whales, the ice itself, or, increasingly, by human beings—from ship traffic, undersea explosions, and Navy sonar.

If sounds travel differently along temperature channels, the seasons of the year could also be considered to be separate channels changing sound perception. After a big snowstorm, the city is noticeably quiet, the snow snatching the din and burying it under its chilly cloak. Packets of snow occasionally flop noiselessly from lamppost heads to the ground below. Few cars roam the street, except the snowplows grittily scraping the asphalt under their wheels. Boots squeak as they carry the weight of bodies over a sidewalk of snow.

My footsteps, quiet in sneakers, were reflecting the spring. We descended the stairs at a subway entrance—the very subway that had rumbled below us earlier. Before Lehrer and I said our good-byes, we lingered in the anteroom of the subway, struck by the sheer number of noises in the space: the clunk of the turnstiles, the snippets of quickly passing conversation, broadcast announcements accompanied by impressive static. When a train actually arrived, it brought its own reverberant broadband rumble, the squeak of its brakes, a swarm of noisemaking commuters, and the whirr of its accelerator. Those entering the station yielded to those leaving, and then the tide turned again. Turnstiles *ding*ed at a prodigious rate, recording the paying fares.

"No one bothered to make that consonant at all," I reflected, listening to the different turnstile tones overlapping.

"Minor second," Lehrer responded in a flash, describing what we were hearing. He whistled it. "People don't like the minor second."

There is a solid scientific basis for this aversion. The pitch of a sound is its most audible frequency of vibration, but that particular vibration is just one of many produced at the same time with any sound. A note played on a piano, for instance, may be heard as one note, but it "includes" many other pitches that help make up the sound we hear. An experienced musician may be aware of these pitches; the rest of us are likely not. The series of pitches hidden within one note are called overtones, and they correspond to other notes on the piano. Hit a middle-C and it vibrates at 262 hertz most loudly. But the note at 524 hertz, the C an octave up, rings out as well. This hidden vibration is the first overtone. The fifth, a G, is next, followed by the fourth, the major third, the minor third, and so on. You might not hear these overtones, but you are surely aware of them: an octave sounds pleasing to our ears, as does a fifth or a third. When one gets to the outer borough of the overtone sequence, though, the sounds are more dissonant. The minor second is well in the outer boroughs. Similarly, the tritone, an augmented fourth or diminished fifth, is so dissonant and unnerving that it was thought to be the work of darker powers, and it came to be called *diabolus in musica,* the "devil's interval." In the Middle Ages it was prohibited in music.

I wondered if this minor second was having any long-term psychological effect on the transit workers stuck in the underground booths.

One of the old uses of the word *silence* netted and pinned forever to the page in the *Oxford English Dictionary* is the nineteenth-century's "a want of flavour in distilled spirit." I thought of this that night as I sat down to listen to the audio recording of my walk with Lehrer. Back in the silence of my office at home . . . wait. There was not silence but *relative* silence. I knew that a few blocks away, a highway hummed. There were regular sounds of apartment living coming out of the back windows my office overlooks. Clothes languidly swished in a warm-water cycle nearby. And the sounds of the day left a ringing in my ears, representing all the sounds we *hadn't* heard outside. Our brains make sound out of silence. *Noise* seems to be the flavor we are designed for.

As I transcribed the recording I made of our conversation on the walk, I was struck by all the noise the recorder, with its high fidelity and indifferent attention, picked up that I had missed at the time. It captured and preserved its own rhythmic banging against my leg as I strode. It noticed my sniffing, an indication of the chill I was collecting as the walk went on. I was surprised to hear on the tape how often the wind rode in to wash out any other sounds. Once, the curls of a laugh rose above it; other times, it erased everything else. I listened for any extraneous sounds of Lehrer: snapping snaps, sighs, a whistle while he inhaled. He was silent. At the end of the tape, we said our good-byes, and the sounds of the city swallowed him up.

Taking a walk entirely for the purpose of listening, I had still missed many sounds. But something else had happened. What I heard had morphed from noxious urban noise into being the characteristic, flavorful clatter of my city. I enjoyed the roar of traffic and the buzz of flies; I looked at pigeons hoping they would coo; I stared down passersby, silently egging them on to hum or cough. I counted squeals and squeaks and squawks and measured them against whines and whistles. Each sound felt invited, a pleasure. Welcome, sound.

"The only true voyage . . . would be not to visit strange lands but to possess other eyes, to see the universe through the eyes of another, of a hundred others, to see the hundred universes that each of them sees, that each of them is."

(Marcel Proust)

A Dog's-Nose View

"A beagle pulling on a long leash trotted by and unceremoniously defined the corner of the trash pile by urinating on it."

This entire project sprang from a walk with a dog; it seemed apt that it end with one. I spent sixteen years walking with (and informally studying) Pumpernickel, a curly haired, sage mixed breed. Through her choices, the subjects of her attention, what she balked at or lunged toward, I began to see her world. By minding her attention, seeing what she saw from two feet off the ground, and observing how much she seemed to *smell* her way through the world, my own perception was changed. I began to see how horrible a long block with no trees or lampposts was: where could one receive word, through the markings of other dogs, who has been around? Where could one leave word oneself? Despite my never once attempting to communicate with others by peeing on the street, I picked up Pump's aesthetic preference for streets with a lively set of street furniture, trees, and other curbside paraphernalia.

During her life, we developed a wide variety of walks together geared to what I imagined her view of the world to be. There were *into-the-wind* walks, during which she kept her eyes closed into slits and her nose in the air, nostrils working mightily. We took *smell walks*: instead of racing to take a walk defined by me for its length or its destination, we loitered at every place she wanted to smell, as she inhaled her view with her nose. As she grew older, we took walks that were largely episodes of sitting, in a field with ample olfactory vistas and plenty of dogs upwind. Most dog walks are done to allow the animal to pee or to get exercise. While those are sound reasons for a walk, what about walks to see the world? To interact with other dogs? What about walks to smell new smells?

Because humans are not smell-centered, we have difficulty imagining how rich in odors the world is. That is a constraint of our eyes: the picture they paint is so vivid that we assume there is no other way to make sense of the world but as a series of things to see. For most other terrestrial mammals, though, on four legs and with their noses near the ground, the world is perceived through odors. Kenneth Grahame, in *The Wind in the Willows,* introduces the genial Mole to school us: "We others," he writes, "who have long lost the more subtle of the physical senses, have not even proper terms to express an animal's inter-communications with his surroundings . . . and have only the word 'smell,' for instance, to include the whole range of delicate thrills which murmur in the nose of the animal night and day, summoning, warning, inciting, repelling . . . those caressing appeals, those soft touches wafted through the air."

Mole must lead us stump-nosed, blunt-seeing humans to imagine what it might be like to "see" in this way through metaphors: metaphors from sound (murmur), tactile sense (appeals, touches), and evocations of emotion (thrills, inciting, warning). We can come up with a vivid description of how a place we visited *looked*; but how it *smelled*? We are left with vague comparisons ("like a summer's day") that are evocative but not specific; names that tell us nothing about the quality of the scent (the smell of garlic or fresh bread); or superficial quality words (foul, lovely, delicious, spicy). What smells are very good at is beckoning memories forth: a whiff of pipe tobacco reminds me of the smell of the inside of my father's desk when I was a child and he was still a smoker, of the sound of his footfalls and the jangle of the change in his pants pockets, of what it felt like to have him listen to me and smile. The smell, like the memory, is entirely personal. It cannot be shared with the ease that an image, rendered in ink or oils, can be experienced by hundreds or millions of viewers.

By now, it is well known that dogs are "good" at smelling. As we humans open our eyes and see the world, dogs come out of sleep with both nostrils working. A dog's nose is remarkably well made for this task. The inside of the nose is a labyrinth of tunnels lined with specialized olfactory receptors waiting for an odorant molecule—a *smell*—to land on them. In the back of the nose is an "olfactory recess" separated from the main respiratory pathway by a bony plate, allowing smelling to be distinct from breathing, and letting odors loiter for a long time to be considered. Though we tend to think that only some things are smelly—a spring bloom, a trash can, a new car, a bus's exhaust—just about everything has a scent. Anything with molecules that can be "volatile," that can evaporate into the air and travel toward a receptor in someone's nose, smells.

The dog nose has *hundreds of millions* of receptors in that nose; they even have a second kind of nose above the hard palate of their mouth, called a vomeronasal or Jacobson's organ. Molecules such as hormones that do not stir the receptors of the nose to fire may find a rousing welcome here. All animals house hormones, which are involved in bodily and brain activities, and those hormones we emit, called pheromones, are detected by the vomeronasal organ. This is how a dog could detect another dog's stress or sexual readiness in a spray of her urine left on the ground.

Dogs are called macrosomatic, or keen-scented, while humans are called microsomatic, or feeble-scented. It is not for lack of equipment, though: almost 2 percent of our genome, the entire blueprint for making a human being, is dedicated to coding for olfactory receptors. Think of it! One out of every fifty genes is committed to making cells that can detect smells. So smells are important to us. Without smells in our lives, we become desperately unhappy—foods are not enjoyable, the environment is flattened—while some smells bother us excessively.*

But for much of the day, we go about our business un-smellily: we do not smell overmuch. For humans, odors tend to be either enticing or repugnant, alluring or foul, evocative or evaded. To a dog, the world is terrifically smelly—but not in the way we think of smelliness. To the dog, smells are simply information. Their world has a topography wrought of odors; the landscape is brightly colored with aromas.

---

* Smelling through the nose is "orthonasal olfaction." There is also "retronasal olfaction": from the mouth, into the nose from the back. That is why if you plug your nose when you eat, it is hard to identify what the food is that you are lolling around on your tongue.

Biologically, the human nose works in the same way as the dog's. Odors are swept into the far reaches of the nose and land in receptors—a few million of them. But that is hundreds of millions fewer than the dog bears.* The difference in number of cells translates into a difference in kind. Dogs detect odors at one or two parts per trillion, unimaginably more sensitive than we are. One part mustard, one trillion parts hot dog: dogs can detect the mustard.

To begin to understand what a city block really smells like, there seemed to be one clear course of action: ask a dog. So it happened that one day I set to taking a walk around the block for this book with Finnegan, the earnest, playful black dog in our home now. I began by asking Finnegan about his interest in accompanying me, in showing me the odors of our block. From the way he was plopped languidly on the sofa, head relaxing off its edge, he did not look inclined. But on my second request, he leapt up, consented to having his leash snapped on, and trotted out our door alongside me.

Finn pushed out into the fresh air with enthusiasm. I followed him. Then we . . . stopped. It had occurred to me to ask *his* preference in our walking route, so instead of pulling him left (parkward) or right (cityward) when we exited the building, I stopped on the steps. Finn, ever cooperative, stopped as well. He perched on the top step, projecting his snout proudly ahead of him. As a steady, light stream of people walked by, they pushed air out of the way as they passed, occasioning plenty of sniffing by Finn. If someone so much as turned in his direction, he ducked

---

* How receptors and the brain code the odors as distinctive smells is a live question for science. There is not one receptor for a single odor, nor is any one receptor activated by just one odor. There is no single receptor for roses, nor for coffee, nor for the smell of a baby's head. An odorant molecule fits in many receptors; and many receptors fire to many odors.

his head and let his tail wiggle his body with anticipation and excitement.

I waited for him to make a move. Between passersby, his body was still, only his head reacting to the activity on the street. The day was especially windy, and a sad old flag on a building across the way whipped around its pole. Finn perked his ears at the snap of the cloth, the bang of the flag rope against the pole. A sound Scott Lehrer could use for a shot of a seaside New England cottage hit by an ocean breeze, I thought. Our urban wind carried the sounds of someone hollering down the block, and tumble-weeded a plastic bag, belly full of air, along the tops of the parked cars.

We stood on the steps for several minutes. At last, I realized that should I not start us moving, we would not be having a walk at all, but a rousing "stand." Were Finn any other kind of animal, he might have bolted as soon as we got outside. So I chose a direction and began walking. As we set off, I watched Finn's attention. My audio recorder was again useless here, as it had been with my son. Instead, I would have to let Finn tell me what he saw by observing where he went, where he loitered, how his ears bent into focus, and how his tail measured his mood.

Straightaway, he sneezed, then licked his nose. I had to think that this was not significant, a reflexive reaction to a pollen tickling him. Later, I would rethink this. Finn pranced along by my side. He held his head high, and it gently bounced up and down with his stride. His gaze lightly touched the wall to our left, a garage door closing, a dog passing on our right. A driver honked a loud honk; Finn did not pause, but his eyes narrowed and his ears flattened against his head. Pressing down his ears should make the sound quieter, if not absent—the canid equivalent of our covering our immobile ears with our hands.

It was not long before he stopped outright. He licked his

nose again. A squat, unimpressive baluster caught his interest. It appeared to be made of poured concrete and held up an iron railing: a short skirt worn by the building to protect it from us. Finn peered at it, nose millimeters away from the surface. He even touched the surface, moistening it with small nose prints. I tried to follow his nose-gaze. I could see a palimpsest of messy splashes of drying liquid, some more messy or more dry than others.

This was, of course, the motherlode for dogs: other dogs' urine. Visible generations of urine splotches lay one (roughly) atop the other. After some satisfying-looking sniffing, he moved to the next urine post. And the next. I noticed with some chagrin that there appeared to be a half dozen balusters ahead of us before we reached the corner. Given his renewed attention at each, I got the distinct impression that to him they were not at all alike. Each told tales of different visitors, some well fed, some ready for sex, some aggressive, some ill. Maybe some sad, longing, suspicious, or delighted.

I began to imagine the sidewalk as a place that conceivably held traces of other people's passage—of their mood and health and habit. In what form I might see those traces was another question. *Other people's trash* was the first thing that came to mind, unhappily: in a city, there is always evidence of others' passage by the things they let drop through their fingers. But there are many more subtle cues. The fog of warm air that hits me as I pass a parked car tells me that someone quite recently turned off the ignition and left. The disruption of fallen petals or leaves on the sidewalk works like reverse tea leaves to tell the story of how many people have swept by. Look up when you see a flurry of cigarette butts on the ground and you are bound to see the entrance to a commercial building. (And it is likely after lunch break.) Some years ago I began noticing, then collecting, stray single gloves or mittens lying forlornly on the ground, displaced from the hands they had been warming. These melancholy creatures, always frozen in an awkward or pleading pose, indicated recent passage of someone busily doing something requiring a free hand. I found more right gloves than left, probably a reflection of the overwhelming right-handedness of people, and the inclination to remove a right glove to do something requiring dexterity: take out one's wallet, punch in a phone number, retie a shoe.

I did not know more than this about the people who had passed, shedding their gloves. Certainly, they now had chilly hands. But were they happy or sad, old or young, healthy or ill? Did they live nearby, were they passing through, did they walk with someone or alone? Apart from the difference between a child's mitten and an adult's leather glove, any personal details eluded me. I did not yet have the perceptual ability to determine who those recent passersby were—though I suspected that information was there to be discovered. As Finn would soon tell me, the dog can see it.

One thing puzzled me about Finn's baluster examination. Once I saw what he was sniffing, the graffitied sprays and splashes were easy to spot. But Finn did not always go directly to the message. He sniffed around it, as though not sure where it was. A dog's vision, though not nearly identical to ours, surely lets him see what I saw here. Finn could see the urine mark, but he was "scanning" the area, just as we scan a scene with our eyes. To see a scene is not to stare fixedly at one point; it is to open our eyes to everything in front of us, looking to and fro. Similarly, to *smell* a scene, Finn approached it from the side, from above, sniffing the air to see if the artist who concocted this particular odor splotch was anywhere nearby. A dog can smell something different in each noseful—and there *is* something different there to smell. This taught me something about smells: they are not at fixed points, nor are they static and unchanging. They are a haze, a cloud, spreading out from their source. Viewed as odors, the street is a mishmash of overlapping object identities, each crowding into the next's odorous space.

I leaned in closely to watch Finn's sniffing. He stopped at once, of course, possibly wondering why I was giving him the eye. What I did see was that he was sniffing *fast*: dogs can sniff up to seven times a second. Humans sniff about once every two seconds. If you try hard, you can do a good run of a dozen sniffs, but then you must stop to breathe, and in exhaling, all that good scented air gets expelled. Should you want to avoid smelling something, give a good strong exhale from your nose. If you are out of its cloud when you next inhale, your olfactory receptors will be none the wiser.

Not only do each of Finn's nostrils pull in odors, they collect a sampling of different slices of the world, which may allow dogs a kind of stereo olfaction. Just as we humans locate the source of a sound by unconsciously and instantly calculating the difference in its loudness hitting our left and right ears, a dog can gauge the difference in a smell's strength between his left and right nostrils. And I was happy to learn that by watching dogs' nostrils very, very carefully, researchers have found that dogs use their right nostril first when smelling a new but nonaversive scent (food, people), and then switch to the *left* nostril once it becomes familiar. By contrast, both adrenaline and the sweat of veterinarians (yes, the researchers collected vet sweat) prompted a bias toward sniffing with the *right* nostril. These nostrils, and the olfactory cells they lead to, send information to the same sides of the brain: right nostril, right hemisphere. The researchers conclude that right-nostril activity is associated with stimulating an arousal response, of aggression, fear, or other strong emotion. The left nostril, like the left hemisphere, is involved in calming experiences. In theory, if you looked closely, you could see if a dog considered you friendly or not by watching which nostril is sniffing.

All this sniff rumination got me back to Finn's sneeze. Starting our walk, he sneezed a good sneeze. After I had interrupted
his sniffing, we resumed walking, and he sneezed again. He was
cleansing his palate. Sneezing is a dog's way of clearing everything out of the nose, so the next good stench can be inhaled. It is
the dog's version of the polite, throat-clearing cough timed to end
one conversation and move to another, or the self-conscious *ahem*
done to break the silence in an elevator or other closed social space.

Similarly, by licking his nose, he was readying it to catch things
to be smelled. You may have noticed that the world outside your
door smells brightly new after a rain, when the ground is wet—
and especially so in summer, when every surface is well baked
and warm to the touch. Those molecules of odor that have settled
on the ground, latent odor traces, are unlikely to be detected by
a passing nose. But warm air—warmed by the sun or from the
inside of a dog nose—makes odors volatile and more likely to be
sniffed. And wet air (or noses) allow for better absorption of an
odor. This is also why Finn may lick or nose-print a surface: he is
not trying to eat it; he is attempting to get the odor closer to the
vomeronasal organ, where it can be smelled further.

Although we had resumed walking, it was at a slow pace. We made
regular stops for Finn to sniff the ground, an errant hubcap, or a
paper bag on the sidewalk, or to stand and sniff into the wind. What
olfactory fireworks must reach his nose on a brisk wind! Smells not
just from our street, but from around the corner, from down the
hill. Scents from New Jersey! Scents from great heights, from the
past, from the place we were walking toward.

At this pace, I began noticing things on our route I had never
noticed before: small faucets attached to sides of buildings; brass
pegs in the sidewalk that are, I subsequently learned, part of a

national registry of such pegs;* the difference in the ratio of shade to sun on the north and south sides of the street. After stopping at each block's fireplug, I realized some had sentinels: short guard posts flanking the fireplug. I suspected these represent a historical glimpse of unhappy automobile/fireplug interactions. I began looking a little too closely at the innumerable spots on the sidewalk (look! they're there!): black bruises that on examination are darkened, smushed gum or splattered liquid.†

At a tall apartment building, something caught Finn's attention at the entrance, three short steps above street level. I followed his gaze. With much fuss, two people were settling a large, older gentleman standing in the doorway into a wheelchair. It looked difficult and exhausting for all involved. Seeing us looking, the man gaped back at us. I smiled and, being a human being, turned away out of politeness. Surely this man did not want me staring at his difficulty in sitting down. But Finn was transfixed. Not only did he continue to stare, he locked his legs, settling his weight on his heels when I encouraged him onward. As the leash became taut between us, I looked back at Finn. He was certainly being impolite.

But, of course, no dog is polite or impolite. It is we who attribute these characteristics to them. Dogs are perfectly culturally

* These "geodetic survey marks" are all over the city. The first were placed in New York in the early nineteenth century as part of a land survey. Each one's coordinates—altitude, longitude, and latitude, and distance from other marks—is noted, and one can look to see if these numbers have changed over time as buildings settle or waters rise. The marks are set in stable places, where they can be found much later—on public buildings, monuments, in bedrock—and have been made of steel, brass, rock, or other material resistant to decay or rust. Though the survey marks still have their original use, there are also entirely non-official geodetic treasure hunts on which visitors collect sightings.

† As a long-time city walker, I have done some examining of these spots. While the prevailing view is that they are all spent gum, covered with city grime, the teardrop-shape of some suggest a droplet—as of a sticky liquid or a phlegmy sputum. When I began seeing the spots on the asphalt where buses stop for passengers, I realized that they were caused by some viscous liquid or oil that the engine perspired while it rested.

ignorant. Despite their neat insinuation into our homes, they do not notice or concern themselves with our customs. Perhaps a dog may learn to "not stare" if an owner punishes him each time he does, but not necessarily: the dog may just learn *watch out for your owner, she's coming for you*. Politeness is a human concept, and it is at best bizarre to imagine that dogs have it.

On the other hand, I could feel, and I suspect the wheelchaired man could feel, the fixedness of Finn's gaze as discomfiting. I knew Finn was just looking, but I felt I needed to relieve the man of being watched, even if only by a dog.* It is a testament to the power of the dog's gaze that we can be unnerved by it, as though the dog were seeing us for who we really are. Both Finn and my son, in their ill-mannered staring, have done more than any psychologist or sociologist to make me more aware of how material gaze is.

When I convinced Finn to move on, I thought to pay attention to where other dogs we encountered on the street were gazing. Nearly all were more interested in getting their noses into Finn's nether regions or wagging face-to-face than in staring at me. Often, though, a dog looked at me—or maybe smelled me. It felt like an invitation. The dog's gaze is simply human.

One dog, an energetic brown-and-white houndy type, galloping toward us against the restraint of the owner he was pulling along, seemed to smell particularly interesting to Finn—and Finn to him. They wagged mightily at each other, tails high in the air, the wags taut and vigorous, then set to an intensive sniff dance. I call it a dance because they moved *together,* like long-term dance

---

* To be sure, he was likely just *smelling,* but the eyes follow the direction the nose points, just as our nose sticks out at the person at whom we look (but we are not "nosing" the poor fellow).

partners, doing some behaviors at once, and others in response to each other: first, mutual sniffing of the low bellies; then back upright, faces close; then a circle step, caused by each trying to get his nose right at the base of the other's tail. I smiled up at the person at the end of the dog's leash, which seemed appropriate as our dogs were getting familiar. She was tall, wearing a raincoat on an unrainy day. Her hair looked expensively cut, but her face was weary, harried. She barely managed a smile back. I thought about what information Finn was getting about her dog with his sniffs: mood, opinions, disease? My Philadelphia physician Bennett Lorber sniffs the tissue samples of his patients. We humans, trained sufficiently, can detect the scent of illness. When physical exams were more literally physical and less mediated by machines, it was common for trained doctors to identify disease in their patients by smell. What were charmingly called "lunatics" in the nineteenth century were said to smell "like yellow deer or mice" (that presupposes that one knows what those animals smell like; perhaps once you get the chance to smell a lunatic, it becomes obvious). Typhoid smells like freshly baked brown bread; the measles, of "fresh-picked feathers"; scabies is moldy; gout, like whey; tuberculosis, reminiscent of stale beer; diabetics, unbearably sweet, like rotted fruit.

Abruptly, the dog bolted and the two of them, wafting their odors in their wake, headed off to the next entertainment. Finn sniffed after them, then turned and trotted away. I refrained from sniffing after the woman. For a few minutes, no one passed us on the sidewalk. Finn took to conducting a detailed examination of the objects of the street. He poked his nose into all sorts of openings. Low basement windows abound in my neighborhood, I learned through following him, and each seemed to have its own currents of dog-alluring scents. Spaces between cars were exciting, as they allowed sniffs of the filaments of odors from the other side of the street. We spent a lot of time with lampposts. I would characterize most of Finn's behavior as *merrily interested,* but as we approached a large Dumpster parked by the sidewalk, I got a taste of his alarm, too. A plastic tarp over the Dumpster had come loose from its moorings and slapped against itself. It was a distinctly different sound than the whip of the yellow "do not cross" tape surrounding a wet square of concrete nearby. Both seemed to spook Finn with their air-snapping and whipping movements in the wind. But he was brave. He held his ground, leaned as far forward as he could while keeping all four feet planted, and inched his nose ever closer to the mysterious tape. Ten seconds—seventy sniffs— later, he determined it was harmless, and even dull, and we moved on. I listened for the other sounds of wind on the street. I tried to listen with the ears of a sound engineer. The round-leaved trees rustled differently than large oak leaves—and both were distinct from the sough of small linden leaves. Finn did not seem to attend to these one whit.

He had something else in mind. Suddenly, after a long slow ramble, he was pulling me, his nose in urgent pursuit. We wound up at the stairs outside a short apartment building. Every week, I watch spellbound as his nose leads him on a wending course to locate the handful of well-slobbered tennis balls that have been waiting in a field of ivy since we visited the prior week, but this time his nose seemed to have led him astray. There was no ball. There was nothing. Only a still, closed door in our face.

Three minutes later, we were on the stairs to greet a woman I recognized from morning dog walks, leading her charge out for a bit of midday relief. She had, she explained, just returned home. I goggled a bit and tried to explain to her our presence on her stoop, while Finn happily wiggled. Shortly, he was ready to move on, and it was I who wanted to loiter and think about how he knew where she lived.

I should not have been at all surprised. Buildings do not typically wear prominent evidence of their tenants, but each person leaves tracks, individual odors in our footprints, even in the smells that radiate from us into the air we move through. Catch an elevator just after it has dropped off a perfumed rider or a smoker and you see what I mean: the evidence of her presence still hangs in the air. Whether trained in tracking or not, dogs can detect our individual odors, and even the direction in which we have gone. Each step we leave has, over time, a slightly different quantity of odor than the one before and after it. The newest step is the smelliest; the oldest is the least smelly. For tracking dogs, five steps is plenty to determine direction through this change of odor concentration.

Finn saw this woman's recent return through her steps. The city block, for him, was covered with evidence of familiar and unfamiliar people and dogs passing by. Each time I step out my door, I see more or less the same block. No wonder Finn stops when we exit: it is a wholly new street, wearing odors of the six hours since we were last outside, waiting to be sniffed in.

A long stretch with nary a tree guard nor lamppost nor fireplug to visit, and we were moving along at a decent clip. Even while I aimed to observe what Finn observed, I found myself mostly observing Finn. He was, after all, a part of the city block, I reasoned—as were all the other dogs we routinely pass. I focused on his bearing. He held his tail high, a friendly sickle curved over his back. He was doing a very particular kind of walk. Dogs, like us, can launch into any of a variety of strides, from *walk* and *pace,* to *trot* and *amble,* and, in a pinch, *gallop*. Between balusters, Finn *walked*: his left rear foot gently chased his left front foot, which started his right rear foot chasing his right front foot. This walk is considered "sloppy" by trackers: the footprints walking dogs leave do not directly register one on top of another; instead, the right front and left rear slightly overlap, leaving a distinct mark for each pawprint. Watching Finn walk, his hips swaying slightly as he moved, I felt that "sloppy," technical or not, was the wrong word for this stride. Maybe *languorous* or *unconcerned*. It was an easy, carefree movement that likely took as much energy as my putting one foot in front of another.

In this long empty stretch, though, Finn downright *trotted*. In a trot, the rear legs catch up with the front; each stride finds a dog with the feet on one side touching toes while the feet on the other side are spread as far apart as possible. When I really run with Finn, he is forced to *gallop,* a stride during which, for a moment, no leg is on the ground. Finn's gallop has his rear legs pushing together to launch him forward. On one street, a dog approaching us was *pacing*: the legs on one side moved together, followed by the legs of the other side. It made him rock from side-to-side, a comic gait for a dog to wear. Indeed, walking with the pacing dog was a man with his hands in his pockets, the dog's leash slung around his wrist. Striding without swinging his arms, he seemed to "pace," too. Evan Johnson, watching gaits with me, observed that the gaits of mammals and reptiles are unalike: in mammals, the upper back and shoulders typically move in opposition to the pelvis; reptiles are back-and-forth, moving the legs on one side of the body at a time. This pair looked positively reptilian.

Finn and I approached the start of our walk, which was also its end. Recognizing the building, or its stairs, or the smell of the flanking balusters (I knew not which), he headed toward the door without hesitation. Again I paused, this time to see if Finn's gaze looked different to me at the end of a walk than at the beginning. I hardly got the chance. A small child tottered over, delight on her face and a bonnet on her head. Her mother had a hand on a stroller and another on a phone; her mind was elsewhere. Finn lifted his head and simultaneously turned his body to face the youngster. I heard the implied "Doggie!" as the girl reached for Finnegan's head. At this he ducked, moved away, and the mother suddenly reached over and snatched her child back.

Finn looked up at me balefully. I commiserated. We like to touch dogs. But do dogs like to be touched? Yes and no. There has not been much research into the dog's tactile perception, but studies have been done with horses and humans. In both species, tactile sensitivity is not the same throughout our bodies. We know that our fingertips, lips, and genitals can be extremely sensitive while parts of our back and legs are relatively insensate to simple touch. (This, too, matches areas where we are more or less disturbed by accidental public bodily contact.) Horses have, it turns out, a high sensitivity on the sides of their bellies—right about where a rider's legs fall. They can react to pressures lighter than humans can detect. This might explain why some horses seem unresponsive to a rider: they may be getting too many tactile signals for any one to be meaningful. Dogs, too, probably have highly sensitive areas, and would prefer not to be touched everywhere, or pet hard. There is evidence that rhythmic, firm strokes are relaxing for horses and dogs—but each dog has his own tactile body map. Look at how a dog touches other dogs, and where he licks himself: that might indicate areas of special sensitivity. If one's whole body is involved in experiencing the world, the "personal space" we feel must be mapped directly from it.

• • •

My walk with Finnegan had been an ordinary walk: very little of moment had happened. Nothing one would bother to report to someone waiting for you at home. But, watching Finn, what counted as momentous changed: I saw how our world was colored with scent. Our block was a patchwork of smells, and the story of its day was readable in it. Through minding his attention, I remembered the smell of childhood, ripe as the smell of crayons, the must of an old book, the smell of a new car. I saw the array of balusters, windows, and detritus at dog height. I noticed *myself* in the scene—and that I had been blindly stumbling through my walk to work, my walk to the store, my walk to the car, missing the details that Finn detected.

Finn and I stepped inside and settled down together on the couch. I closed my eyes and smelled his fur: the top of his head smelled like fast-moving rivers; the curl of his ears evoked a warmed window seat. I could feel him sniffing me back.

"You know my method.
It is founded upon the observation of trifles."

(Sherlock Holmes)

Seeing It

"As it turns out, I was missing pretty much everything."

I plopped on the floor and rummaged under the bench by our front door, feeling for my shoes. I needed walking shoes. Today I would return, alone, to my first route around the block, walk it again, and see what I saw.

Since the time I took that first walk, the city was substantively unchanged. Sure, some buildings were erected, a few were felled; many trees were lost in storms, a handful were planted. There were more bicyclists on the streets and more people decrying bicyclists on the streets. In our neighborhood, a grocery store opened and a half dozen restaurants closed. But it was the same space, the same block, the same city.

I hoped that *some*thing had changed. The likeliest thing would be me.

•   •   •

It rained. This struck me as a deterrent to a walk, but then I brightened: umbrella sound! I stepped outside, experimenting with how sound was changed with an umbrella raised above my head. A satisfying pitter-plitter of light raindrops on the skin of the umbrella should have made things louder, but the umbrella seemed to slightly temper the noises of the street. Everything was just as loud, but the local noise of the rain predominated my experience. I pulled up the hood of my raincoat. This blocked nearly all street noise and introduced me to my noisy breathing. The sounds of my movement—a foot landing on the concrete, the press of my leg against my rain jacket, the rustle of the fabric between arm and body—was translated up to my ears.

I decided to forsake both hood and umbrella and simply get wet. Taking the posture of someone coming out of her apartment and greeting the day (only with a notebook in hand), I began to walk.

A sudden wave of panic overtook me. This all looked *very familiar*. There, the cherry tree; this, the neighboring bricked building; that, the fence, the ivy, the street, the street traffic. It looked just as it always did, on every one of my daily walks. The scene was not cinematic. I did not have the eyes of a child, nor an artist. I smelled nothing.

As I stood reflecting on this unfortunate situation, my gaze idled at the building. Its bottom story was covered in—could it be limestone? I stepped closer. The stone looked raked, corduroyed, and resembled concrete more than limestone. Then I saw the *O*. And a flamboyantly big *C*. I peered closer, my eyes adjusting. The surface was entirely made of sea sediment: shells, ancient fossils. The *O*, looking capital, was accompanied by many lower-case *o*'s: each probably a disk of an ancient crinoid. The *C* was serifed with an abundance of small spongelike vessels. Scattered broken shells and feathery spines lay around them. The closer I looked, the more the surface revealed itself to be fractally patterned—from unbroken shells, to pieces of shells, to imprints where pieces may have laid.

Now this was more like it. I'd lived in this building for six years and never had noticed the population of sea creatures resting by the entryway.

The limestone face was decorated with patches of moisture from the rain. They ran horizontally, spreading toward each other from the edges between stones. A splotchier wet spot was definitely contributed by a dog. I could see where a windowsill plant had been overwatered, the streaks of dirt-laden water spreading south.

Behind me sounds registered: I heard tires, a sticky-wet slipping over the surface of the asphalt like tape being unpeeled from its roll. A series of birds whistled, one twittering, another sending a declarative, six-whistle message.

It was a new street.

My eye caught sight of something a few yards down the street. I nearly leapt toward it, rudely lunging right in front of someone happening to walk by and not anticipating nearly-leapers. The object of my lungely leaping was a gaping sidewalk crack, unfilled with mortar. I kneeled and peered in. Inside lived dozens of tiny, hopeful two-leafed plants pushing up toward the light. None bore the mark of an insect. Between them were stuffed uncountable elm seeds, dried and colorless, limp with dampness. The slit between sidewalks told the story of the season: late spring, the plants cycling through their frenzied growth and reproduction. The lack of detritus—cigarette butts, bits of paper—within it told the story of the block: well tended.

Above my head, a flurry of birds seemed to fly right into the brick wall of a tall apartment building. Another chased them in, and I realized that they had flown directly into the small space, maybe two inches wide, between adjacent buildings. Heads poked out, tails were vainly ruffled. Occasionally a bird sprang forth into the air like a brick come alive. Grass and twigs and pieces of paper were packed into the space, forming an apartment building of nests. A row of overhanging brick served as a balcony, where a male, resplendent in black and bright brown feathers, seemed to sharpen his beak like a knife on a whetstone.

A door was propped open on a nearby building; a gaggle of men stood around, apparently assigned to bring in a handful of washing machines glumly waiting on the sidewalk. One of the men followed my gaze and smiled. "There's gotta be a nest in there!" he offered, happily. Oh yes, it's a building's full, I said. Maybe the birds were moving in their own appliances. "Bird refrigerators!" he said. We exchanged greetings and I walked on, not ready to leave the sight of these crafty birds but pushed by awareness of the perfection of a pleasant, and not over-long, exchange with a stranger to leave the scene.

After that the sights came fast and furious. Caterpillars of soft green seeds lay sodden on the ground, accompanied by small, green . . . caterpillars. A truck grumbled by, advertising its business in cacophonous yellow lettering. It banged over a metal plate put down by someone working under the street. Three orange cones nearby had all fainted dead away. I remembered walking with my son on this street looking for orange things when *orange* had been an early word that he liked to get his mouth around. (*Purple* things, so much fun to say, are especially hard to find; but orange was surprisingly common.) On the corner, a long tree limb, stripped of branches, stood upright in a trash can. I looked up at a nearby tree, half expecting to see its glow of satisfaction on having finally cleaned house. A large brown dog, waist high, peered at the stick as it rounded the corner. He was walked by a woman hidden underneath an umbrella; as she passed, a waft of shampoo told me she had recently washed her hair. The dog turned to me with deep full eyes; I smiled. As if in response, he nosed me right on my elbow, leaving a wet smudge. Behind her, a young fellow, umbrella-less, leaning deeply to his right as he thumbed a message on a phone, swerved right off the sidewalk.

A gate was ajar. It opened onto the private parking behind a building. A wall within was lined with ivy curlicuing up and out. No one was inside. I took a quick look around me, and I ducked in.

That was only the first half-block of my final walk around the block. A simple walk had become unrecognizably richer. In the nineteenth century, skilled anatomists might boast of being able to identify an animal—and even reconstruct it—from the evidence of a single bone. The animal that is the city is similarly traceable from small bits of evidence. Part of seeing what is on an ordinary block is seeing that everything visible has a history. It arrived at the spot where you found it at some time, was crafted or whittled or forged at some time, filled a certain role or existed for a particular function. It was touched by someone (or no one), and touches someone (or no one) now. It is evidence.

The other part of seeing what is on the block is appreciating how limited our own view is. We are limited by our sensory abilities, by our species membership, by our narrow attention—at least the last of which can be overcome. We walk the same block as dogs yet see different things. We walk alongside rats though each of us lives in the dusk of the other. We walk by other people and do not see what each of us knows, what each of us is doing—captured instead by the inside of our own heads.

My original block—and every block—is impossibly dense with sights and sounds. What allowed me to see the bits that I would have otherwise missed was not the expertise of my walkers, per se; it was their simple interest in attending. I selected these walkers for their ability to boost my own selective attention. An expert can only indicate what she sees; it is up to your own head to tune your senses and your brain to see it. Once you catch that melody, and keep humming, you are forever changed.

My initial walk now felt like the imprimatura for an oil painting: the very first layer of paint on a canvas, which lends something to future layers but will eventually be obliterated by them. In some paintings, even heavy, Rembrandtian oil paintings, there are gaps where the base layer spread on the new canvas shines through, where it has not yet been altered by layers of oils and inks and colors. Those peeks at the imprimatura are not moments of laziness; the meaning of the gaps changes because the context around them has changed. The bit left unpainted is now surrounded by smears of pinks and reds that form the nose, or the ear, or the eye of the subject of the portrait; the unpainted bit becomes the nostril, or the inner ear, or the corner of the eye—and will never be just a base layer again. My initial walk was this negative space changed by layers of walks hence.

The result of these walks on my head is tangible: they refined what I can see. My mind can prepare my eyes to spontaneously find a leaf gall, to hear an air conditioner's hum, to smell the sickly sweet smell of garbage on a city street (or the fragrance of my own soap on my face, instead). It can tune to the sounds of my own breath, the feel of my heartbeat, or the shifts of my weight as I walk and negotiate sidewalk space. I can feel my hip bones rotating in their sockets as I walk, my arms swinging in rhythm with my legs. I can hear the conversation behind me, in front of me, in a passing car—or just the jingle of my dog's tags as he strides alongside me down the street. For me, walking has become less physical transit than mental transportation. It is engaging. I have become, I fear, a difficult walking companion, liable to slow down and point at things. I can turn this off, but I love to have it on: a sense of wonder that I, and we all, have a predisposition to but have forgotten to enjoy.

There could be an exhaustion in being told to look, to pay attention, to *be here now*: one might feel put upon, as though being chastised for being neglectful. Nearly all the people I walked with—some of whom were, in essence, professional attenders or lookers—reproached themselves for not paying good enough attention.

Do not sag with exhaustion. There is no mandate; only opportunity. Our culture fosters inattention; we are all creatures of that culture. But by making your way through this book—by merely picking it up, perhaps—you, reader, are in a new culture, one that values looking. The unbelievable strata of trifling, tremendous things to observe are there for the observing. *Look!*

Sources

CHAPTER EPIGRAPHS

"You can observe a lot":

Y. Berra, *The Yogi Book* (New York: Workman Publishing Company, 2010).

"To find new things":

This is widely attributed to Burroughs, but I have yet to find the original source. An early variant published in *Nature,* vol. 42, 1949, goes "If you would see new things under the sun, the way to go today is the way you went yesterday." The sentiment is the same, but which words he said remain a mystery.

"To see is to forget":

via L. Weschler, *Seeing is Forgetting the Name of the Thing One Sees: Over Thirty Years of Conversations with Robert Irwin* (Berkeley, CA: University of California Press, 2008).

"The world is full of obvious things":

A. C. Doyle, *The Hound of the Baskervilles* (Ontario, Canada: Broadview, 2006), p. 75.

Sources

"'tis very pregnant":

W. Shakespeare, *Measure for Measure,* act II, scene I.

"It matters not where or how far you travel":

H. D. Thoreau, *The Journal, 1837–1861* (New York: New York Review of Books, 2009), entry on May 6, 1854.

"We must always say what we see":

Le Corbusier, *Le Corbusier Talks with Students From the Schools of Architecture,* trans. P. Chase (New York: Princeton Architectural Press, 1999).

"What is life but a form of motion":

G. Santayana, "The Philosophy of Travel," in *The Birth of Reason and Other Essays* (New York: Columbia University Press, 1995), p. 5.

"look, with all your eyes, look!":

J. Verne, *Michael Strogoff* (play) (New York: Samuel French & Son, 1881), p. 57.

"Sound comes to us":

H. Schwartz, *Making Noise: From Babel to the Big Bang & Beyond* (New York: Zone Books, 2011), p. 50.

"The only true voyage":

M. Proust, *In Search of Lost Time, Vol. 5: The Captive* (New York: Random House, 1993), p. 343.

"You know my method . . .":

A. C. Doyle, "The Boscombe Valley Mystery," in *The Adventures of Sherlock Holmes and the Memoirs of Sherlock Holmes* (New York: Penguin, 2001).

AMATEUR EYES

Fechner and James on attention:

W. James, *Principles of Psychology,* vol. 1, ch. 11, "Attention" (New York: Dover, 1890/1950).

Sources

"hold the image still as one would with a camera":

S. Carson, M. Shih, and E. Langer, "Sit Still and Pay Attention?", *Journal of Adult Development 8* (2001): 183–188.

"blooming, buzzing confusion":

William James's famous words, in *Principles of Psychology* (p. 488). In his later *Some Problems of Philosophy: A Beginning of an Introduction to Philosophy* (New York: Longmans, Green, and Co., 1916), though, he attributes them to someone else (unnamed).

on attention generally:

R. Parasuraman, ed., *The Attentive Brain* (Cambridge, MA: MIT Press, 1998); and S. Kastner and L. G. Ungerleider, "Mechanisms of Visual Attention in the Human Cortex," *Annual Review of Neuroscience 23* (2000): 315–341.

selective attention:

S. Yantis, "The Neural Basis of Selective Attention: Cortical Sources and Targets of Attentional Modulation," *Current Directions in Psychological Science 17* (2008): 86–90.

MUCHNESS

on the experience of childhood:

A great stab at imagining this is attempted by developmental psychologist Charles Fernyhough, in *A Thousand Days of Wonder: A Scientist's Chronicle of His Daughter's Developing Mind* (New York: Avery, 2009).

synesthesia:

R. E. Cytowic, *Synesthesia: A Union of the Senses* (New York: Springer-Verlag, 1989) and *The Man Who Tasted Shapes* (New York: Putnam, 1993).

"gloomy" 3:

A. R. Luria, *The Mind of a Mnemonist* (Cambridge, MA: Harvard University Press, 1987).

Sources

"drab shoelace" of h, "weathered wood" a:

V. Nabokov, *Speak, Memory* (New York: Putnam, 1966).

sensorium commune:

U. Muëller, "The Context of the Formation of Heinz Werner's Ideas," in J. Valsiner, ed., *Heinz Werner and Developmental Science* (New York: Plenum, 2005), pp. 25–55.

curly lines as happy:

J. Valsiner, ed., *Heinz Werner and Developmental Science* (New York: Kluver Academic, 2005).

theory of synesthesia:

Since individual synesthetes' subjective experiences are rarely identical (Nabokov thought the colored alphabet blocks he was given to play with were colored "all wrong"), some researchers think that the notion of loss of differentiation is insufficient to explain synesthesia. Cytowic, for instance, suggests "polymodal combination" in the limbic system.

on natural synesthesia:

F. Gonzalez-Crussi, *The Five Senses* (San Diego: Harcourt Brace Jovanovich, 1989).

aboriginal sensible muchness:

James, *Some Problems of Philosophy: A Beginning of an Introduction to Philosophy* (New York: Longmans, Green, and Co., 1916), p. 50.

Cézanne on spheres, cones, and cylinders:

L. Birch, *How to Draw and Paint Animals* (London: David & Charles UK, 1997).

Froebel on spheres, cones, and cylinders:

Pratt Institute Monthly, 1904.

on the coherence of the natural world:

D. L. Ruderman, "The Statistics of Natural Images," *Network: Computation in Neural Systems* 5 (1994): 517–548.

SOURCES

neophilia:

J. S. Bruner, "Nature and Uses of Immaturity," *American Psychologist* 27 (1972): 687–708.

"whelp(ing) whole litters of new objects":

L. Halprin, *Cities* (New York: Reinhold Publishing Corporation, 1963), p. 51.

standpipes:

C. Delafuente, "It's no hydrant, but this hardware plays a critical role in fires," *New York Times,* August 26, 2007.

on animism:

J. Piaget, *The Child's Conception of the World* (London: R. & K. Paul, 1926/1951).

on animate-inanimate distinction in childhood:

G. Hatano, "Animism," in R. A. Wilson and F. Keil, eds., *The MIT Encyclopedia of the Cognitive Sciences* (Cambridge, MA: MIT Press, 1999), pp. 28–29.

keeping flowers company:

Piaget, *The Child's Conception of the World.*

MINERALS AND BIOMASS

hexagonal Roman roads:

M. G. Lay, *Ways of the World: A History of the World's Roads and of the Vehicles That Used Them* (New Brunswick, NJ: Rutgers University Press, 1992).

Clochán na bhFómharach:

http://www.nationaltrust.org.uk/giants-causeway/history/.

weathering of buildings:

M. Mostafavi and D. Leatherbarrow, *On Weathering: The Life of Buildings in Time* (Cambridge, MA: MIT Press, 1993).

Sources

stair erosion:

J. Templer, *The Staircase: Studies of Hazards, Falls, and Safer Design* (Cambridge, MA: MIT Press, 1992).

on gingko:

"Introduction to the Ginkgoales," http://www.ucmp.berkeley.edu/seedplants/ginkgoales/ginkgo.html.

horticulture books:

e.g., P. Henderson, *Handbook of Plants and General Horticulture* (New York: Peter Henderson & Company, 1910).

on Central Park:

R. Rosenzweig and E. Blackmar, *The Park and the People: A History of Central Park* (Ithaca, NY: Cornell University Press, 1992).

on Manhattan schist:

C. Merguerian and C. J. Moss, "Structural Implications of Walloomsac and Hartland Rocks Displayed by Borings in Southern Manhattan," in G. N. Hanson, ed., *Thirteenth Annual Conference on Geology of Long Island and Metropolitan New York,* 1996, p. 12.

on expertise:

A. Diderjean and F. Gibet, "Sherlock Holmes—An Expert's View of Expertise," *British Journal of Psychology 99* (2008): 109–125.

brains of dancers watching dancers:

B. Calvo-Merino, D. E. Glaser, J. Grèzes, R. E. Passingham, and P. Haggard, "Action Observation and Acquired Motor Skills: An fMRI Study with Expert Dancers," *Cerebral Cortex 15* (2005): 1243–1249.

on chessmasters' recall:

F. Gobet and H. A. Simon, "Recall of Random and Distorted Positions: Implications for the Theory of Expertise," *Memory & Cognition 24* (1996): 493–503; and P. Chassy and F. Gobet, "Measuring Chess Experts' Single-Use Sequence Knowledge: An Archival Study of Departure from 'Theoretical' Openings," *PLoS One 6* (2011): e26692.

SOURCES

fusiform face area:

M. Bilalic, R. Langner, R. Ulrich, and W. Grodd, "Many Faces of Expertise: Fusiform Face Area in Chess Experts and Novices," *Journal of Neuroscience 31* (2011): 10206–10214.

Sacks and prosopagnosia:

O. Sacks, *The Mind's Eye* (New York: Knopf, 2010).

on schist:

D. C. Roberts, *A Field Guide to Geology—Eastern North America* (New York: Houghton Mifflin, 2001).

geology in NYC:

J. Kiernan, *A Natural History of New York City: A Book for Sidewalk Naturalists Everywhere* (New York: Houghton Mifflin, 1959).

limestone:

information on limestone and its residents retrieved from http://academic. brooklyn.cuny.edu/geology/powell/613webpage/NYCbuilding/IndianaLime stone/IndianaLimestone.htm.

MINDING OUR Qs

children learn a word every two hours:

M. Tomasello, *Constructing a Language: A Usage-Based Theory of Language* (Cambridge, MA: Harvard University Press, 2005), p. 50; and L. Fenson, et al., "Variability in Early Communicative Development," *Monographs of the Society for Research in Child Development 59* (1994): 1–185.

inscriptions in Pompeii:

W. S. Davis, *Readings in Ancient History: Illustrative Extracts from the Sources* (Boston: Allyn and Bacon, 1913).

on lettering:

paulshawletterdesign.com.

Sources

New York City's architectural style:

N. White, E. Willensky, and F. Leadon, *AIA Guide to New York City* (New York: Oxford University Press, 2010).

hunger to pursue visual stimuli that give us pleasure:

I. Biederman and E. A. Vessel, "Perceptual Pleasure and the Brain," *American Scientist 94* (2006): 249–255.

pregnant ampersand:

www.aiga.org/lettering-grows-in-brooklyn.

6-8 Delancey Street:

J. Mendelsohn, *The Lower East Side Remembered and Revisited: A History and Guide to a Legendary New York Neighborhood* (New York: Columbia University Press, 2009).

"shoes for abnormal feet":

Advertisement, *Jewish Frontier,* vol. 18, 1951, p. 43.

locally famous robbery:

H. P. Jeffers, *Commissioner Roosevelt: The Story of Theodore Roosevelt and the New York City Police, 1895–1897* (New York: Wiley, 1996).

"disorderly house":

Report of the Special Committee of the Assembly Appointed to Investigate the Public Offices and Departments of the City of New York and of the Counties Therein Included, vol. 2 (Albany, NY: James B. Lyon, 1900), p. 2002; and R. Zacks, *Island of Vice: Theodore Roosevelt's Doomed Quest to Clean Up Sin-Loving New York* (New York: Doubleday, 2012).

Tetris study:

R. Stickgold, A. Malia, D. Maguire, et al., "Replaying the Game: Hypnagogic Images in Normals and Amnesics," *Science 290* (2000): 350–353.

Sources

INTO THE FOURTH DIMENSION

"if you're ever bored or blue":

M. Kalman, *The Principles of Uncertainty* (New York: Penguin, 2007).

"no two human Umwelten are the same":

J. von Uexküll, "A Stroll Through the Worlds of Animals and Men," in C. H. Schiller, ed., *Instinctive Behavior: The Development of a Modern Concept* (New York: International Universities Press, 1934/1957), pp. 5–80.

"nude, shamed look":

A. Kazin, *A Walker in the City* (New York: Harcourt Brace Jovanovich, 1951), p. 78.

personal space:

H. Hediger, *Wild Animals in Captivity* (London: Butterworth, 1950).

judgments about people:

M. Bar, M. Neta, and H. Linz, "Very First Impressions," *Emotion* 6 (2006): 269–278.

sclera and width-height ratio of eye:

H. Kobayashi and S. Kohshima, "Unique Morphology of the Human Eye," *Nature* 387 (1997): 767–768.

neurobiology of vision:

N. J. Emery, "The Eyes Have It: The Neuroethology, Function and Evolution of Social Gaze," *Neuroscience and Biobehavioral Reviews* 24 (2000): 581–604.

neuropsychology of attention:

R. Datta and E. A. DeYoe, "I Know Where You Are Secretly Attending! The Topography of Human Visual Attention Revealed with fMRI," *Vision Research* 49 (2009): 1037–1044.

SOURCES

newborns babies' interest in gaze:

T. Farroni, G. Csibra, F. Simion, and M. Johnson, "Eye Contact Detection in Humans from Birth," *Proceedings of the National Academy of Sciences 99* (2002): 9602–9605.

eye contact and attachment:

K. S. Robson, The Role of Eye-to-Eye Contact in Maternal-Infant Attachment," *Journal of Child Psychology and Psychiatry 8* (1967): 13–25; and A. J. Guastella, P. B. Mitchell, and M. R. Dadds, "Oxytocin Increases Gaze to the Eye Region of Human Faces," *Biological Psychiatry 63* (2008): 3–5.

eye contact generally:

A. Senjua and M. H. Johnson, "The Eye Contact Effect: Mechanisms and Development," *Trends in Cognitive Sciences 13* (2009): 127–134.

eyes and art:

M. F. Marmor and J. G. Ravin, *The Artist's Eyes: Vision and the History of Art* (New York: Abrams, 2009), pp. 125–127.

never complains about waiting for the subway:

G. K. Chesterton wrote something similar about boys in railroad stations in *On Running After One's Hat.*

canonical "creative brain":

Ö. de Manzano, S. Cervenka, A. Karabanov, et al., "Thinking Outside a Less Intact Box: Thalamic Dopamine D2 Receptor Densities Are Negatively Related to Psychometric Creativity in Healthy Individuals," *PLoS One 55* (2010): e10670.

streetlights:

"Lighting," *NYC Department of Transportation Street Design Manual,* 2010. http://www.nyc.gov/html/dot/html/about/streetdesignmanual.shtml.

Sources

FLIPPING THINGS OVER

categories of insect sign:

C. Eiseman and N. Charney, *Tracks and Sign of Insects and Other Invertebrates: A Guide to North American Species* (Mechanicsburg, PA: Stackpole Books, 2010).

"people stood overwhelmed with awe":

Quote from the *Wabash Plain Dealer* in D. E. Nye, *Electrifying America: Social Meanings of a New Technology, 1880–1940* (Cambridge, MA: MIT Press, 1992), p. 3.

on invertebrate attraction to lights:

C. Bruce-White and M. Shardlow, "A Review of the Impact of Artificial Light on Invertebrates," (2011), retrieved from http://www.buglife.org.uk/.

ants in the medians:

www.livescience.com/11068-ant-oases-nyc-street-medians.html.

search images:

S. J. Shettleworth, *Cognition, Evolution, and Behavior* (New York: Oxford University Press, 1998).

blue jays trained to look for camouflaged moths:

J. Alcock, *Animal Behavior,* 9th ed. (Sunderland, MA: Sinauer, 2011).

olfactory search images:

V. O. Nams, "Olfactory Search Images in Striped Skunks," *Behaviour 119* (1991): 267–284; F. R. Cross and R. R. Jackson, "Olfactory Search-Image Use by a Mosquito-Eating Predator," *Proceedings of the Royal Society B 22* (2010): 3173–3178; and I. Gazit, A. Goldblatt, and J. Terkel, "Formation of an Olfactory Search Image for Explosives Odours in Sniffer Dogs," *Ethology 111* (2005): 669–680.

Sacks' first Tourette's patient:

http://blog.ted.com/2009/09/qa_with_oliver.php.

SOURCES

the "clay pitcher search image":

J. von Uexküll, "A Stroll Through the Worlds of Animals and Men," in C. H. Schiller, ed., *Instinctive Behavior: The Development of a Modern Concept* (New York: International Universities Press, 1934/1957).

visual search in the brain:

M. P. Eckstein, "Visual Search: A Retrospective," *Journal of Vision 11* (2011): 1–36.

radiologists, satellite image analysts, and fishermen:

Eckstein, "Visual Search."

THE ANIMALS AMONG US

Cooper's hawks:

W. A. Estes and R. W. Mannan, "Feeding Behavior of Cooper's Hawks at Urban and Rural Nests in Southeastern Arizona," *The Condor 105* (2003): 107–116.

great tits:

H. Slabbekoorn and M. Peet, "Birds Sing at a Higher Pitch in Urban Noise: Great Tits Hit the High Notes to Ensure That Their Mating Calls Are Heard Above the City's Din," *Nature 424* (2003): 267.

song sparrow:

W. E. Wood and S. M. Yezerinac, "Song Sparrow (*Melospiza melodia*) Song Varies with Urban Noise," *The Auk 123* (2006): 650–659.

peppered moth:

J. Alcock, *Animal Behavior,* 9th ed. (Sunderland, MA: Sinauer, 2011).

"North American primate":

"Raccoons Attack in Los Angeles," interview with J. Hadidian, November 24, 2006, retrieved from http://www.npr.org/templates/story/story.php?storyId=6534152.

SOURCES

raccoon population numbers:

J. Hadidian, S. Prange, R. Rosatte, et al., "Raccoons *(Procyon lotor),*" in S. D. Gehrt, S. P. D. Riley, and B. L. Cypher, eds., *Urban Carnivores: Ecology, Conflict, and Conservation* (Baltimore: The Johns Hopkins Press, 2010), pp. 35–47.

raccoon reaching in trash bag:

Ibid.

raccoon hands:

I. D. Walker, "A Successful Multifingered Hand Design—the Case of the Raccoon," in *Proceedings of the IEEE/RSJ International Conference on Intelligent Robots and Systems,* 1995, 186–193.

Latin name and the history:

M. Pettit, "The Problem of Raccoon Intelligence in Behaviourist America," *British Society for the History of Science 43* (2010): 391–421.

raccoon "knavery," greed:

H. B. Davis, "The Raccoon: A Study in Animal Intelligence," *The American Journal of Psychology 18* (1907): 447–489.

Coolidge's raccoon Rebecca:

"Coolidge 'Coon' Gets Ribbon and Is Now Named Rebecca," *New York Times,* December 25, 1926; and "Coolidge Returns to the White House from His Vacation," *New York Times,* September 12, 1927.

Easter egg roll:

"President's Wife Attends the Easter Egg-Rolling," *New York Times,* April 19, 1927.

raccoons . . . four-inch space:

J. Hadidian, personal communication, December 21, 2010.

starlings and Shakespeare:

S. Mirsky, "Shakespeare to Blame for Introduction of European Starlings to U.S.," *Scientific American* (May 23, 2008).

Sources

expectation about what we will see:

C. Summerfield and T. Egner, "Expectation (and Attention) in Visual Cognition," *Trends in Cognitive Science 13* (2009): 403–409.

inattentional blindness:

D. J. Simons and C. F. Chabris, "Gorillas in Our Midst: Sustained Inattentional Blindness for Dynamic Events," *Perception 28* (1999): 1059–1074.

"cued-target detection task":

R. T. Marrocco and M. C. Davidson, "Neurochemistry of Attention," in R. Parasuraman, ed., *The Attentive Brain* (Cambridge, MA: MIT Press, 1998), pp. 35–50.

rats' ever-growing teeth:

A. F. Hanson and M. Berdoy, "Rats," in V. T. Tynes, ed., *Behavior of Exotic Pets* (UK: Blackwell Publishing, 2010) pp. 104–116.

pigeon owl deterrents:

J. Hadidian, ed., *Wild Neighbors: A Humane Approach to Dealing with Wildlife* (Washington D.C.: Humane Society Press, 2007).

thigmotaxic:

M. R. Lamprea, F. P. Cardenas, J. Setem, and S. Morato, "Thigmotactic Responses in an Open-Field," *Brazilian Journal of Medical Biological Research 41* (2008): 135–140.

rat smudges:

Hadidian, ed., *Wild Neighbors.*

rat whiskers:

Hanson and Berdoy, "Rats."

rat vocalizations:

Ibid.

SOURCES

rat play:

L. W. Cole, "Observations of the Senses and Instincts of the Raccoon," *Journal of Animal Behavior 2* (1912): 299–309.

rat grooming:

C. C. Burn, "What Is It Like to Be a Rat? Rat Sensory Perception and Its Implications for Experimental Design and Rat Welfare," *Applied Animal Behaviour Science 112* (2008): 1–32.

rat home range:

Hadidian, ed., *Wild Neighbors.*

rat control same since Middle Ages:

Hadidian, ed., *Wild Neighbors.*

rat neighborhoods (Baltimore):

L. C. Gardner-Santana et al., "Commensal Ecology, Urban Landscapes, and Their Influence on the Genetic Characteristics of City-Dwelling Norway Rats *(Rattus norvegicus),*" *Molecular Ecology 18* (2009): 2766–2778.

rats like grids:

"Rats Say: Manhattan Rules!" interview with David Eilam, *Science Daily,* January 13, 2009.

flock-swooping:

M. Ballerini, et al. "An Empirical Study of Large, Naturally Occurring Starling Flocks: A Benchmark in Collective Animal Behaviour," *Animal Behaviour 76* (2008): 201–215; and H. Pomeroy and F. Heppner, "Structure of Turning in Airborne Rock Dove *(Columba livia)* Flocks," *The Auk 109* (1992): 256–267.

pigeon gliding:

D. Larson, U. Matthes, P. E. Kelly, et al., *The Urban Cliff Revolution: Origins and Evolution of Human Habitats* (Ontario, Canada: Fitzhenry & Whiteside, 2004), p. 29.

Sources

cliffs and their ecology:

D. W. Larson, U. Matthes, and P. E. Kelly, *Cliff Ecology: Pattern and Process in Cliff Ecosystems* (Cambridge, UK: Cambridge University Press, 2000).

"concrete and glass versions":

Larson, Matthes, and Kelly, *Cliff Ecology,* pp. 247–248.

Heat Island effect:

EPA.gov: "The annual mean air temperature of a city with 1 million people or more can be 1.8–5.4°F (1–3°C) warmer than its surroundings. In the evening, the difference can be as high as 22°F (12°C)." "On a hot, sunny summer day, roof and pavement surface temperatures can be 50–90°F (27–50°C) hotter than the air." http://www.epa.gov/heatisld/index.htm.

A NICE PLACE (TO WALK)

platoon:

W. H. Whyte, *City: Rediscovering the Center* (New York: Doubleday, 1988).

walking pace:

R. L. Knoblauch, M. T. Pietrucha, and M. Nitzburg, "Field Studies of Pedestrian Walking Speed and Start-up Time," *Transportation Research Record 1538* (1996): 27.

Highway Capacity Manual:

Transportation Research Board of the National Academies, 2010.

fish schooling rules:

B. L. Partridge, "Internal Dynamics and the Interrelations of Fish in Schools," *Journal of Physiology 144* (1981): 313–325.

swarm intelligence:

L. Fisher, *Perfect Swarm: The Science of Complexity in Everyday Life* (New York: Basic Books, 2009).

SOURCES

"step and slide":

M. Wolff, "Notes on the Behaviour of Pedestrians," in A. Birenbaum and E. Sagarin, eds., *People in Places: The Sociology of the Familiar* (New York: Praeger Publishers, 1973), pp. 35–48.

sociology of pedestrian behavior:

E. Goffman, *Behavior in Public Places: Notes on the Social Organization of Gatherings* (New York: Free Press, 1963); Wolff, "Notes on the Behaviour of Pedestrians"; and Whyte, *City.*

anticipatory head movements:

R. Grasso, P. Prévost, Y. P. Ivanenko, and A. Berthoz, "Eye-Head Coordination for the Steering of Locomotion in Humans: An Anticipatory Synergy," *Neuroscience Letters 253* (1998): 115–118; and T. Imai, S. T. Moore, T. Raphan, and B. Cohen, "Interaction of the Body, Head, and Eyes During Walking and Turning," *Experimental Brain Research 136* (2001): 1–18.

Mormon crickets and desert locusts:

I. Couzin, "!@#$% Traffic: From Insects to Interstates," lecture, World Science Forum, New York, 2009.

serotonin and swarms:

M. L. Anstey, S. M. Rogers, S. R. Ott, et al., "Serotonin Mediates Behavioral Gregarization Underlying Swarm Formation in Desert Locusts," *Science 323* (2009): 627–630.

jaywalking:

P. D. Norton, *Fighting Traffic* (Cambridge, MA: MIT Press, 2008).

the "veerers," "runners," etc.:

M. B. Lewick, "The Confusion of Our Sidewalkers and the Traffic Problems of the Future in the Erratic Pedestrian," *New York Times,* August 3, 1924.

"Nobody likes to be looked at":

Ellen Langer, personal communication, June 1, 2010.

Sources

one person can, in theory, "move" the other:

Idea from I. Couzin, "!@#$% Traffic."

Hans Monderman and the "naked street":

T. McNichol, "Roads Gone Wild," *Wired,* December 2004.

cost of a penny:

http://www.usmint.gov/faqs/circulating_coins/index.cfm?action=faq_circulating_coin, retrieved July 31, 2012.

looking at path while walking:

T. Foulsham, E. Walker, and A. Kingstone, "The Where, What and When of Gaze Allocation in the Lab and the Natural Environment," *Vision Research 51* (2011): 1920–1931.

history of sidewalks:

A. Loukaitou-Sideris and R. Ehrenfeucht, *Sidewalks: Conflict and Negotiation Over Public Space* (Cambridge, MA: MIT Press, 2009).

sidewalk composition:

http://www.infrastructurist.com/2010/02/22/the-sidewalks-of-today-and-tomorrow-is-concrete-our-only-option/.

Bureau of Incumbrances:

Arthur F. Cosby, compiler, 1906–1908 Code of Ordinances of the City of New York.

fluid dynamics:

Couzin, "!@#$% Traffic"; and L. F. Henderson, "On the Fluid Mechanics of Human Crowd Motion," *Transportation Research 8* (1974): 509–515.

"please, just a nice place to sit":

W. H. Whyte, "Please, Just a Nice Place to Sit," *New York Times Magazine,* December 3, 1972.

Sources

movable chairs:

Whyte, *City.*

THE SUGGESTIVENESS OF THUMB-NAILS

Sherlock Holmes and Dr. Bell:

T. A. Sebeok, *The Play of Musement* (Bloomington, IN: Indiana University Press, 1982).

"the importance of sleeves, the suggestiveness of thumb-nails":

A. C. Doyle, "A Case of Identity," in *The Adventures of Sherlock Holmes and the Memoirs of Sherlock Holmes* (New York: Penguin, 2001).

"nail abnormalities":

R. S. Fawcett, S. Linford, and D. L. Stulberg, "Nail Abnormalities: Clues to Systemic Disease," *American Family Physician* 69 (2004): 1417–1424.

gait:

J. Perry, *Gait Analysis: Normal and Pathological Function* (Thorofare, NJ: Slack Inc., 1992).

an infant's walking and falling:

K. E. Adolph, "Learning to Move," *Current Directions in Psychological Science* 17 (2008): 213–218.

stance and swing of step:

Perry, *Gait Analysis,* p. 5.

gait can go wrong:

http://library.med.utah.edu/neurologicexam/html/gait_abnormal.html#03.

breed standards for gait:

American Kennel Club standards, retrieved from http://www.akc.org.

Sources

bad breath:

B. E. Johnson, "Halitosis, or the Meaning of Bad Breath," *Journal of General Internal Medicine 7* (1992): 649–659; and B. Lorber, "Bad Breath and Pulmonary Infection," *American Review of Respiratory Disease 112* (1975): 875–877.

Laënnec's sound catalog:

H. Schwartz, *Making Noise: From Babel to the Big Bang & Beyond* (New York: Zone Books, 2011), pp. 210–212; and J. L. Andrews and T. L. Badger, "Lung Sounds Through the Ages," *JAMA 241* (1979): 2625–2630.

mirror neurons:

G. di Pellegrino, L. Fadiga, L. Fogassi, et al., "Understanding Motor Events: A Neurophysiological Study," *Experimental Brain Research 91* (1992): 176–180.

brain activity of expert dancers:

B. Calvo-Merino et al., "Action Observation and Acquired Motor Skills: An fMRI Study with Expert Dancers," *Cerebral Cortex 15* (2005): 1243–1249.

anthropomorphic measurements:

L. G. Farkas and I. R. Munro, *Anthropometric Facial Proportions in Medicine* (Springfield, IL: Charles C. Thomas, 1987).

SEEING; NOT SEEING

"hear the grass grow and the squirrel's heart beat":

G. Eliot, *Middlemarch* (New York: Oxford University Press, 2008).

gaze and conversation:

C. L. Kleinke, "Gaze and Eye Contact: A Research Review," *Psychological Bulletin 100* (1986): 78–100.

eyes and improv:

K. Johnstone, *Improv: Improvisation and the Theatre* (New York: Routledge, 1981).

SOURCES

million-colored landscape

J. D. Mollon, "Color Vision: Opsins and Options," *Proceedings of the National Academy of Science 96* (1999): 4743–4745.

neural reorganization:

D. Bavelier and H. J. Neville, "Cross-Modal Plasticity: Where and How?", *Nature Reviews Neuroscience 3* (2002): 443–452.

Brodmann's map:

S. Kastner and L. G. Ungerleider, "Mechanisms of Visual Attention in the Human Cortex," *Annual Review of Neuroscience 23* (2000): 315–341.

Thurber and a blue Hoover vacuum:

V. S. Ramachandran and S. Blakeslee, *Phantoms in the Brain: Probing the Nature of the Human Mind* (New York: Harper Perennial, 1999).

on odor perception of blind:

O. Sacks, *The Mind's Eye* (New York: Knopf, 2010), p. 233.

on cane work:

National Research Council, "The Cane as a Mobility Aid for the Blind," 1971; and A. Serino, M. Bassolino, A. Farnè, and E. Làdavas, "Extended Multisensory Space in Blind Cane Users," *Psychological Science 18* (2007): 642–648.

echolocation in the blind:

B. N. Schenkman and M. E. Nilsson, "Human Echolocation: Blind and Sighted Persons' Ability to Detect Sounds Recorded in the Presence of a Reflecting Object," *Perception 39* (2010): 483–501.

John Hull:

Sacks, *The Mind's Eye;* J. Hull, *Touching the Rock: An Experience of Blindness* (New York: Pantheon, 1991).

Sources

peripersonal space:

Serino et al., "Extended Multisensory Space"; S. Blakeslee and M. Blakeslee, *The Body Has a Mind of Its Own: How Body Maps in Your Brain Help You Do (Almost) Everything Better* (New York: Random House, 2007).

blindfold fMRI study:

L. B. Merabet et al., "Rapid and Reversible Recruitment of Early Visual Cortex for Touch," *PLoS One 3* (2008): e3046.

blindfold study in room:

O. Yaski, J. Portugali, and D. Eilam, "The Dynamic Process of Cognitive Mapping in the Absence of Visual Cues: Human Data Compared with Animal Studies," *The Journal of Experimental Biology 212* (2009): 2619–2626.

winds in cities:

K. Pryor, "The Wicked Winds of New York," *New York Magazine,* April 24, 1978, 35–40.

"so preocupplied with cell phones":

Sacks, *The Mind's Eye,* p. 199.

1969 mobile phone study:

I. D. Brown, A. H. Tickner, and D. C. Simmonds, "Interference Between Concurrent Tasks of Driving and Telephoning," *Journal of Applied Psychology 53* (1969): 419–424.

unicycling clown:

I. E. Hyman, Jr.; S. M. Boss; B. M. Wise et al., "Did You See the Unicycling Clown? Inattentional Blindness While Walking and Talking on a Cell Phone," *Applied Cognitive Psychology 24* (2010): 597–607.

information in voices:

P. Belin, P. E. G. Bestelmeyer, M. Latinus, and R. Watson, "Understanding Voice Perception," *British Journal of Psychology 102* (2011): 711–725.

SOURCES

Belgian Federal Police force blind officers:

D. Bilefsky, "A Blind Sherlock Holmes: Fighting Crime with Acute Listening," *New York Times,* October 29, 2007.

THE SOUND OF PARALLEL PARKING

the first sound:

R. M. Schafer, *The Soundscape: Our Sonic Environment and the Tuning of the World* (Rochester, VT: Destiny Books, 1994), p. 15.

sounds in the womb:

M. C. Busnel, C. Granier-Deferre, and J. P. Lecanuet, "Fetal Audition," *Annals of the New York Academy of Sciences 662* (1992): 118–134; and S. Tyano and M. Keren, "The Competent Fetus," in *Parenthood and Mental Health: A Bridge Between Infant and Adult Psychiatry* (New York: Wiley Online, 2010).

diesel sounds:

Extrapolated from various sources, such as *Diesel Technology: Report of the Technology Panel of the Diesel Impacts Study Committee* (Washington, D.C.: National Academy Press, 1982).

infrasonic sounds of the giraffe:

Research by E. Muggenthaler, in D. Feldman, *Why Do Pirates Love Parrots?* (New York: Harper, 2006).

lo-fi soundscape; "music is sounds":

R. M. Schafer, *The Soundscape.*

noises as "tumbled about in confusion":

H. L. F. Helmholtz, *On the Sensations of Tone as a Physiological Basis for the Theory of Music,* trans. A. J. Ellis (London: Longmans Green and Co., 1875), p. 8.

interruptedness of sound:

Schwartz, *Making Noise,* p. 239.

Sources

fingernails on a chalkboard:

C. Reuter and M. Oehler, "Psychoacoustics of Chalkboard Squeaking," *162nd Acoustical Society of America Meeting,* San Diego, California, 2011.

otoacoustic emissions:

D. T. Kemp, "Exploring Cochlear Status with Otoacoustic Emissions: The Potential for New Clinical Applications," in M. S. Robinette and T. J. Glattke, eds., *Otoacoustic Emissions: Clinical Applications* (New York: Thieme, 2002), pp. 1–47.

otoacoustic emission signatures:

M. Swabey, S. P. Beeby, A. Brown, and J. Chad, "Using Otoacoustic Emissions as a Biometric," *Proceedings of the First International Conference on Biometric Authentication* (2004), pp. 600–606.

keynote sounds:

R. M. Schafer, *The Soundscape.*

auditory restoration:

L. Riecke, F. Esposito, M. Bonte, and E. Formisano, "Hearing Illusory Sounds in Noise: The Timing of Sensory-Perceptual Transformations in Auditory Cortex," *Neuron 64* (2009): 550–561.

on bats:

C. Moss and A. Surlykke, "Probing the Natural Scene by Echolocation in Bats," *Frontiers of Behavioral Neuroscience 4* (2010): 1–16.

physical reactions to sound: Homer, David, et al.:

F. Gonzalez-Crussi, *The Five Senses* (San Diego: Harcourt Brace Jovanovich, 1989), pp. 38–44.

self-similarity:

M. N. Geffen, J. Gervain, J. F. Werker, and M. O. Magnasco, "Auditory Perception of Self-Similarity in Water Sounds," *Frontiers in Integrative Neuroscience 5* (2011): 15; and W. J. Davies, "The Perception of Susurration: Envelopment in Indoor and Outdoor Spaces," *18th International Congress on Acoustics, Kyoto,* 2004.

Sources

firs sob and moan:

Or so wrote Thomas Hardy in *Under the Greenwood Tree or the Mellstock Quire: A Rural Painting of the Dutch School.*

cricket pulse rate and temperature:

S. D. Martin, D. A. Gray, and W. H. Cade, "Fine-Scale Temperature Effects on Cricket Calling Song," *Canadian Journal of Zoology 78* (2000): 706–712.

sounds as warfare:

U.S. Department of Defense Non-Lethal Weapons Program, http://jnlwp. defense.gov.

automatic doors in science fiction:

The director of *The Empire Strikes Back* did just this. M. Chion, *Audio-Vision: Sound on Screen* (New York: Columbia University Press, 1994), p. 12.

henbane: "swift as quicksilver":

W. Shakespeare, *Hamlet,* act I, scene V.

elephants . . . infrasounds are resilient to weakening:

K. McComb, D. Reby, L. Baker, et al., "Long-Distance Communication of Acoustic Cues to Social Identity in African Elephants," *Animal Behaviour 65* (2003): 317–329.

medical effects of infrasound:

G. M. Foy, *Zero Decibels* (New York: Scribner, 2010), pp. 6–7.

breathing noises:

Chion, *Audio-Vision,* p. 36.

insides likely vibrated to this growl:

Foy, *Zero Decibels,* p. 35.

SOURCES

effects of children's laughing and crying:

E. Seifritz et al., "Differential Sex-Independent Amygdala Response to Infant rying and Laughing in Parents Versus Nonparents," *Biological Psychiatry 54* (2003): 1367–1375.

antinoise in London:

Schwartz, *Making Noise,* pp. 143ff.

noises of 500 BC, seventeenth-century London, and twentieth-century New York:

E. Thompson, *The Soundscape of Modernity: Architectural Acoustics and the Culture of Listening in America, 1900–1922* (Cambridge, MA: MIT Press, 2002).

not all air (or water) is alike:

J. W. Bradbury and S. L. Vehrencamp, *Principles of Animal Communication,* 2nd ed. (Sunderland, MA: Sinauer Associates, 2011).

animal sound communication:

Ibid.

fin whales:

R. Payne and D. Webb, "Orientation by Means of Long Range Acoustic Signaling in Baleen Whales," *Annals of the New York Academy of Sciences 188* (1971): 110–141.

humans' noise interference underwater:

M. L. Melcon et al., "Blue Whales Respond to Anthropogenic Noise," *PLoS One 7* (2012): e32681.

overtones:

D. J. Levitin, *This Is Your Brain on Music: The Science of a Human Obsession* (New York: Penguin, 2006).

diabolus in musica:

M. Kennedy, *The Concise Oxford Dictionary of Music* (Oxford: Oxford University Press, 2004).

Sources

A DOG'S-NOSE VIEW

"We others, who have long lost":

K. Grahame, *The Wind in the Willows* (New York: Charles Scribner's Sons, 1960), pp. 80–81.

on the dog nose:

G. S. Settles, D. A. Kester, and L. J. Dodson-Dreibelbis, "The External Aerodynamics of Canine Olfaction," in F. G. Barth, J. A. C. Humphrey, and T. W. Secomb, eds., *Sensors and Sensing in Biology and Engineering* (New York: Springer, 2002), pp. 323–336.

on receptors in the dog nose:

S. Firestein, "How the Olfactory System Makes Sense of Scents," *Nature 413* (2001): 211–217. For more on perceiving smells, see also http://bigthink.com/users/stuartfirestein.

on dog sniffing:

B. A. Craven, E. G. Paterson, and G. S. Settles, "The Fluid Dynamics of Canine Olfaction: Unique Nasal Airflow Patterns as an Explanation of Macrosmia," *Journal of the Royal Society Interface 7* (2010): 933–943.

nostril lateralization:

M. Siniscalchi, R. Sasso, A. M. Pepe, et al., "Sniffing with the Right Nostril: Lateralization of Response to Odour Stimuli by Dogs," *Animal Behaviour 82* (2011): 399–404.

geodetic survey marks:

http://celebrating200years.noaa.gov/survey_marks/welcome.html#look; and F. W. Koop, "Precise Leveling in New York City," a report of the City of New York Board of Estimate and Apportionment, 1909–1914.

smells of disease:

M. Shirasu and K. Touhara, "The Scent of Disease: Volatile Organic Compounds of the Human Body Related to Disease," *Journal of Biochemistry 150* (2011): 257–266; and "Odor as a Symptom of Disease," *New York Medical Journal 69* (1899): 103.

SOURCES

tracking via footsteps:

P. G. Hepper and D. L. Wells, "How Many Footsteps Do Dogs Need to Determine the Direction of an Odour Trail?" *Chemical Senses 30* (2005): 291–298.

dog gaits:

C. M. Brown, *Dog Locomotion and Gait Analysis* (Wheat Ridge, CO: Hoflin Publishing, 1986).

sloppy tracks:

P. Rezendes, *Tracking and the Art of Seeing: How to Read Animal Tracks and Sign* (New York: HarperCollins, 1999).

horse tactile sensitivity:

C. A. Saslow, "Understanding the Perceptual World of Horses," *Applied Animal Behaviour Science 78* (2002): 209–224.

SEEING IT

Rembrandtian paintings:

This idea comes from James Elkins's description of a Rembrandt portrait: http://www.jameselkins.com/index.php?option=com_content&view=article&id=227.

Acknowledgments

One of the pleasures of this project was simply that it allowed me to engage in long conversations with people while walking. Most of my fellow walkers were complete strangers, yet for some reason were willing to spend a few hours with me wandering along city streets in sometimes less than ideal weather. It was surprising that they were. A few even took trains long distances to do so. I am extraordinarily grateful: why did they do it? I'll never know, but I'm tickled and in their debt. Many thanks to all the people with whom I walked, only some of whom are represented in these pages: Adrian Benepe, Bill Buchen, Andrew Dolkart, Charley Eiseman, Arlene Gordon, John Hadidian, Sidney Horenstein, Jonathan Jezequel, Maira Kalman, Fred Kent, Ellen Langer, Terry Leto, Bill Logan, Bennett Lorber, Benjamin Miller, Helen Mirra, Bill Oldham, Catryna and Whitney North Seymour, Paul Shaw, Fiona Shea, Ogden Horowitz Shea, Eliza Slavet, and Mark Woods (whose very approach to the city was partial inspiration for this book, and with whom I would walk anywhere). I am especially grateful to Maira Kalman for sharing with me not only on foot, but also through her fabulous illustrations, what she saw on the street.

ACKNOWLEDGMENTS

I do not only thank, but also tickle the ears of Finnegan, Pumpernickel, and now Upton, for taking me walking around the block three times a day for thousands upon thousands of days.

Colin Harrison can date an antique map from twenty paces. He observes people in restaurants, on trains, on the street, and notes their mannerisms and when they cough. He has theories about the gummed spots on sidewalks. In other words, he is, clearly, the perfect reader of this book; how fortunate for me that he is also my editor. My only regret about the book's completion is that we will not get to have three-hour-long conversations about it with regularity. I am ever appreciative. Thanks, too, to everyone at Scribner for following me down this block, especially Nan Graham, Susan Moldow, Roz Lippel, Kate Lloyd, Kelsey Smith, Jason Heuer, Lauren Lavelle, and Brian Belfiglio.

I am always happy to say that my agent is Kris Dahl. I am thankful for her wisdom, the utter lack of nonsense in her manner, and her boosterism. She and Laura Neely manage to be supportive while also getting me to change my course in a way that will make a book better.

Even before the walking began in earnest, many people contributed ideas or inspiration, including Alison Curry, John Herrold, Daniel Hurewitz, Oliver Sacks, Andy Tuck, Abraham Verghese, Catherine Wing, and especially my parents Elizabeth Hardin and Jay Horowitz, and my brother, Damon. My parents are often my first and best readers. My brother can kill a bad idea with an eyebrow-raise, but will kick and punch and help promote a good idea to the moon. Thanks for every one of them.

Ammon Shea is a great walker. Walking is pleasurable to me in the way that breathing is: it is a part of life, and at moments I especially savor it. Walking with Ammon can't be beat. Sitting, he helped me snag slippery facts and turn a good phrase. I wrote this book with Ammon in mind, as I do most things. I goggle, bemused, at his picklesomeness. Much thanks, for all.

Index

aboriginal sensible muchness, 26
acclimation, 30–31, 110
Adobe Garamond, 57
adrenaline, 84, 249
Africa, 135
algae, 106, 134
alignment in walking, 146, 150, 173
American Museum of Natural
    History, 41–42
ampersands, 63, 68–69
amygdala, 179–80, 234n
anaerobic infections, 162, 176, 178
animals:
    attraction and, 99, 104, 111, 126,
        134, 146
    avoidance and, 110, 117 127, 129,
        131–32, 145–46, 150, 225
    search image in, 107–9, 124
    sensory world of, 77
    swarms of, 146, 150–51
animate city, 15
animism, 37–39
animistic error, 38

antidepressants, 151
ants, 94, 97, 103, 105, 145–46
aphids, 97, 99–100, 104
arms, 198, 200
    swinging of, 163, 173, 256, 264
Art Deco, 63
Arthropoda, 94
articulation of sound, 222
artificial intelligence, 146
Art Moderne, 63
Art Nouveau, 70–71
asphalt, 6, 27, 42, 46, 156, 220–21, 238,
    251n–52n, 261
attention, 1–4, 9–15, 65, 126, 146, 150,
    160, 188n
    absence of, 2–3, 9, 14, 24, 45,
    123–24, 181, 189, 265
    cell phones and, 206–7
    children and, 26, 31, 35–36, 38, 258
    dogs and, 241, 246–47, 251–52, 263
    evolution and development of,
        10–11, 26, 83
    expectation and, 122–23

Index